Women in China's Long Twentieth Century

Women in China's Long Twentieth Century

GAIL HERSHATTER

Global, Area, and International Archive
University of California Press
BERKELEY   LOS ANGELES   LONDON

The Global, Area, and International Archive (GAIA) is an initiative
of International and Area Studies, University of California, Berkeley,
in partnership with the University of California Press, the California
Digital Library, and international research programs across the
UC system. GAIA volumes, which are published in both print and
open-access digital editions, represent the best traditions of regional
studies, reconfigured through fresh global, transnational, and thematic
perspectives.

University of California Press, one of the most distinguished university
presses in the United States, enriches lives around the world by
advancing scholarship in the humanities, social sciences, and natural
sciences. Its activities are supported by the UC Press Foundation and by
philanthropic contributions from individuals and institutions. For more
information, visit www.ucpress.edu.

University of California Press
Berkeley and Los Angeles, California

University of California Press, Ltd.
London, England

Library of Congress Cataloging-in-Publication Data

Hershatter, Gail.
    Women in China's long twentieth century / Gail Hershatter.
        p.   cm.
    Includes bibliographical references and index.
    ISBN-13: 978-0-520-09856-5 (pbk.: alk. paper),

    1. Women—China—Social conditions—20th century.
2. Women—Employment—China.   3. Sex role—China.
4. Women and communism—China.   5. Feminism—China.
I. University of California, Berkeley. Global, Area, and International
Archive.   II. Title.
HQ1767.H47   2007
305.40951'0904—dc22   2006029808

Manufactured in the United States of America

15   14   13   12   11   10   09   08   07
10   9   8   7   6   5   4   3   2

The paper used in this publication meets the minimum requirements of
ANSI/NISO Z39.48–1992 (R1997) (Permanence of Paper).

For Grace

Contents

Introduction

The study of women in twentieth-century China has expanded so quickly since the mid-1980s that a state-of-the-field survey becomes outdated in the time it takes to assemble and write one. This burgeoning area of inquiry draws its inspiration and approaches from many sources outside "the China field," a realm no longer hermetically sealed within exclusive logics of sinology or area studies. Research about Chinese women has been enriched by the growth of women's studies abroad and in China; by debates about gender as a category of analysis and its uneasy relationship to sex and sexuality; by conversations inside established scholarly disciplines about gender's entanglement with politics, migration, nation building, and modernity; by discussions across the disciplines about agency, resistance, subjectivity, and voice; and by several waves of refigured Marxism in the wake of feminist activity, socialism's demise, and the development of postcolonial scholarship. During the same period, China's reform and opening have changed the conditions for scholarly work by both foreign and Chinese scholars. Gender has appeared at the center of new debates in the Chinese press, within the state, and among emergent groups such as women's studies scholars, social workers, legal experts, and labor analysts. Available sources and opportunities for research and fieldwork in China have expanded for both Chinese scholars and foreigners, giving rise to scholarly conversations that sometimes intersect and sometimes trace utterly separate trajectories.

To complicate this endeavor further, writing about women routinely crosses disciplinary boundaries. For China, the disciplines that investigate "women" shift with the period of time under investigation as well as with changing disciplinary norms. Historians, for instance, used to stop at the edge of the People's Republic of China in 1949, at which point the pursuit of knowledge was handed over to social scientists. Now historians often

traverse the 1949 divide, borrowing methods from anthropology and literature. Even now, most studies of women in post-Mao China are produced by
anthropologists, sociologists, and scholars of contemporary literature.

The field being surveyed here, then, ranges within and across disciplines.
The emergence of women's studies has enabled many of these projects, but
not all the scholars discussed herein locate themselves within "women's
studies." This situation of crumbling boundaries presents some not-so-
innocent taxonomical choices: To follow the interdisciplinary practices of
women's studies and risk a runaway bibliography? To draw on categories
of analysis developed outside Chinese contexts, including the categories of
"woman" and "gender" themselves, and risk analytical imperialism? To
stay within the national boundaries of China (but which twentieth-century
boundaries should we choose?) and risk reifying "the nation" as a timeless
entity? To roam through recently imagined territories such as "Greater
China" and risk taking "civilization" or "culture" for granted? To treat the
term "Chinese" as synonymous with Han and risk subimperialism or the
reinforcement of a simplistic Han-minority dyad? To include scholarship
written for a Chinese audience and risk eliding its different conditions of
production? To ignore such scholarship and thereby assume a provincial
"we" as the only ones authorized to speak? To proceed chronologically, as
historians habitually do, and thus assume the familiar signposts of political
change (1911; 1949; 1978) as significant markers in a gendered landscape,
as well as the very habit of thinking causally? To proceed thematically and
thus naturalize categories such as "family" or "work" without attending to
specificities of time and space?

Faced with such questions, I have made choices that are unlikely to
please everyone. My aim is to produce a usable and bounded piece of work,
avoiding telegraphically brief discussion of the materials that are included
while acknowledging the dispersed and overlapping inquiries that shape
the scholarly subject of "Chinese women." This volume is interdisciplinary
but limited, focusing on works produced since 1970 in history, anthropology, sociology, and politics. It does not include most of the fine studies of
gender in literature, film, or the performing arts (see, for example, R. Chow
1991b; Barlow 1993; L. Liu 1994, 1995; T. Lu 1993; Prazniak 1989; Yingjin
Zhang 1994, 1996; Shih 1996; Larson 1998, 2005; Dooling and Torgeson
1998; Berry 1999; Sang 2005). It generally stays within the confines of the
Chinese mainland, both for practical bibliographical reasons and because
mainland political arrangements and gender discourse across the twentieth century have looked significantly different from those in Taiwan,
Hong Kong, and Chinese diasporas, whatever their long-term connections

or contemporary entanglements. Although I cross these boundaries opportunistically when a piece of scholarship on Taiwan or Hong Kong provides conceptual or comparative insight into mainland practices, I have not discussed many important works (see, for example, M. Wolf 1968, 1992; Kung 1995; Pearson and Leung 1995; Ping-chun Hsiung 1996). This book reflects the Han-centered nature of most scholarship on Chinese women, without in any way assuming that this is a satisfactory or permanent situation. Excluded are sourcebooks or translations (see, for example, Croll 1974; Yu-ning Li 1992; Zeng 1993; Lan and Fong 1999), most memoirs or collections of oral histories and interviews (see, for example, Pruitt 1979; Sheridan and Salaff 1985; Zeng 1993; Verschuur-Basse 1996; P. Chang 1997), and earlier surveys of or interpretive guides to the state of the field (see, for example, Anagnost 1989; Jacka 1999; Brownell and Wasserstrom 2002c; Leutner 2002). Also excluded for reasons of space are many of the fine edited collections on East Asia that include one or more essays on women in China (see, for example, Brook and Luong 1997), as well as edited collections on gender across East Asia that include discussion of China (see, for example, E. Chow 2002). By including citations to these works here, I commend them to the reader. Perhaps most regrettably, the review covers only scholarship in English, discussing works by Chinese scholars or work in other languages only when they are available in translation. Fortunately, guides to the growing and complex Chinese scholarship on women have begun to appear (see, for example, Hershatter et al. 1998; C. Ho 1999).

The siren call of chronology guides and seduces every historian, and readers will certainly hear its echoes here. Nevertheless, I have attempted a thematic rather than strictly chronological approach. Much scholarship on twentieth-century Chinese women has been framed by major political events, and has been animated by questions such as these: How did events leading to the fall of the dynasty affect women? How was the status of women deployed by Chinese thinkers to illuminate a need for social and cultural change? What did women contribute to the Chinese revolution, and what did it do to and for them? Are the economic reforms good or bad for women? All of these are surely worthy historical questions, and some of them have contemporary urgency as well. What they tend not to foreground are issues of temporality itself. How can we attend to practices and beliefs, for instance, that perdure across political regimes or that change in ways not easily correlated with the tempo of political events? How can we account for the moments in scholarly practice when particular questions are brought to visibility—shifts in scholarly temporality that have political coordinates? How can we identify master narratives without flattening other story lines? How can we avoid a triumphal progressive narrative wherein we lavish pity and faint praise on our benighted foremothers for their scholarly assumptions? In order to question, rather than assume, the importance of specific political events and the underpinnings of scholarly work, each chapter of the volume roams across the long twentieth century, itself an awkward and artificial category.

This volume builds upon, usually without explicitly crediting, developments in the overlapping fields known as women's studies and gender studies. Assuming the mutability, instability, and historical specificity of gender, it looks at the shaping of a relational category called "woman" and its inhabitants, "women." And although the other of "woman" in a gendered order is most commonly "man," the volume concerns itself primarily with other pairings that dominate writing on women in twentieth-century China: women and marriage, family, sexuality, and gender difference in Chapter 1, women and labor in Chapter 2, and women and national modernity in Chapter 3. I have chosen these categories because the authors surveyed here chose them. Although each pairing has been enormously productive of important scholarship, however, each presents a problem.

The first pairing—women and marriage, family, sexuality, and gender difference—centers on twentieth-century ethnographic and textual materials, and tends to assume a timeless projection backward of certain patterns into the indefinite past, with a huge jolt coming variously in the 1920s, the 1950s, or the 1980s, depending upon one's class and geographic position. Here, timelessness is the problem. The second, women and labor, is largely organized around twentieth-century economic refigurings and political movements, and as yet has done little to create a bridge to the emergent literature on the late imperial (or early modern) period, with its studies by Francesca Bray (1997), Susan Mann (1997), Kenneth Pomeranz (2005), and others suggesting that patterns of women's work were no more timeless than those of marriage. The third, women and national modernity, is the most directly entangled with the grand revolutionary narrative, and the very term "nation" marks it as a modern construct. This story rests on two foundational assertions. The first, made mostly by recuperative feminist historians, was that "women were there, too" as participants in every important revolutionary moment. The second held that women had long been oppressed by "Confucian society" and that only revolution could free them. Tracing this story out, praising the revolution for its successes and holding it accountable for its failures, has produced much innovative scholarship. But the formulation "state shapes women, for good and ill" may have exhausted itself. At the very least, it needs to be joined by attention to a few new questions.

The twentieth-century narrative of revolution is now a bit tattered, and not only because the particular revolution that bisected the twentieth century has done everything but declare itself over. We now know that 1895 did not by itself mark the end of a world; that 1911 was both less of a revolution and more of an extended process than previously understood; that the CCP barely cohered in its early years and subsequently marched off regularly in hundreds of different localized and incompatible directions; that state-building activities were on the shared agenda of the Qing rulers, the revolutionaries who overthrew them, the Guomindang, and the Communists, and so forth. The withering away of a grand twentieth-century revolutionary story must surely raise questions about whether making women the barometer of social crisis or revolutionary success is tenable. It is one thing to note that women, and Woman (as state subject), were regarded as such barometers in the past, by the people whose lives we try to apprehend across time. It is quite another thing to use women, or Woman, that way ourselves. In the final section of this volume, "Afterthoughts," I suggest that we cultivate several alternative habits of mind in thinking about gender in China's recent history.

The scholarship on each theme—women and marriage, family, sexuality, and gender difference; women and labor; and women and national modernity—has moved from an emphasis on the transformative power of the revolution to a reliance on more complex and less linear temporalities. These categories are not cleanly divisible: prostitution, for instance, could plausibly be discussed under all three. Each theme has been the site of important foundational claims on, for, and sometimes by women. Nevertheless, they are all formations whose flexibility and permeability have probably contributed to their longevity, and this volume traces their changing meanings in the scholarship.

A state-of-the-field survey, particularly one by a historian, conventionally makes an attempt to assess changes in the field over time, point out major issues of contention, and sometimes take sides in ongoing arguments. I have done very little of that here for two reasons. First, this is an emergent field of inquiry; it has not been around long enough to generate much debris from abandoned paradigms. One could say that the initial question animating much early feminist scholarship on twentieth-century China—Was the revolution good or bad for women?—no longer compels attention. It has been replaced by inquiries that are more localized (where?), more segmented (which women?), and more attentive to the multiple, contradictory levels of state activity and the unintended but often powerful consequences of state policies. Some newer scholarship openly criticizes earlier feminist frames of reference; a larger group of works quietly departs from them. I regard these newer questions as salutary, but in my opinion the "older" scholarship of the 1970s and 1980s is not superannuated, and we may well return to it seeking answers to different questions from the ones that inspired its authors. Put plainly, little of this scholarship is ready to be consigned to the dustbin of history.

Second, this field has not, or perhaps has not yet, generated internal disagreements as a means of defining itself. Over the past several decades, questions of gender have attracted some of the most talented scholars in the China field, and their work is rich in opinions and interpretations as well as descriptive detail. To date, however, the work has been largely recuperative rather than contentious; the argumentative strain in this scholarship has mostly been directed to other audiences. To the wider China field, this scholarship says that "women were there, too" and posits that attention to gender dynamics and gendered language can reconfigure our most basic assumptions about what counts as a twentieth-century event. To scholars who work on gender in other locations, it offers both an assertion of historically specific difference and a refusal to categorize "Chinese women" as a unified, timeless, or ineluctable Other. Perhaps a state-of-the-field survey a decade from now will be organized around explosive controversies; such a development might even mark a maturing of the field. But for purposes of this book, I have decided not to pronounce any question safely past or any assertion profoundly misguided. Rather, I have attempted to map areas where the scholarship is thickest; note areas of fragmentation or silence; and demonstrate, if only through the accretion of some 650 citations, that the study of women in China's recent past is an extraordinarily productive field of inquiry.

This book began its life as an essay in the *Journal of Asian Studies* 63.4 (November 2004), 991–1065, and an earlier form of the Afterthoughts appeared in Hershatter 2005b. I thank Wendy Brown, Christopher Connery, Tony Crowley, Susan Glosser, M. Grace Laurencin, Susan Mann, Randall Stross, Ann Waltner, Wang Zheng, and an anonymous reader for their encouragement and suggestions. Remaining gaps, gaffes, infelicities, and idiosyncratic judgments are my responsibility. Thanks also to Sasha Welland for introducing me to the paintings of Yu Hong, and to Yu Hong for permission to reproduce her work on the cover.

1. Marriage, Family, Sexuality, and Gender Difference

China has long been portrayed by Chinese and foreigners both as the home of a thoroughly entrenched patriarchal family system and as a place where the 1949 revolution and the post-Mao reforms massively rearranged marriage, family, and affective life. The scholarship reviewed here introduces nuance and local variation into this picture, and redraws some sections of it altogether. Patriarchy and gender hierarchy (the term favored in scholarly discussion more recently) are locally variable, mediated by other sorts of ties, and at the same time extremely adaptable to the successive environments of revolution and reform, flourishing in new venues even as the old ones disappear. Revolution and reform from the final years of the Qing dynasty to the present have been both corrosive and preservative of family arrangements, reconstituting gender relations in ways that can be distressingly predictable or intermittently surprising. Across the long twentieth century, key meanings of modernity have been worked out in public discussions—official, intellectual, pop-cultural, and overlapping—about marriage, family, sexuality, and gender difference.

MARRIAGE

The story of Chinese marriage practices in the twentieth century has often been told as a transformation from family-based oppression to limited individual choice—or in another register, from feudalism to socialism—with the PRC's 1950 Marriage Law marking an important, if ultimately incomplete, moment of progress. Every piece of this story has been called into question by recent scholarship. Courtship practices and discussions about love and attraction have indeed changed across the twentieth century, but the temporality of these changes is uneven and not easy to classify. Women's transition into married life turns out to be more partial, less traumatic, and more varied than we have usually acknowledged. The Marriage Law produced more long-term effects than its feminist critics realized and was used in ways unforeseen and not endorsed by its authors. If marital satisfaction receives more public discussion than it used to, so does marital discord.

Courtship and Wedding Practices

Social spaces in which young people might meet one another proliferated in urban areas during the Republican period, expanding significantly in towns and villages after 1949, particularly in the 1960s and 1970s (Davin 1988; Gates 1999; Y. Yan 2002). Nevertheless, Sulamith Potter and Jack Potter (1990) note considerable constraints on contacts between young men and women in 1970s and early 1980s Guangdong. In a study of the politics of marriage from the early 1960s to the mid-1970s, based on policy documents, case studies in the press, and a small number of interviews, Elisabeth Croll (1981) found a range of parental involvement in the marriage choices of their children, with parents often initiating a match in rural areas and consenting to their children's choices in urban areas. These types of parental action were generally regarded as compatible with free-choice marriage. Through the end of the Mao years and well into the reform era, parental participation in mate choice continued in both urban and rural settings, although senior generations no longer had unilateral control (Parish and Whyte 1978; Honig and Hershatter 1988; Selden 1993; Whyte 1993; X. Zang 1999; Y. Yan 2002; Yuen, Law, and Ho 2004; Friedman 2006). Mothers appear to have exercised more influence in their children's marriages and family relations in general than did fathers (X. Zang 1999; Jankowiak 2002). During the collective period, officials attempted unsuccessfully to discourage betrothal and its attendant gifts, with their connotations of family exchange and the purchase of women. Attempts to encourage courtship had more effect in urban than in rural areas (Croll 1981).

The rearrangements in rural life caused by collectivization affected marriage choice, but not always in the way that policy makers intended. Croll (1981) suggests that because the geographical mobility of peasants was limited during the collective period, in contrast with the Republican era, primary kin groups retained a great deal of influence over rural marriage negotiations. William Parish and Martin Whyte (1978) find that during the collective period, bride price (at least in Guangdong) became far more important than dowry, enough to cover much of the expenses of the bride's family and leave enough surplus to help bring in a wife for the son. They link the increase in bride price to women's increased work in the fields, which made the acquisition of rights to women's labor more valuable.

The notion of an ideal spouse, which did not necessarily overlap with that of an ideal affine, emerged during the collective period. Political and socioeconomic standing, although sometimes in conflict, were both considered important (Croll 1981). In rural areas, migration was strictly controlled, some locales were better off than others, and marriage was generally patrilocal. Marriage migration was one of the few ways that women could move out and up, and women's mate choice was profoundly influenced by spatial hierarchy (Lavely 1991), a trend that intensified in the reform period (C. Fan and Huang 1998; C. Fan and Li 2002; L. Tan and Short 2004).

Since the 1980s, discussions of compatibility, affect, and intimacy have loomed large in public discussions of courtship (Honig and Hershatter 1988). The spread of television and foreign programming have also shaped village social imaginaries and notions of desirability and appropriate behavior (Y. Yan 2002). Yunxiang Yan (2002, 2003) further finds that changing expectations of courtship have been shaped importantly for both young men and women by periods of migrant labor outside the village. Under the post-Mao reforms, he notes that young men are valued for the ability to articulate emotions and to make money, and young women for beauty, adornment, and a sweet temperament (see also Hooper 1984; Honig and Hershatter 1988; Jankowiak 1993, 2002; Yuen, Law, and Ho 2004).

Yan (2002, 2003) also suggests that among the youth of rural North China, love, intimacy, and premarital sex have become the focus of courtship. Autonomy in mate choice, the main courtship issue among young rural people soon after 1949, is no longer particularly controversial. In Fujian in the 1990s, according to Sara Friedman (2000, 2005, 2006), state enforcement of minimum marriage ages has encouraged young couples to get to know one another, and even to cohabit, prior to marriage. Yan and Friedman both find widespread acceptance of premarital sex between engaged couples, although Friedman adds that speaking about sexual activity and sexual pleasure may incur social disapproval. Other scholars find that female virginity has continued to be valued in a bride, even as premarital sex has become more common (Whyte 1990; X. Zang 1999). Yan (2002, 2003) notes that young women, supported by their fiancés, have taken initiative in dating, determining marital gifts, and deciding when the newly married couple should separate households.

Many of the reform-era changes in mate choice and wedding practices were already under way in the Mao years, and urban bureaucratic structures continued to shape the lives and marriage calculations of young people and their parents well into the reform period (Whyte 1990). These included the possession of a coveted urban residence permit, which limited access to the "urban public goods regime" (Solinger 1999) and was as difficult to obtain in new boomtowns such as Shenzhen (Clark 2001) as in more established cities. Nevertheless, the reform era involved new considerations in the search for an ideal spouse. Men from poor rural areas were willing to enter uxorilocal marriages (marriages into the household of the wife's family) to women in prosperous peri-urban areas, while women from poorer inland provinces began to marry out to coastal areas, leading to bride shortages in their regions of origin (Davin 1997, 1999). In the Pearl River delta, some migrant women entered into long-term liaisons with Hong Kong men in a practice of "cross-border polygyny" (Lang and Smart 2002). Among urban Shanghai women in the 1990s, James Farrer (2002) finds pressure to marry up the social scale defined in the terms of the market economy. Since women are the first to be laid off when enterprises downsize, they look to men for material security while simultaneously stressing the importance of emotional expressiveness and connection in making a good match. At the same time, young men under increased pressure to provide for a future wife also need to know how to demonstrate romantic feelings.

Urban women have begun to entertain the possibility of transnational upward mobility through marriage to foreign citizens. In such transactions, Chinese women may represent "traditional" values of support and nurturance to bride-seeking men from other Asian nations (Clark 2001), while overseas Chinese and foreign men represent the possibility of modernity and wealth to urban Chinese women (Ong 1999; Erwin forthcoming). Anxieties about Chinese masculinity and the ability of Chinese men to "master" transnationality by marrying and satisfying white women are aired in popular media productions, eliding the role of Chinese women altogether (Erwin 1999).

Until the 1980s, rural marriage rituals, although somewhat modified from pre-Liberation practices (fewer sedan chairs or religious observances, less elaborate wedding feasts), continued both to feature the transfer of gifts between families and to occasion official exhortations to frugality (Croll 1981). In the reform era, both bride-price and dowry costs have escalated dramatically, often requiring contributions beyond the couple themselves (M. Johnson, Parish, and Lin 1987; Honig and Hershatter 1988; Ocko 1991; Siu 1993; Whyte 1990, 1993; Pasternak and Salaff 1993; Bossen 2002). A disapproving state has framed this development as a resurgence of old customs in a time of new prosperity (Honig and Hershatter 1988; Potter and Potter 1990). Croll (1994) links rising bride prices to the increased need for family labor: when one family gains a daughter-in-law's labor, another loses a daughter's economic contributions. Potter and Potter (1990) attribute more elaborate and expensive weddings to the need to cement kinship ties, which became newly important in the early years of the reforms. Whyte (1990) has determined, however, that the rise in wedding costs in Chengdu began in 1970, well before the current reform-era rise in incomes. Helen Siu argues that the increase in marital payments in the Pearl River delta is no longer about transfers of wealth or declarations of prestige involving the bride's and groom's families but, rather, comprises "the intense and rapid devolution of property to the conjugal couple at the time of marriage itself" (1993: 170). Yunxiang Yan (2002, 2003) confirms this conclusion for rural north China. Here the old practice of marital payments has taken on new meanings, marking the changing relationship between senior generations and their children.

In urban Xi'an, Maris Gillette (2000a, 2000b) notes the adoption during the 1990s of elaborate, rented Western-style wedding gowns among Hui (Muslim) Chinese as well as the Han majority. The selection and display of these gowns is an occasion for brides to define themselves as modern and cosmopolitan through consumption. Gillette also argues that urban Hui women's willingness to wear these gowns bespeaks a lesser degree of involvement with formal Islamic religious practice than that of men.

Revisiting Women's Transition into Married Life

Descriptions of marriage practices across the twentieth century, among both elites and the less affluent, have focused on the patriarchal, patrilocal, and patrilineal features of marriage. Scholars have paid particular attention to the disjuncture marking a woman's move from her natal to marital family (M. Wolf 1972, 1985; Johnson 1983). Much feminist scholarship has explored the disadvantages of this practice for young rural women: it uprooted them from childhood social networks, made them temporary and therefore less-valued members of their natal households, subjected them to a wrenching transition and a period of extreme vulnerability to husbands and in-laws, and in the postrevolutionary period placed constraints on their ability to develop political and social networks that would support them in leadership roles (M. Wolf 1972, 1985; Johnson 1983). At marriage, Rubie Watson (1986) tells us, rural women literally lost their childhood names and were known henceforth mainly by kinship terms, denying them the full personhood attainable by men. Margery Wolf's now-classic (1972) concept of the uterine family, in which women built affective ties to their own children while improving their standing by contributing to the patriline of their marital families, remains an important exploration of daily coping strategies under conditions of patrilocality. Her analysis (1975) of suicide statistics among newly married women in early-twentieth-century Taiwan is a grim reminder that the transition from daughter to daughter-in-law was fraught with emotional and physical danger.

From the Republican period to the present, Croll (1995) argues, girls have anticipated and undergone a major rupture in their lives at the point of marriage. She speculates that this gives rise to a crucial feature of gender difference, "female-specific concepts of both measured and fantasy time" (1995: 6), which has alienated women from political change, itself imagined to take place in linear time advancing toward a glorious future. The cluster of scholarly work on twentieth-century marriage reviewed here, however, read alongside recent work on marriage practices in the late imperial period (Ko 1994; Mann 1997), indicates that we need "to revise what has been portrayed as the lonely, subjugated predicament of women in a major marriage," and acknowledge that women have "contributed their part in shaping marital expectations and the content of accompanying rituals" (Siu 1990: 50).

Marriage practices have not been uniform. In work that ranges from the late imperial period to the recent past, Hill Gates (1989, 1996a) argues that a petty-capitalist mode of production centered on family businesses led to regionally variable marriage forms in which families sought to maximize the returns on young women's labor, and in some cases to commoditize women outright. Arthur Wolf (1975) describes high rates of minor, or "little-daughter-in-law," marriage as reflected in northern Taiwan population registers. He and others find that some version of minor marriage was practiced, if not as commonly, in the Pearl River delta and other areas, where it was associated with poverty (A. Wolf 1975; R. Watson 1994; Hayes 1994).

Arthur Wolf also uses data from Taiwan to discuss uxorilocal marriage, which he argues led to weaker conjugal bonds and higher divorce rates than major marriage (A. Wolf 1975). Uxorilocal marriage, however, has not always been regarded as an inferior practice, as Weijing Lu (1998) suggests in her study of mobility-conscious elites in the lower Yangzi during the eighteenth century. In rural Yunnan, Laurel Bossen (2002) finds that uxorilocal marriage has been practiced for generations without stigma, and that in the reform period it has enabled men to expand their political and economic influence via both natal and marital kinship networks.

Marjorie Topley (1975) describes nineteenth- and early-twentieth-century marriage resistance among women in silk-producing areas of the Canton delta. She links lifelong refusal to marry, as well as various forms of delayed marriage, to employment possibilities for unmarried women in sericulture. Spinster sisterhoods emerged among working women who swore not to marry, announced their vows in rituals similar to those of marriage, and often resided in spinster houses, contributing support to the families of their brothers (Sankar 1984, 1985; Jaschok 1984). When the silk industry collapsed during the depression of the 1930s and the subsequent Japanese invasion, many of these women migrated to Hong Kong and southeast Asia, became domestic servants, and joined Daoist or Buddhist vegetarian halls in which they passed their retirement. Their relationships with one another were sometimes sexual (Sankar 1985).

Janice Stockard (1989) describes a widespread and accepted pattern of delayed-transfer marriage in the Canton delta in which women remained in their natal families for variable but sometimes lengthy periods after marriage, visiting their husbands' families on ritual occasions and contributing to the economy of their natal households by working in the silk industry. In contrast to Topley, she argues that this was not marriage resistance, but rather an alternative set of marriage practices supported by the woman's family and regarded as proper behavior. By the turn of the twentieth century, it could shade over into forms of sanctioned marriage resistance in which a woman negotiated a compensation marriage so that her husband could acquire a secondary wife. Siu (1990) points out that delayed-transfer marriage was practiced in this area well before the advent of mechanized silk production, and that it was common among elite families who had no direct need for their women to generate income. In her reading, delayed-transfer marriage, accompanied by large dowries, was a means for elite families to distinguish themselves from commoners in a process by which earlier non-Han customs "were creatively fused with Confucian practices" (Siu 1990: 52). In the early twentieth century, Siu hypothesizes, delayed-transfer marriage was adapted into a form of marriage resistance by silk-producing women. Studies of women's writings in southern Hunan (Silber 1994; Chiang 1995; F. Liu 2004) suggest that a form of delayed-transfer marriage may have been practiced there as well, and that there too the practice may have been an indicator of non-Han origins or influence. In southeastern Fujian, a variant of the same practice has persisted well into the 1990s in spite of assiduous state attempts to discourage it during the collective period (Friedman 2000, 2006).

Structures of affect and their change over time remain particularly opaque in the scholarship on women, but much of what we do know concerns a woman's transition into marriage. In a study of women's expressive culture in the early-twentieth-century Pearl River delta, Rubie Watson

(1994) describes girls' houses, where girls took up residence from about age ten until marriage. There young women learned "bridal laments, funeral dirges and embroidery styles" (1994: 39), religious and work songs, festival customs, and sometimes literacy skills. Through bridal laments, young women reaffirmed their existence as sisters and daughters, mourned the forthcoming separation from natal family, and actively participated in their own transformation into wives (R. Watson 1996). These laments some-times describe marriage and a woman's separation from family in terms of death and war (Martin 1988). Elizabeth Johnson (1988) points out that weddings and funerals are occasions at which women, but not men, are permitted to articulate their feelings, and the feelings they express deal with concerns specific to their position as women in the family. In her study of women's funeral laments in a New Territories Hakka village in the mid-1970s, Johnson (1988) notes that a woman may take the occasion of lamenting a deceased relative to mourn her own fate and criticize others (including the deceased) for their treatment of her, while presenting her own virtues, much as women do in Hakka bridal laments (Blake 1978). Such laments were orally transmitted and few of them survive. Potter and Potter (1990) found that laments were no longer sung in the Guangdong village where they conducted research in the 1980s, but that marriage was still defined as a wrenching experience for women.

At marriage a bride left friends as well as family. The "women's script" *(nüshu)* written and sometimes sung by women in southern Hunan prior to 1949 (Silber 1994; Chiang 1995; F. Liu 2004; L. Zhao 2004) records *laotong* (lit., "old same") relationships between girls and young women, describing them as formally negotiated non-kin pairings between age-mates from different villages. They were expected to last a lifetime, and their interrup-tion at marriage added to the pain of departure from a network of girlhood attachments. Silber contends that "a reading of village exogamous marriage solely in terms of the way it changes a bride's relationship to her natal fam-ily slights the importance of non-kin social arrangements" (1994: 49). This point is reinforced by descriptions of girls' houses and women's friendships in the delayed-transfer marriage area (Stockard 1989; R. Watson 1994) and the women's *dui pnua* networks of coastal Fujian (Friedman 2006), which permitted affective networks among girls of the same age to flourish. Put another way, formulaic expressions of antipathy to marriage (McLaren 1996, 1999; F. Liu 2004) may well have expressed reluctance to part from peers as well as natal families.

Texts written in women's script yield other messages as well. McLaren (1996, 1998, 1999) finds in them an oral transmission of a women's culture, reinterpreting Confucian norms for women, in which tales of women's abduction feature heroic endurance, virtue, and resistance to male intimidation. Fei-wen Liu (2001) uses *nüshu* and *nüge*, women's songs, to explore the ways that widows negotiated the demands of fidelity to a dead husband and the practical need to produce a son through remarriage or acquire one through adoption.

Ellen Judd's research in north China (1989) calls attention to a practice that was and is far more widespread than delayed-transfer marriage: postmarital dual residence, in which a newly married woman goes back and forth between her natal family *(niangjia)* and marital family, often spending the majority of time in her natal family until her first child is born and continuing to visit frequently even beyond the death of both her parents. Unlike patrilocality but like the uterine family, this fluidity of residence is not given formal articulation; it exists in the interstices of patrilocality and does not actively challenge it. Nevertheless, it is crucial to understanding how women negotiate the profound transition required by patrilocal marriage. As Judd points out, visits to the *niangjia* also secure a daughter's ongoing aid and caregiving for her aging parents, even if her obligations are less than those of a son. On occasions such as the Dragon Boat Festival, Mayfair Yang (1994) finds that gifts exchanged by married women and their natal families play an important role in expanding relationships between villages and lineages. Xiangqun Chang notes the crucial role of non-agnatic (i.e., women-linked) kin in providing social and material support in a famous Jiangsu village, creating networks that combine "the functions of banks and insurance policies" (1999: 172). Potter and Potter (1990) describe networks of women who have married from one village into another, then helped to arrange matches for younger women from the same natal village, while Judd (2005) notes that such matchmaking contributes directly to women's networks.

Marriage Law and Its Discontents

Free-choice marriage was a major theme of the New Culture Movement, which began in 1915 (K. Johnson 1983; McElderry 1986; Z. Wang 1999; Glosser 2002, 2003), and was later codified in Guomindang law (Davin 1976; P. Huang 2001a, 2001b). The Guomindang attempted rural reform campaigns against underage marriages and extravagant weddings through the 1940s, but these were limited in geographic scope and effectiveness (Gilmartin and Crook 2005). In their rural base areas from the 1930s on, including the Jiangxi Soviet and the Shaanganning border region, the Chinese Communist Party (CCP) promulgated marriage reform—freedom of marriage, abolition of purchased brides, minimum marriage age, and divorce under certain specified conditions—as a means to mobilize young men and women and bring women into work outside the household (Belden 1970; Davin 1973, 1976; C. Hu 1974; Hua 1984; Walker 1978). Implementation of all these measures proved difficult throughout the base area period. Peasant men—and their mothers—complained bitterly about the divorce policy of the Communists; in practice, it was subsequently discouraged by local cadres, although it was more commonly permitted again during the Civil War period of the late 1940s (K. Johnson 1983; Hua 1984). When the intellectual agenda of family reform collided with peasant desires, Kay Ann Johnson (1983) and Judith Stacey (1983) have argued, the CCP deferred to the peasants, beginning a series of compromises in party (and later state) policies about women. Arranged marriage remained near-universal in the rural areas and was the dominant form throughout China during the Republican period (Croll 1981).

The 1950 Marriage Law of the PRC abolished "feudal marriage" and "marriage by purchase" and established freedom of choice as a fundamental principle (Meijer 1971; Davin 1976; Ono 1989; Croll 1981; K. Johnson 1983; Stacey 1983; Ocko 1991). The law also asserted the rights of adults to divorce at will. Croll (1981) identifies this intervention as an attempt to transform marriage from an exchange of women between groups, controlled by senior generations, to a personal relationship between individual and equal partners. Friedman adds that the state's emphasis on conjugality was intended to draw married women (and men) out of kinship networks and into "the more encompassing intimate community of the socialist nation" (2005: 313; see also 2006). This important juncture in the transfer of power from older to younger generations helped empower young women in particular, as described by Yunxiang Yan (2003) and others (see, for example, Diamant 2000b).

The radical nature of the changes proposed in the Marriage Law can be partially indexed by the depth of resistance to them. Just as before 1949, these provisions were difficult to implement in rural areas. State authorities soon found that they led to serious resistance on the part of parents and prospective parents-in-law (Davin 1973, 1976; Croll 1981; K. Johnson 1983). A man and his parents, having acquired a wife and daughter-in-law at considerable expense, were disinclined to lose their investment through divorce. Mothers-in-law were among the most vociferous opponents of the Marriage Law. Kay Ann Johnson (1983) argues that that the party-state advanced its marriage reform agenda very tentatively. Aside from a one-month period of intensified publicity for the Marriage Law in March 1953, party officials soon backed away from attempts to enforce the law, particularly when it engendered conflicts with the priorities of land reform and collectivization (Croll 1981). Divorce spiked briefly in 1953 with the campaign to publicize the Marriage Law, remained low throughout the rest of the Mao era, and began to rise with the advent of the economic reforms (Honig and Hershatter 1988; X. Zang 1999).

Recent research by Neil Diamant (2000a, 2000b) takes issue with this earlier scholarship, however, arguing that peasants in particular made active use of the Marriage Law and that its implementation was more protracted and more disruptive of social order than previously understood, extending well beyond the party's campaign. Drawing on local court records and government work reports, he traces the effects of the law up through the Cultural Revolution. Peasants, in spite of the "feudal thinking" attributed to them by the PRC state and most feminist scholarship, appeared less concerned with questions of social standing and privacy than urban dwellers and more willing to seek divorces aggressively. Diamant names the law's main beneficiaries as young rural women and high-level male officials, who acquired younger, more sophisticated wives. Older people, poor men, and soldiers were the losers, in spite of recurrent party-state attempts to protect the marriage stability of military personnel.

Most scholarship on the Marriage Law has tended to assume a high degree of internal unity on the part of the party-state. Where scholars have seen resistance, they have traced it along an assumed fracture between state and society. In addressing assertions by earlier scholars, as well as Chinese government pronouncements, that "the state" had liberated women, they have complicated the picture by suggesting that the state was inconstant in its efforts and that society was full of resisters, particularly local cadres and mothers-in-law (K. Johnson 1983; Stacey 1983; M. Wolf 1985). Yet as Diamant (2000a, 2000b) cogently argues, "the state" was not a uniform entity, and enterprising peasants in particular made effective use of the range of different agencies and jurisdictions to whom they could appeal for divorce. He further notes that the law set into motion effects that state officials could not control, and that local interests could work in favor of marriage reform as well as against it. Where earlier work highlighted the ways in which marriage reform conflicted with land reform, Diamant contends that Marriage Law reform took much of its language and methods from land reform, rather than being undermined by it. Furthermore, women exercised more agency in this situation than the older scholarship suggests. Judd (1998, 2002) corroborates this point, finding that older rural women interviewed in the late 1980s remembered little about the Marriage Law but could retell in some detail how individual women had managed to leave marriages, with the state playing an "indirect, enabling role" in support of women's agency (2002: 7).

Whereas Diamant focuses on the unintended and apparently quite disruptive effects of the Marriage Law, Susan Glosser (2003) argues that the law was intended to bring the domestic realm into closer relationship with the state, not to disrupt it. It was not primarily a means to raise women's status; its central concern was the state's relationship to society. The CCP, she notes, made nation building an explicit part of a couple's marital duties, codifying the May Fourth idea that a reformed family would lead to a strong nation. Philip Huang (2005) characterizes divorce law practice in the 1960s and 1970s, with its focus on a mediation process that forcefully encouraged marital reconciliation, as a core component of what he calls "Maoist justice."

The Marriage Law was successful in raising the age of marriage, broadening a practice that had begun in urban China during the Republican period. By the 1930s, only about 10 percent of urban women were under age fifteen at marriage, and the percentage continued to decline in the PRC (X. Zang 1999). In rural areas, the collective era saw a rise in marriage age to the early twenties (Selden 1993), although there were still eight million new marriages of women under fifteen in 1990, with the number falling to half that four years later (X. Zang 1999: 275).

In 1980 the state promulgated a new Marriage Law, which eliminated references to older practices such as concubinage and raised the age of marriage to twenty-two for men and twenty for women. It made no major departure from the approach of the earlier Marriage Law, but it did mark the beginning of a new round of public education aimed at persistent rural practices such as arranged marriage and bride-price payments (Croll 1985c). Implementation of new articles of divorce in 1990 made divorces easier to obtain (P. Huang 2005). Further revisions to the law in 2001 explained marital property rights and legislated against marital violence (Farrer and Sun 2003; M. Chen 2004). In the reform era, women as plaintiffs have used the courts mainly in marriage and family cases. In a pattern echoing Diamant's findings for the 1950s, intellectuals appeared more reluctant than workers to sue for divorce (Woo 2002).

The Question of Marital Satisfaction

In the reform period, discussions of love, marriage, and sexuality were no longer closely monitored by state authorities, except where criminal activity was involved. Cautionary tales in the popular press discussed prostitution, rape, domestic violence, sexual harassment, concubinage, and other "neotraditional forms of oppression" (X. Xu 1996: 384; see also Jaschok, Milwertz, and Ping-chun Hsiung 2001). But popular journalistic literature *(jishi wenxue)*, radio call-in shows, advice columns, gossip, and personal stories also took up situations where the moral stance was less clear: the search for romantic love (Hooper 1984; Honig and Hershatter 1988; Y. Chen 1994; X. Xu 1996; Farrer 2002), satisfaction or the lack thereof in marriages, and extramarital affairs (Xu 1996; Parish and Farrer 2000; Farrer and Sun 2003; Yuen, Law, and Ho 2004; McDougall 2005; Friedman 2006).

Popular discourse on marriage encompassed a profusion of contradictory themes (Parish and Farrer 2000): women were reportedly both more mercenary and more romantic than men when seeking a mate; husbands were both privileged and henpecked. Drawing on Chinese social surveys from the late 1980s and early 1990s, Parish and Farrer found that when wives' incomes approached those of their husbands (a situation they found to be widespread in urban families), they had more control over household purchasing decisions and stronger beliefs in gender equality. As an urban wife's income increased, so did the time her husband spent on household chores, although her satisfaction with the domestic division of labor did not necessarily rise.

Popular writings, hotlines, and call-in radio programs directed at both urban and rural audiences devoted serious attention to compatibility, sexual satisfaction within marriage and detailed instructions about how to achieve it, and the menace of adultery and how to prevent it (Honig and Hershatter 1988; Jankowiak 1993; Evans 1995, 1997, 2002; X. Xu 1996; Erwin 2000, forthcoming; Farrer and Sun 2003; McDougall 2005). Sexological research, with both statistical and ethnographic components, became a legitimate field of scholarly inquiry (D. Liu et al. 1997; Hershatter 1996; Farquhar 2002). Discussions of middle-aged and older widows in the media urged them to abandon "feudal" attitudes and embrace romance, remarriage, and sexual knowledge and activity, even as ethnographic evidence suggested that the attitudes and practices of older women were quite varied (Shea 2005). Many of these marriage and sexuality discussions highlighted women's purported differences from men in patterns of emotional and sexual satisfaction, and their simultaneous dependence upon men, who alone could provide that satisfaction (X. Xu 1996; Evans 1997, 2000).

By the 1990s, extramarital love was a common theme in news stories and television dramas. Interviews with men and women in Shanghai suggest that participants in such affairs understood them as a product of social change, a legitimate expression of romantic feelings unsullied by material concerns, and a sexual exchange involving indirect compensation from the man to the woman (Farrer and Sun 2003). In this analysis generational differences are more salient than gender differences, shaping relationships to both labor and marriage markets. Although men and women both stressed the centrality of sexual passion in discussing extramarital relationships, they also understood participation in sexual affairs to be a gendered exchange in which, in Farrer and Sun's phrase, "men trade money for sex, and women sex for money" (Farrer and Sun 2003: 16). Such affairs coexisted with a code of family responsibility in which philandering spouses often made significant compromises in order to keep their conjugal households together. Both men and women saw sexual satisfaction as important, but the significance of extramarital affairs in media accounts was gendered in ways that paralleled mate choice for marriage: women sought affairs with men of higher status, while men looked for young and beautiful partners (Farrer and Sun 2003).

As in the Republican period, both male and female anxiety about deception and trickery by sexual partners acted "as public allegories of social relations in the market society" (Farrer and Sun 2003: 17). Devotion to constancy and idealism in romance became a critique of slippery market morality, and irony in storytelling about sex became a means of coping with the storyteller's inability to reach unattainable moral standards.

Equally a topic of public discussion was the rise in divorces, almost two-thirds of which were initiated by women, often on grounds of incompatibility or the desire for greater fulfillment (X. Xu 1996; Parish and Farrer 2000; Xiong 2004). At the same time, divorce was often portrayed as disadvantageous to women, particularly when it was preceded by a man's extramarital involvement with a younger, more attractive "third party." Women's Federation officials and emergent women's organizations found themselves divided over whether to push for punitive measures against men and their "third-party" partners, or to encourage women to leave unsatisfactory relationships as a sign of self-respect (Honig and Hershatter 1988; X. Xu 1996; Farrer and Sun 2003).

FAMILY

Much sociological literature (usefully surveyed in X. Zang 1999) takes the family or household rather than women or gender relations as the unit of analysis. The findings in this literature, nevertheless, have profound implications for the analysis of women's lives. They suggest important temporal lags but not fundamental divergence between urban and rural patterns.

Overall, this literature on the family indicates that whereas the state may not have transformed marriage and family practices by edict, state policies on collectivization and decollectivization have contributed to long-term changes in rural household composition and relationships. Younger women are among the chief beneficiaries of these changes; older women, perhaps, are the neglected remainder.

Household Composition and Family Power

The extended or joint family—patrilocal, patrilineal, and multigenerational—remained a powerful ideal at least until the establishment of the PRC (Croll 1985a). A woman's status in the family rose with the birth of children, particularly sons (Croll 1985a, 1994), who formed the core of her affective life and old-age support—her uterine family—even as they reproduced the patriline (M. Wolf 1972). Nevertheless, in spite of the power of this cultural ideal and its practice by those who could afford it, joint families did not predominate in the Republican period. Croll (1985a) offers a brief survey of the literature establishing this point.

During the New Culture Movement, radical critics blamed the patriarchal joint family for many of China's ills, saying that it thwarted individual development, promoted a slave mentality, perpetuated generational and gender hierarchies, monopolized people's loyalties, and prevented interest in wider social and national issues (Schwarcz 1986; Glosser 2002, 2003). Nuclear families built on free-choice companionate marriage were promoted in May Fourth and New Culture writings as the key to both individual happiness and the building of a strong nation. Although the desired form of the family had changed, Republican-era writings reinscribed its centrality to social order. They closely linked equality for women to family reform and national regeneration, but primarily reflected the economic and identity concerns of urban educated men (Glosser 2002, 2003).

From the New Culture period through the 1930s, the family envisioned by educated male reformers depended heavily on a gendered division of labor in which women's domestic roles were written into modernity. In 1930s urban periodicals such as *Family Weekly* [Jiating xingqi], the nuclear family became the site of modern urban consumption, the cornerstone of economic health, and the place where women contributed to the nation by creating a comfortable and nurturing environment for husband and children (Glosser 1995, 2003). Emphasis on the home, however, did not always connote a desire for the modern. The Ningbo community in Shanghai, a native-place group prominent in the business elite as well as in white-collar and artisanal jobs, prided itself through the 1940s on a cult of domesticity in which women did not go out to work, which Ningbo people explained by reference to Confucian womanly virtues (Mann 1994).

Across the twentieth century, nuclear families have become the dominant urban family form (Whyte and Parish 1984; Jankowiak 1993; X. Zang 1999). In rural areas, meanwhile, the revolution brought enough stability that more poor men could afford to marry, resolving the rural family crisis brought on by years of war and class stratification (K. Johnson 1983; Stacey 1983). From the 1950s on, collectivization undermined households as units of production and inheritance while leaving the practice of virilocal marriage intact (Croll 1985a; K. Johnson 1983; Selden 1993; Y.Yan 2003). Throughout the collective period, family heads lost a degree of economic control, and family division became easier (Pasternak and Salaff 1993; Diamant 2000b; Y. Yan 2003). Mark Selden (1993) finds nuclear families and smaller family size to be the pattern in rural northern China during the collective era; Parish and Whyte (1978) cite similar findings for Guangdong in southern China. Yet even as the composition of the household slowly changed, the network of extended male kin remained important in ways that both facilitated collectivization and disadvantaged rural women. Collectives generally comprised groups of male relatives and their households, reconstituting lineage ties and making it difficult for women to attain positions of responsibility, especially because women continued to marry out of their natal communities (Diamond 1975; K. Johnson 1983; Stacey 1983).

In spite of the long ascendance of the nuclear family, Whyte (1993) finds patrilocal residence rising again in several urban areas under the reforms, perhaps because of changing economic pressures. Under socialism and its successor, market socialism, people have needed family and an extended web of family connections to help negotiate jobs, housing, and access to services. Thus, urban parents have sometimes remained involved in the postmarital living arrangements of their children, even as their role in mate choice has diminished. Meanwhile, under the reforms, neolocal residence (establishing a new residence separate from either family after marriage) is increasing in the countryside, as is delayed childbearing, bringing urban and rural practices into closer alignment (Selden 1993; X. Zang 1999; Riley 1997). In wealthy areas of the countryside such as Zhejiang, women have been demanding construction of a mansion for neolocal residence as a condition of marriage (Sargeson 2004). Selden (1993), however, also notes a rise in stem and joint families among rural entrepreneurs, perhaps paralleling Whyte's findings among urban families. And Croll describes the formation of what she calls "the aggregate family" (1994: 173), an arrangement in which patrilateral or affinal networks of kin living separately pool resources and labor to maximize opportunities. Although families may be dividing more rapidly than before, she suggests, the division is not complete; families who cook separately may own property jointly and cooperate in economic activities.

Household division means, among other things, that mothers-in-law and daughters-in-law no longer routinely live together as they did before 1949 and in the early years of collectivization. Daughters-in-law have more independence, although if they work outside the home, the mother-in-law often becomes the primary provider of child care. In general, Judd (1994) observes, household division at marriage contributes to the increasing power of the younger generation, and is partly a shift in generational rather than gendered power.

Yunxiang Yan (2003) also sees a rural shift in power since 1949 to younger generations, who enjoy a degree of autonomy that their elders never experienced. With the rise of the rural conjugal family, involving increased intimacy and joint decision making by married couples, he describes a "waning of the patriarchal order" (Y. Yan 2003: 218; see also Sargeson 2004) and the emergence of an ethos of individual development in which emotion, personal desires, familial affection, and the expression of opinion are emphasized. This shift, Yan suggests, has particularly changed the lives of young rural women. In a major challenge to many anthropologically based social histories, Yan urges scholars to rethink the "corporate model" of the Chinese family, which stresses its economic functions, and to pay more attention to individuals and their relationships within families, particularly in heretofore relatively opaque rural households.

The shift in social emphasis from family to conjugal ties is not uniformly celebrated. In urban areas, elderly women worry about insufficient retirement income and rising health-care costs (Y. Liu 2004). Although the 1980 Marriage Law requires that both sons and daughters take responsibility for the care of aging parents, documents from the collective era and more recent accounts of rural fieldwork frequently mention complaints by the elderly that their children provide insufficient material or emotional support (Siu 1993; Diamant 2000b; Hershatter 2003, 2005a; Shea 2005). It appears that previous expectations of reciprocal support between generations are under challenge, to the general disadvantage of the older generation (Y. Yan 2002, 2003; Sargeson 2004)—a majority of whom are widowed women. Yan calls this a "crisis of filial piety" (Y. Yan 2003: 218). He suggests that the state—through its policies of deemphasizing the family's functions, promoting marriage and family reform, installing formal bureaucracies to replace rule by kinship networks, and constraining the

development of nongovernmental social organizations—has unintention-
ally contributed to "the formation of the uncivil individual" responsible
only to himself or herself (2003: 16).

Women, Law, and Family Property

For the first two decades of the Republican period, civil law continued to
be based on the Qing code, taking the patrilineal family as the social unit,
until the Guomindang Civil Code of 1929–30 established the importance
of the individual for legal purposes (P. Huang 2001a, 2001b). Women in
the Qing code were granted what Huang calls "passive agency" to endure
or resist abuse, and were sometimes held criminally liable if their resistance (to rape, for example) was deemed insufficient. In contrast, the new
Guomindang law regarded women "as fully autonomous and active agents"
(P. Huang 2001a: 11), able like men to control their own marriage choices,
inherit property (Bernhardt 1999), and seek divorce. Patrilineal succession,
which the Guomindang lawmakers regarded as "feudal," was no longer to
be a valid basis for legal claims to property. Instead, for legal purposes, kinship was to be organized into "relatives by blood" (maternal and paternal
alike), "relatives by marriage," and spouses (Bernhardt 1999).

Kathryn Bernhardt (1994; see also Croll 1980) finds that in urban China
the law substantially increased women's access to divorce, even though a
gap existed between code and practice. Divorce was available by mutual
consent and on the grounds of spousal and familial cruelty, desertion, and
adultery. In protecting the rights of concubines not to be expelled, however,
the law also made it difficult for wives to get rid of concubines without
divorcing their husbands.

Huang argues that the Republican code as well as custom and legal
practice deprived women of protection even as it granted them new rights.
Working as a prostitute, being sold without overt coercion, or remarrying
as a widow, for instance, were assumed to be a woman's choice, regardless
of the material constraints or actions by relatives that might have put her
in these situations. Furthermore, the Guomindang code's stipulation that
husbands and wives had an obligation to cohabit was sometimes used to
force unhappy or abused wives to remain with their husbands rather than
taking refuge in their natal homes (P. Huang 2001a, 2001b). Similarly,
Bernhardt (1999) shows that daughters, in spite of equal inheritance rights
(see also Ocko 1991), found these rights undercut when fathers continued
the widespread social practice of dividing their property among their sons
prior to their deaths. In the Republican period, women brought into mar-

riage some property of their own, including personal goods, gifts, and previously earned income. The Guomindang Civil Code of 1930 gave women the right to manage this property independent of their husbands (Ocko 1991). Yet although married women might maintain some control over cash gifts they received at marriage and might augment this fund with earnings from waged work or sidelines, their claims on family property were limited (R. Watson 1984).

Widows, deprived by the code of the right to designate a patrilineal successor for their husbands, found themselves with reduced custodial control over family property; now they were just one among many possible heirs and were often pitted against their own children. Widowed daughters-in-law were in even worse straits, with neither custodial nor inheritance rights (Bernhardt 1999). No one has studied the situation of widows in the PRC, but Christina Gilmartin (1990) notes that widows in reform-era rural China still had difficulty claiming family property.

Although the Marriage Law of 1950 allowed women to hold formal title to land, effective control of a family's landholdings remained with heads of household, who were usually male (Diamond 1975; Bossen 1999). Women were equally entitled to family property (sharing that right with their brothers in natal families and their husbands in marital families), but since the main form of property after collectivization was housing and household goods and since women married out, in practice inheritances generally went to sons. In short, women had little control over property (Davin 1988, 1989). Women who attempted to claim their land after a divorce were often met with violence (Davin 1976). Parish and Whyte (1978) found that in cases of divorce in rural Guangdong during the collective era, wives did not fare well in issues of child custody or property division.

The Marriage Law of 1980 strengthened the community property status of all goods acquired during a marriage (Ocko 1991). A new inheritance law passed in 1985 specified protection of the inheritance rights of daughters, including married ones (Davin 1988; Ocko 1991), although its actual effects on inheritance practices have not been studied.

Marriage itself, Jonathan Ocko (1991) argues, moved in the twentieth century from a form of family property first to a form of personal property in which a marriage "belonged" to the married couple even if the husband had greater rights than the wife, then (after 1949) to a form of social property in which the state had a primary stake. Tensions between the notions of personal and social property continue to shape state approaches to divorce (Diamant 2000b; P. Huang 2005).

Birth Planning and the One-Child Family Policy

Fertility rates for the early twentieth century have been estimated at five to six births per woman (Banister 1987). Missionaries decried female infanticide, but disagreed as to its prevalence (B. Lee 1981). The Republican penal code and other government regulations outlawed infanticide, but rural fieldwork reports from the 1930s often found lopsided sex ratios that pointed to preferential treatment of sons, if not direct infanticide of girls (B. Lee 1981). In periods of social upheaval, such as the Japanese invasion and the Civil War, demographic data suggest that female infanticide or neglect of girl babies rose (Banister 1987). The Marriage Law of 1950 reiterated the prohibition on infanticide (B. Lee 1981), and census data indicate that female infanticide and neglect decreased in the early years of the PRC (Banister 1987).

From the mid-1950s on, party-state planners mentioned population as an important area of policy-making, with an emphasis on health and welfare (Kane 1985; T. White 1994; Greenhalgh and Winckler 2005). In the 1950s, women within the party argued against an unalloyed pronatalist policy and for access to birth control and abortion (T. White 1994). Access to abortion was eased, although not without objection from health-care providers concerned about the strain on the medical system (Tien 1987). By the middle of the decade, the top party leadership, worried about rapid population growth, endorsed birth control, but this approach was soon transformed into a doctrine of state-controlled birth planning (Banister 1987; T. White 1994; Greenhalgh and Winckler 2005).

In the first two decades of the PRC, most state efforts in the countryside centered on improving women's reproductive health through the training of midwives (Davin 1975b, 1976; Banister 1987; J. Goldstein 1998), rather than on family planning. Fertility planning was encouraged but was generally voluntary, with decision making left to the family (Croll 1985b; Banister 1987). The rural health infrastructure set up in the 1960s during the Cultural Revolution made it possible for the first time to deliver IUDs, tubal ligations, and more rarely vasectomies to the rural population (Chen 1985; Banister 1987). Collectivization offered no particular economic incentive to limit family size (Davin 1985; Bianco and Hua 1988; for a somewhat different view, see Salaff 1973, 1985), but rural interviews suggest that birth control was greeted with relief by women exhausted by the demands of large families (Pasternak and Salaff 1993; Hershatter 2002, 2003, 2005a). By the 1970s, the government had begun a national effort to lower the birth rate via a policy of "later, longer, fewer," and the 1970s saw a dramatic reduction in the birth rate, even prior to the one-child campaign (Parish and Whyte 1978; Chen 1985; Croll 1985b; Banister 1987; Tien 1987; Greenhalgh and Winckler 2005). But until the late 1970s, state-sponsored birth planning continued to be framed primarily in terms of women's liberation, health, and the education of children, rather than national survival (Potter 1985; Greenhalgh 1990).

In 1979, the Chinese government moved to the goal of one child per Han family (Croll 1985a; Davin 1985; Kane 1985, 1987; Banister 1987; Greenhalgh 1990; Greenhalgh and Winckler 2005), with more children allowed to non-Han families (Pasternak and Salaff 1993). The government argued that if drastic steps were not taken to limit fertility, the needs of a burgeoning population would not be met, national development strategy would be undermined, and terrible suffering would result (Potter 1985; Croll 1985a; Tien 1985, 1987; Bianco and Hua 1988; Potter and Potter 1990; Greenhalgh 2003). The policy was crucially shaped by government visions of "achieving wealth, modernity, and global power through selective absorption of Western science and technology" (Greenhalgh 2003: 164; see also Greenhalgh and Winckler 2005), in this case the development of a population science linked to politics. Birth planning was mentioned as a state concern and a citizen's duty in the 1978 and 1982 Constitutions, the 1980 Marriage Law, and the 1992 Law on the Protection of Rights and Interests of Women, but its implementation has been based on local laws and regulations rather than on a national population law (Tien 1987; Milwertz 1997). Fertility rates, which in 1971 had been 5.442, dropped by 1980 to 2.238 (P. Chen 1985; Banister 1987). By 1993, the national leadership was able to claim that the birth rate had fallen below replacement levels, to 1.9 births per woman (Greenhalgh, Zhu, and Li 1994; Greenhalgh 2001). By the mid-1990s it ranged from about 1.8 to 2.0 children per woman (Greenhalgh and Li 1995), and held steady at approximately 1.7 for the next decade (Hesketh, Li, and Zhu 2005). From the late 1970s on, abortion played an important role in this decline, although contraception and sterilization were arguably more important—abortion rates were below those of Eastern Europe (Tien 1987) and, as of the early 2000s, well below those of the United States (Hesketh, Li, and Zhu 2005). Some abortions were performed on unmarried women, who were not formal targets of the birth planning campaign and did not have regular access to birth control (Tien 1987).

The success of this policy in the cities has been attributed to several factors. The state could provide effective incentives and penalties in the urban environment (Croll 1985b; Tien 1987; Milwertz 1997). Urban families live in crowded housing conditions (Banister 1987; T. White 2003), rely on pensions in addition to children for old-age support (Davis-Friedmann 1985; T. White 2003), and have devised mobility strategies relying on education and work connections rather than on extended family ties (Salaff 1973, 1985; Kane 1985, 1987; Croll 1985a, 1985b; Milwertz 1997). Urban women who work in family businesses (Gates 1993) and women more generally who find the rising costs and effort of raising children quite demanding (Milwertz 1997) have been quite explicit about their desire to limit childbearing. Many of them would prefer a less restrictive policy of two children, with one boy and one girl as an ideal configuration (Gates 1993; Milwertz 1997). Cecilia Milwertz (1997) finds that any given woman might express conflicting opinions, depending upon whether she felt herself to be speaking from her own perspective, that of her child, her family, or the nation. Yet overall, urban families are regarded by scholars as having made the "demographic shift" in which unlimited childbearing no longer improves chances for survival and upward mobility.

In the countryside, by contrast, the one-child policy collided with the re-emergence of the household as a fundamental unit of production; the dismantling of rudimentary collective welfare guarantees; the emergence of peasant households wealthy enough to pay hefty fines for excess births; and a general weakening of state control over peasant mobility, income, activities, and its own local branches (Wasserstrom 1984; Potter 1985; Croll 1985c; Davin 1985; Davis-Friedmann 1985; Dalsimer and Nisonoff 1987; Greenhalgh 1990, 1993; Potter and Potter 1990; T. White 2003). Since viri-locality continued to be the dominant marriage pattern through collectiv-ization and decollectivization, farming families had immediate practical reasons to value sons over daughters, who would leave the family and the community at marriage (Robinson 1985). With the weakening of the col-lective, families expected to rely almost exclusively upon their sons for old-age support, although the Marriage Law of 1980 held sons, daughters, and grandchildren alike responsible for care of the elderly (Potter 1985; Mu 1999). Potter (1985) suggests that peasants regarded not having enough sons for old-age support to be a moral as well as a practical failure, making the attainment of happiness impossible. In some areas, reform-era land contracting practices meant that when a daughter married out, her family lost her land allotment, further strengthening the preference for sons (Judd 1994; Bossen 2002).

The disturbing results of these conflicting pressures and desires have been well-documented in a substantial body of scholarship. Local state authorities, required to meet birth planning quotas mandated at higher levels, intermittently adopted draconian and coercive measures—fines, late-term abortions, sterilization, insertion and monitoring of IUDs—to enforce birth planning goals (Potter 1985; Croll 1985a; Davin 1985; Banister 1987; Bianco and Hua 1988; Potter and Potter 1990; Greenhalgh 1994; Greenhalgh and Winckler 2005). In rural areas, enforcement initially fell to the women's team leaders, although party and local government leaders increasingly participated in birth planning committees, a sign of the importance that the state attached to this campaign (Davin 1985). In the early years of the one-child policy, some cadres responsible for birth planning were targets of community retaliation (Wasserstrom 1984; Banister 1987; Bianco and Hua 1988; Greenhalgh and Winckler 2005). Women fled their local areas to conceal pregnancies, and families as well as local officials underreported births (Banister 1987; Greenhalgh 1994; T. White 2003). Women were also subjected to spousal and family abuse for giving birth to girl children (Wasserstrom 1984; Croll 1985c; Tien 1985; Anagnost 1988; Honig and Hershatter 1988; Bianco and Hua 1988; Gilmartin 1990), leading to a belated but energetic state attempt to educate rural masses both about who carries the Y chromosome and about the legal rights of women and children (Wasserstrom 1984; Croll, Davin, and Kane 1985; Tien 1985; Anagnost 1988; Honig and Hershatter 1988; Croll 1994, 1995).

Other peasant reactions to the policy included refusal to pay fines, bribery of officials, and refusal to contracept, generally by removing IUDs (Wasserstrom 1984; Bianco and Hua 1988; Davin 1990; Greenhalgh 1993, 1994; Greenhalgh and Li 1995; Bossen 2002). They also included formal and informal adopting out of girls, or what Greenhalgh and her colleagues call "the feminization of adoption" (Greenhalgh 1994; Greenhalgh, Zhu, and Li 1994; K. Johnson 2004), abandonment (K. Johnson 1993, 1996, 2004; K. Johnson, Huang, and Wang 1998), and female infanticide or selective neglect (Banister 1987; Hom 1992; Croll 1994). Research in Guangdong, however, suggests that female infanticide was regarded as immoral and uncivilized, something that happened in "remote areas" (Potter 1985; Potter and Potter 1990). By the 1990s ultrasound followed by sex-selective abortion had become the preferred strategy to ensure that families would be able to try again for a son (Greenhalgh, Zhu, and Li 1994; Greenhalgh and Li 1995; Chu 2001; Eckholm 2002; T. White 2003; Hesketh, Li, and Zhu 2005; Greenhalgh and Winckler 2005). In the past few years, farmers have also begun to use the courts to appeal excessive enforcement of the policy (T. White 2003).

Since the advent of the one-child campaign, national and regional population statistics show disturbing imbalances in reported sex ratios at birth. In the 1953 and 1964 censuses, prior to the birth planning campaigns, the ratio was close to "normal," conventionally set at 106:100 (K. Johnson 1993). But by 1989, it was 113:100 and in 2000 117:100 (Greenhalgh and Li 1995; Eckholm 2002; see also Banister 1987). The imbalance characterizes both urban and rural China (Hesketh, Li, and Zhu 2005), but is often much higher in rural counties and in certain provinces: in 2000 a ratio of more than 120:100 was reported in Guangdong, Guangxi, Hunan, Hubei, Shaanxi, and Anhui, with Hainan Island reporting a rate of 135.7:100 (Eckholm 2002). The sex ratio for second-order births was 151.9:100 in 2000 (T. White 2003). By the mid-1990s, so-called missing girls were estimated to total more than 1 million per year (K. Johnson 1996, 2004); Croll mentions a total estimate of the missing as 40 million (1995: 164; see also Croll 2000).

Official pronouncements generally represented these facts as a sign of backwardness or remnants of feudal thinking among the rural masses, with little attention to the ways in which rural reform policies directly contributed to these patterns or the broader issues of how "cultural values" are made and remade under shifting historical circumstances (Wasserstrom 1984; Anagnost 1988; Honig and Hershatter 1988; K. Johnson 1993; Greenhalgh and Li 1995). Such backwardness then became the target of local campaigns aimed at both stopping the violence and reinforcing the birth planning quotas (Anagnost 1988).

Abandonment of female infants has been estimated at several hundreds of thousands yearly, and is associated with high mortality rates (K. Johnson 1993, 1996; K. Johnson, Huang, and Wang 1998). In Hunan and Hubei, infant abandonment, reportedly common prior to 1949, has reemerged (K. Johnson 1993, 1996, 2004). In Hunan alone, 16,000 abandoned children, 92 percent of them girls, were brought to civil affairs offices from 1986 to 1990. Kay Ann Johnson, Banghan Huang, and Liyao Wang (1998) found that in 237 families who had abandoned children, almost 90 percent of those abandoned were girls; the small number of abandoned boys were often ill or disabled. Second and third daughters with no brothers were the most likely to be abandoned; families usually did not abandon the first girl born to them, and many left children at the doorsteps of people who might be likely to adopt them.

Kay Ann Johnson (1996) argues that local cadres, faced with conflicting pressure from higher levels of government and their local communities, monitored family size rather than births, ignoring or sometimes even abetting abandonment that took unwanted children out of their jurisdiction. Welfare centers and orphanages, meanwhile, were inadequate in number and quality to deal with the rising number of foundlings. Legal adoption procedures were so cumbersome—partly because state authorities wanted to block informal adoptions as a way of getting rid of daughters—that many families gave up the effort. When state authorities discussed infant abandonment, they generally proposed punishing the parents for violation of birth planning quotas, rather than attending to the ways in which birth planning itself contributed to the problem, considering the immediate interests of abandoned children, or easing restrictions on adoption. The 1992 adoption law, for instance, allowed only childless couples over the age of 35 to adopt, and families who already had children could be fined for adopting informally, as though they had produced an over-quota birth. The rate of official adoptions nationally remained low, and informal adoptions predominated in spite of the penalties. Difficulties in obtaining household registrations for adopted children meant that the (mostly female) children who survived abandonment and were adopted did not have full legal protection or access to social services. Nevertheless, many abandoned girls were apparently informally adopted, partly in order to provide families who already had sons with a desired daughter as well (K. Johnson 1996, 2004; K. Johnson, Huang, and Wang 1998). In 1998 a revised adoption law was passed, lowering the age of prospective adoptive parents to thirty and removing the requirement that they be childless if adopting abandoned children (Families with Children from China 1999; K. Johnson 2004).

As third-order births became less common, second-order births were the most vulnerable to sex selection (Chu, 2001; Hesketh, Li, and Zhu 2005). In an unnamed county in central China in 2000, Junhong Chu (2001) found that almost half of pregnant women used ultrasounds to determine the sex of the fetus, usually in the second trimester or later, and 92 percent of all families who already had a daughter opted for an abortion if they learned that a fetus was female. This may not be atypical, since by that time ultrasound-B machines were common in county and township hospitals, family planning stations, and private clinics. Technically illegal, the practice of using ultrasound for sex determination is almost impossible to regulate, and skewed sex ratios have spread along with ultrasound machines from coastal to inland provinces. While most of the women surveyed felt that sex-selective abortion was unfair to girls, they did not regard it as immoral, arguing that life begins at birth (Chu 2001). As Susan Greenhalgh puts it, "The politics of gender had not so much eased as been pushed back into the period before birth" (Greenhalgh and Winckler 2005: 216–217).

Population policy was not determined exclusively at the center, nor was it impervious to wider changes set in motion by the economic reforms (Bianco and Hua 1988; Greenhalgh 1990, 1993; Greenhalgh and Winckler 2005). Over the course of the 1980s and into the early twenty-first century, state birth-planning goals were modified repeatedly, with initiatives taken by different levels of government at different moments (Banister 1987; Davin 1990; Potter and Potter 1990; Croll 1994; Greenhalgh 1994; Greenhalgh and Winckler 2005). Susan Greenhalgh and Edwin Winckler (2005) have characterized these changes as follows: A Maoist approach combining central planning and periodic intensive campaigns was, paradoxically, only fully applied to birth planning in the era of Deng Xiaoping. Under Jiang Zemin, and particularly from 1993 to 2003, the government continued to try to manage population growth, but increasingly turned to law rather than direct intervention as the preferred means. Since Hu Jintao's accession to power in 2003, the emphasis has been on coercion rather than rewards, and on social policies intended to decrease reliance on children for old-age security.

Behind these changes lay a complex process of political negotiation with the rural population. Even during an initial period of coercive enforcement and local resistance from 1979 to 1983—when women were pressured into coerced abortions and tubal ligations, while families who proceeded with an out-of-plan pregnancy had their houses sealed—the conditions under which a family could have a second child were steadily expanded. The period from 1984 to 1987 was one of negotiation and state accommodation in which two children were permitted—sometimes more children were allowed if both were girls—in an effort to enable each family to have a son. When fertility surged in the late 1980s and early 1990s, the policy tightened. At some points, families with only one child, if it was a son, were not permitted to try again, while families with a daughter could attempt to have a son after four years. The major change was not in rules but in consistency of enforcement (Davin 1990; Greenhalgh 1990, 2001; Greenhalgh, Zhu, and Li 1994; Greenhalgh and Li 1995; Greenhalgh and Winckler 2005). Not until 2002 was a national Population and Family Planning Law put into effect (T. White 2003).

By the early 1990s, state practices were much more refined than the coercive roundups of a decade earlier, giving more attention to women's health and reproductive choice. In Shaanxi, party secretaries were brought into birth planning work; provincial funds enabled better pay for birth planning cadres, with pay tied to performance. These cadres established Birth Planning Associations (*jihua shengyu xiehui*), with monthly study sessions. For families with two or more children, sterilization and IUD insertion were linked to regular gynecological exams and carried on at predictable intervals. Localities began to offer old-age pensions for couples with two daughters. Families who refused to pay fines for second or third births outside the plan found their "excess" children ineligible for crop land or housing land at marriage until the fines were paid. At the same time, the development and diversification of the rural economy in wealthier areas and a rise in per capita income decreased the pressure to have more sons and increased the emphasis on educating children to take advantage of new economic opportunities (Greenhalgh, Zhu, and Li 1994). In addition, wealth opened up options for families who did decide to have more children. In 2000, one study in central China found that couples with a girl could buy a second-birth permit for 4,000 yuan. Couples with a boy, while officially not allowed a second child, could often pay the local government about 12,000 yuan to register a second child after he or she was born (Chu 2001).

In the course of the 1980s and 1990s, then, a policy that had begun as gender neutral—one child per family—became deeply inflected by gender preference: a son for as many families as possible (Davin 1990; Greenhalgh and Li 1995; T. White 2003; Greenhalgh and Winckler 2005). Resistance was gender specific as well: when the policy was enforced more strictly, the sex ratio of reported births became more unbalanced. Boys were also breastfed longer, prefiguring a pattern of discrimination against girls "in cultural attention, social investment, and economic opportunity" (Greenhalgh and Li 1995: 633)—one which echoes, disturbingly, the practices common before 1949 (Croll 1985a). In short, sex ratios, adoption, and breastfeeding, which had been relatively gender neutral in the first decades of the PRC, all became active sites of gender discrimination during the reform period.

Susan Greenhalgh and Jiali Li (1995) point to a lack of nuanced attention paid to these matters among demographers, using the China case to call for a feminist demography and attention to reproduction as social and political rather than "natural" and private. Likewise, Sharon Hom suggests that female infanticide must be understood not as a private and proscribed act of violence, but as part of a systemic devaluation of female life that also includes forced abortion, abuse of wives who bear daughters, and giving male offspring preferred access to food. She terms this "social femicide" (1992: 260).

How many children a woman should bear and the disposition of an individual pregnancy have not been understood in Chinese discussions as a woman's individual reproductive choice or as a religious issue but, rather, as a matter that affects and is legitimately affected by the family and the state (Potter 1985; M. Wolf 1985; Potter and Potter 1990; Greenhalgh 1994; Wong 1997). Whereas earlier writing on this topic presented rural women as caught between the conflicting demands of the family for more children and the state for fewer (M. Wolf 1985), recent scholarship (see, for example, Greenhalgh and Li 1995; Milwertz 1997) suggests that the major conflict is between the party-state and society as a whole, with women generally aligned with their families. This does not mean, however, that women have no opinions on the matter. Greenhalgh and others have argued that the reproductive desires of village women are not driven by an undifferentiated cultural preference for more offspring, but are finely calibrated to create a family whose gender and age structure will satisfy a mix of practical and affective needs: old-age support, income maximization, and emotional intimacy. The rising costs of raising children, bringing in brides for sons, and building houses for sons and their families all constrained the desire for many children in the reform-era countryside (Greenhalgh 1994; Greenhalgh and Li 1995; Mu 1999; Chu 2001). Junhong Chu (2001) suggests that since ultrasound and sex selection allow families to have a son with fewer births, desire for large families has waned. In central Shaanxi, Greenhalgh and Li found that 86 percent of the nearly 1,000 women they surveyed wanted two children: a boy to carry on the family line, support his parents in their old age, and bring in income through his labor, and a girl (though this was a weaker preference) to provide company and affection (Greenhalgh and Li 1995; see also Greenhalgh 1993; K. Johnson, Huang, and Wang 1998; K. Johnson 2004). Adoptive families gave similar reasons, seeking girls to provide emotional connections rather than to become daughters-in-law or household servants, as was often the case in female adoptions before 1949 (K. Johnson, Huang, and Wang 1998; K. Johnson 2004). Some interviewees implied that multiple sons would only fall to fighting over who was responsible for parental support. Unfilial behavior of all sorts, including economic neglect, was a frequent complaint of aging parents, as was divisive behavior by daughters-in-law (Greenhalgh, Zhu, and Li 1994; Greenhalgh and Li 1995; Hershatter 2005a). At the same time, a rise in intravillage marriage has made daughters physically and emotionally more available, although their material obligations to parents are fewer than those of sons.

After 1994, when China participated in the International Conference on Population and Development in Cairo, and 1995, when it hosted the Fourth World Conference on Women (Hershatter, Honig, and Rofel 1996; Z.Wang 1997), the grounds for discussion of population policy within China shifted somewhat. The State Birth Planning Commission began to raise questions about women's health. Researchers in various quarters, while declaring support for the state's determination to limit population growth, voiced increasing criticisms of the deleterious effects of the birth planning program on girls and women, the burden that it placed on women to prevent pregnancy, and the need to improve educational access and women's status as an integral part of birth planning (Wong 1997; T. White 2003). Population researchers suggested a need for improved reproductive knowledge and contraception supply for a growing population of unmarried and sexually active women migrant workers (Z. Zheng et al. 2001). With central government support, various localities experimented with improving the quality of care, an initiative that reduced coercion, improved compliance and sex ratios, and was eventually more widely adopted in the early 2000s with the policy known as Comprehensive Reform. In 2004, Shanghai officially promulgated a two-child rule, although the national government has so far declined to adopt this change more broadly. Meanwhile the Hu Jintao administration has undertaken policy initiatives to support elderly couples who had only one child and to address the sex ratio imbalance (Greenhalgh and Winckler 2005).

In general, like official state discourse, these critics paid more attention to the effects on adult women, which were certainly serious, than to the question of the "missing girls," for which demographic data were not widely reported in China (Greenhalgh 2001). Official publications also contained detailed discussions about the coming marriage crunch for men caused by the shortage of women and about the rise in trafficking of women to compensate for local shortages of brides (Honig and Hershatter 1988; Chu 2001). Most critics appeared to share the state's assumptions that the one-child policy is the only alternative to no policy at all; alternative birth planning policies are little discussed (Greenhalgh 2001).

Tensions in the state apparatus compounded the state's inability to put women's welfare at the center of the birth planning problem. Officials of the All-China Women's Federation mistrusted the State Birth Planning Commission, and were unwilling to assist in a policy that they felt did not represent women's interests (Greenhalgh 2001). At the same time, local women's cadres in rural areas were stuck with the unenviable, psychologically difficult, and sometimes dangerous task of enforcing state birth planning targets (Anagnost 1997)—an arrangement troubling to individual cadres and much resented by the Women's Federation (Potter 1985; Greenhalgh 2001). No government agency was willing or able to take up all aspects of women's reproductive health, especially when that health was itself threatened by the birth planning policy (Greenhalgh 2001).

Outside of Han-dominant areas, state policy moved from no limits on minority births to mandating a limit of two births in urban areas and three in rural areas. Little systematic research has been done on the intersection of state birth-planning policy and local practices in minority areas. One survey of rural Tibet in the 1990s indicates that birth quotas have not been effectively enforced but that rising costs and shrinking land per capita have led many rural families to begin voluntary contraception, although women indicate that they want three or four children if the family can afford it (M. Goldstein et al. 2002).

The valorization of scientific and technical know-how as a sign of modernity has contributed to a telling anomaly: in a nation where the official goal is to limit births to one per family, test-tube babies are celebrated and urban women who do not conceive can find themselves under tremendous pressure to undergo expensive fertility treatments. Handwerker (1995a, 1995b, 1998), in a 1990 ethnographic study of infertile women in Beijing, finds that the demographic surveys conducted in conjunction with the family planning campaign help to create a powerful norm—the fertile woman—from which infertile women deviate. Motherhood remains normative, the defining characteristic of adult womanhood. Childless couples observe that families with one child are eligible for various rewards not available to the childless; one woman told Lisa Handwerker, "the one-child policy is really the 'you must have one-child policy' " (1998: 183). Since 1985, infertility clinics have been established in many hospitals. Male infertility, while acknowledged, is considered shameful and women often protect their husbands by concealing it. Female infertility, in contrast, is scrutinized and often blamed on the woman herself, who may be castigated for her previous sexual history or for pursuing her studies rather than reproduction (Handwerker 1998). Handwerker points out that "the focus on women, not men, perpetuates the idea that the ability and will to reproduce and maintain the integrity of the family and the nation is vested in women" (1995b: 378).

SEXUALITY AND GENDER DIFFERENCE

The works and themes surveyed in this section are far more fragmentary than those treating marriage and families, a circumstance that reflects both habits of scholarship and the availability of sources. Writings about bodies and sexuality draw on the ethnographic, the medical, the nationalistic, and the analysis of a substantial array of writings we might call "anxiety literature," which discuss practices that are no longer acceptable (footbinding) and persons (woman students, homosexuals, prostitutes) whose actions redefine or threaten to disrupt current social arrangements. Writings about gender difference and its relationship to domestic and undomesticated femininity are largely framed by the concerns of the reform era, although a closer look reveals continuities between the Mao years and the reforms.

Bodies and Sexuality

Dorothy Ko has argued in a major recent study of footbinding (2005) that scholars have understood the practice entirely through the agitation against it that began in the late nineteenth century and lasted well into the twentieth. Treating it as emblem and cause of China's weakness and ills, reformers inside and outside the Qing, Republican, and PRC governments sought its abolition in the name of national strength and modernity. Ko asks, instead, that we start from the premise "that footbinding was an embodied experience, a reality to a select group of women from the twelfth to the twentieth centuries" (1), and that we regard it as an ongoing process central to the creation of meanings of gender that changed across time. Although much of her discussion involves earlier periods and is beyond the scope of this review, she begins her exploration with the end of footbinding in the nineteenth and twentieth centuries. She examines the category of "natural feet," introduced by missionaries and taken up by reformers in the 1890s, which helped to "introduce a view of the body as a machine"(5) whose optimal functioning was required of each national citizen. Footbinding then became the Other of modernity, a shameful remnant that had to be overcome in order for a healthy nation to emerge. Women's agency was to be relocated from the daily rebinding of feet to the single heroic act of unwrapping the bindings and striding forth into the world. And yet, as Ko meticulously documents for Shanxi province, the natural foot campaign, pursued as government policy in rural Republican China, met resistance from family patriarchs and village women alike, prompting public sympathy for women harassed by government bureaucrats. During the 1930s, Yao Lingxi, a man of letters living in the treaty port of Tianjin, assembled and published an encyclopedia of footbinding, including photographs, travel accounts, changing fashions in footwear and bindings, poems, letters, songs, memoirs, and interviews. This marked footbinding's final transformation from a woman's daily bodily practice to an object of connoisseurship and obsession by male editors and readers.

Changes in the discourses of human reproduction during the same period were less dramatic. In the imperial era, medical practitioners held reproducing couples and women in particular to standards of moderation and restraint intended to produce healthy offspring (Dikötter 1998; Furth 1999). Women were blamed for birth defects. In the Republican period, social criticism, medical texts, and fiction "maintained earlier preoccupations with reproduction, health, and family continuity while adding the question of what sorts of sexual behavior were appropriate to a modern society" (Hershatter 1996: 80). During the New Culture movement, the scientific study of sexuality was promoted as a modern area of inquiry, giving particular attention to disease and danger. New biologizing discourses, many of them developed by male feminists, reinforced a gender hierarchy in which women were seen as less evolved and intelligent than men. Normatively understood as passive respondents to male sexual activity, they were regarded as dangerous if sexually assertive. Weakened by menstruation, pregnancy, and menopause, prone to hysteria, women were nevertheless held more responsible than men for the reproductive realm (Dikötter 1995).

Republican-era biomedical writers reinforced the importance of fetal education, in which a pregnant woman was exhorted to avoid excitation or acts of imagination in order to produce a healthy child (Dikötter 1995, 1998). Thinkers across the political spectrum joined their counterparts in many other parts of the world in linking eugenics to the future of the race and the nation (Dikötter 1998; Barlow 2004, 2005; Sakamoto 2004). They assigned women substantial responsibility not only for the perpetuation of the family but also for the very survival of China. Frank Dikötter sees the contemporary concern with population quality in the PRC and the 1995 law intended to limit "inferior" births as a continuation of these trends (Dikötter 1998; see also Banister 1987).

Ethnographic work suggests a continuing association among women, reproduction, and danger. Emily Ahern (1975) describes the power and pollution associated with the blood of menstruation and childbirth, as well as the practices of purification and avoidance that contain it. In her more recent work, based on field observations in Taiwan, she suggests that women see birth, death, and the relationship between them in a specifically gendered way, regarding childbirth as closely conjoined to and containing the possibility of death. Funeral rituals performed by women, she notes, sometimes incorporate cloth also used in baby carriers (Martin 1988).

In cities before 1949, transient male foreigners, literati, sojourning merchants, and the working poor sought sexual services in a highly segmented market, and the varieties of working conditions make the unifying label "prostitution" of limited descriptive use. Nevertheless, prostitution was a powerful theme in Republican narratives about modernity. While intellectuals linked prostitution to social disorder, cultural backwardness, and national weakness, popular writings narrated a devolution from the cultured nineteenth-century courtesan (X. Ye 1999; Henriot 1994, 1997; V. Ho 1993; Yingjin Zhang 1999b; C. Yeh 2005) to the diseased streetwalker who worked the streets of Shanghai, Canton, and other expanding cities

(Gronewold 1984; Hershatter 1989, 1991, 1992a, 1993, 1994, 1997; Henriot 1992, 1994, 1996, 1997; V. Ho 1993; Yingjin Zhang 1999b). Such accounts may well be more useful as indicators of elite male anxiety—individual, social, and national—than as accurate renderings of prostitution, but they do convey a sense of the variety of motivations, arrangements, social standing, and regulatory constraints of women in the sex trades. They also delineate the status preoccupation of urban men: guidebooks described how men should conduct themselves properly to avoid humiliation in courtesan houses, thereby demonstrating their masculine urbanity in a changing world where social arrangements were not fixed (V. Ho 1993; Hershatter 1997; C. Yeh 1998, 2005). Individual courtesans sometimes played signifi-cant political roles by virtue of their connections with powerful men (Dong 2005). Under Guomindang law, prostitution was not illegal (P. Huang 2001a: 183), and taxes on prostitution provided revenues for local state-building in many provinces (V. Ho 1993; Remick 2003). Regulating prostitution, how-ever, or better yet eliminating it, became a sign of national recovery and a goal of successive Chinese governments, from various warlord regimes through the Guomindang and the Communists, who came closer to achiev-ing it than their predecessors (Hershatter 1992b, 1992c, 1996, 1997; Henriot 1988, 1995, 1997).

By the mid-1990s, prostitution once again had become a frequent topic in journalism, sexology (D. Liu et al. 1997), sociology, criminology (R. Jiang 1997; Dongchen District 1997; Ouyang 1997; Dazhong Wang 1997; C. Qian 1997; Yanshang Zhang 1997; Jeffreys 2004a, 2004b), and popular literature (Yongshan Li 1997; Niu 1997), with cautionary tales of abduction and vic-timization alternating with stories about the high income, upward mobil-ity, and excitement enticing women into sex work (X. Xu 1996; Hershatter 1997; V. Ho 1998–99; Evans 1997, 2000, 2003). Prostitution also became a regular, if less often discussed, feature of rural life (Friedman 2000, 2006; Yuen, Law, and Ho 2004). State attempts to detain and reeducate prosti-tutes (and occasionally customers) were intermittent and ineffectual (Ruan 1991; Hershatter 1997), although they produced a new web of regulations and procedures, some aimed at preventing state officials from patroniz-ing sex workers (Jeffreys 1997a, 2004a). Some authors see the growth of prostitution as a challenge to repressive state authority (Ruan 1991; V. Ho 1998–99). Others argue that the state has responded in a flexible fashion to the need to delineate new forms of prostitution while regulating new social spaces, and that the police apparatus itself has been transformed in the process (Jeffreys 1997a, 2004a). Whereas some call attention to the rela-tive absence of a discourse of sex work or prostitutes' rights in public discussion (Hershatter 1997), others question whether transnational feminist categories such as these are appropriately applied to contemporary China (Jeffreys 2004a, 2004b).

Research on prostitution extends to minority regions as well. In the rural Tai minority area of Xishuangbanna, Yunnan, Han prostitutes from Sichuan and Guizhou work in disguised brothels including "karaoke bars, hair salons, barbershops, massage parlors, saunas, and bars" (Hyde 2001: 147). Many of them dress like Tai women in order to enhance their erotic allure to visiting Han businessmen who are seeking an exoticized and ethnicized rural idyll even as they pursue an urban, modern pleasure: sex as a consumer good. This is not the only situation in which minority women are eroticized. The Mosuo, based in Yunnan and Sichuan, have achieved notoriety as a "country of women." Christine Mathieu (1999) describes Han views of Mosuo sexuality, with its matrilineality and serial sexual liaisons, as simultaneously alluring, dirty, and primitive. Eileen Walsh (2005) explores Mosuo engagement with ethnic tourism. She suggests that Mosuo participate in but also reshape the commodification of their culture, in a situation where "tourism has reified culture as a gendered consumable" (451). Louisa Schein, in her study of the Miao (1997, 2000), notes that in the 1980s cosmopolitan Han Chinese engaged in "internal orientalism," othering minorities as exotic, erotic, irreducibly rural, and prototypically female, and in the process defining Han men as modern urban subjects. Schein (2000: 285) warns that "for the feminine to be called up again and again where peasant minorities were concerned only reinforced that femininity stood unquestioned as the inferior rank in a vertical social ordering." Cherlene Makley (2002: 579) comments that the "'erotics of the exotic' on the Sino-Tibetan frontier" has been accompanied by a heightened concern with "containing, regulating, and objectifying female sexuality above all," and that Tibetan women carry a "disproportionate burden" (616) of maintaining community morality in a period of accelerating change.

As women's education and companionate marriage became features of the modern ideal in Republican China, women's nonmarital sexual activity, already regarded as a threat to patriarchal power, was criticized on new grounds. This was true not only with respect to prostitutes, but with sexual acts between women as well. Such acts were occasionally described in Republican-era erotic literature (Ruan 1991; Ruan and Bullough 1992). Examining May Fourth-era debates, Tze-lan Sang (2003; see also Damm 2005) finds the introduction of a neologism, "same-sex love" *(tongxing ai)*, which emphasized emotional connection as well as erotic activity. Translations of Western sexological works contributed to a medicalization of same-sex relations. In journals aimed at an urban middle-class readership, women's same-sex erotic activity was portrayed as abnormal and in need of regulation (like female sexuality more generally), although some writers defended intense affectionate attachments between young women. Writers of scientific treatises and fiction regarded same-sex relationships among students (both male and female) as situational rather than biologically determined. Sang notes that these authors expressed more anxiety over same-sex relations between women than men, fearing that increased independence combined with attraction to other women might induce some women not to marry.

Same-sex relationships were not mentioned in sources from the Mao years, at least not in those accessible at this writing. Scattered reportage about lesbian couples began to appear during the reform era, usually as a minor theme in investigations of male homosexual relationships. This material tended to portray lesbianism as a reaction to abuse or neglect by men or as a compensatory form of sexual contact adopted in the absence of male sexual partners (Ruan and Bullough 1992). Fictional works by Lin Bai and Chen Ran explored female homoeroticism (Sang 2003), while less positive treatments in journalistic literature represented lesbians as jealous, lascivious, violent, and generally incomprehensible (X. Xu 1996). An emergent urban network of lesbians centered on Beijing organized a conference in 1998 (He 2001) and began to publish a community newsletter (Sang 2003). Like gay men, they identify themselves as *tongzhi*, appropriating a term which meant "comrade" in the Mao years.

In urban reform-era China, new notions of masculinity and femininity have been marketed through the use of athletes and models. Susan Brownell introduces the term "body culture," including "daily practices of health, hygiene, fitness, beauty, dress, and decoration," as well as the means by which the body is trained and displayed to express a particular lifestyle (Brownell 2001: 124; 1995: 10). During the late imperial period, she notes, gender distinctions (among others) were established via dress, hairstyle, and footbinding. Late Qing reformers and revolutionaries, in agitating against footbinding, also advocated that women engage in physical education (Rankin 1975; Brownell 1995; H. Fan 1997; Yu 2005). Men, too, were exhorted by reformers to abandon older notions of sports as a lower-class activity, and to build up their physical strength as a means of strengthening the nation. This association of modern nationhood with physical fitness intensified during the Republican period (H. Fan 1997; Z. Wang 1999; Yu 2005), and by 1924 China's National Games included sports for women (Brownell 1995). In the Communist base areas in Jiangxi and Yan'an (H.

Fan 1997), and on into the PRC, body culture became more homogeneous (Brownell 1995), linked to military and (in the PRC) working-class ideal types. In the reform period, woman athletes continued to be trained, as they were under Mao, in a sports system that minimized gender difference and produced athletes meant to embody a homogeneous vision of the nation (Brownell 1999, 2001). Because Chinese women athletes have done better than men in international competitions, however, they hold a special place in reform-era Chinese nationalism, even though Brownell (1999) characterizes popular nationalism in China as predominantly about the redemption and strengthening of masculinity. Woman, who in the late Qing and early Republic symbolized China's weakness, became in the 1980s a source of redemption from those earlier humiliations and from the recent Cultural Revolution travails as well. When the Chinese women's volleyball team won the World Cup in 1981, letters from the public praised them for overcoming extreme hardship to gain a victory that helped to vitiate China's national humiliation. Popular responses called this a victory, not for women or even for Chinese women, but for China (Brownell 1995, 1999).

Although the question of women in sports is not framed in gender-specific terms, the success of women athletes is linked in the popular press to women's ability to "eat bitterness," a sign of female virtue and industriousness in revolutionary discourse as well. Where sports commentators see female virtue, however, Brownell (1995, 1999) sees a social logic wherein women, particularly rural women, regard sports as a rare means of social mobility. Hoping that prominence in a sport will make them more desirable marriage partners, women athletes are concerned not to let their skin become too dark or to injure their reproductive health by training during their menstrual periods. Brownell argues that in comparison to American woman athletes, they are less subject to questions about their sexuality (Brownell 1995).

Like athletes, women fashion models are meant to demonstrate that China has arrived in transnational culture, in this case by performing haute couture femininity—and height (5'11" and taller is preferred). Chinese runway models present themselves either as "Western" (expressive, exuberant) or "traditional Oriental" (melancholy, nonthreatening). The contrasting rules for gendered self-presentation of athletes and models notwithstanding, Brownell (1998–99, 2000, 2001; see also Finnane 2005a) sees nationalist rhetoric emanating from sports contests and supermodel competitions alike. She warns (1998–99) that new forms of patriarchy are emerging through the deployment of these women's bodies, even as the athletes and models themselves experience their new opportunities as liberating.

By the turn of the twenty-first century, new venues for socializing—

including discos, social dance clubs, and the Internet—provided opportunities for "sexual play" free of permanent relationships, in which flirtation and sexual activity might be understood within a narrative of romantic love but were assumed not to lead to marriage (Farrer 2000, 2002; Farrer and Sun 2003). James Farrer (2000) exempts karaoke bars from this characterization, because they were often used to build long-term business relationships. He finds that in discos young single men and women honed their skills of self-display and desirability, while in social dance halls middle-aged employees in the state sector enjoyed small intimacies and discreet erotic pleasure, up to and including pre- and extramarital affairs.

In a study of "the rhetoric of sexuality of everyday social interactions" (2002: 3) among young unmarried nonmigrant heterosexual men and women in Shanghai during the 1990s, Farrer describes a rapidly changing and elaborate sexual culture, encompassing not only what people do, but the stories they tell about themselves, their desires, and their motives. He finds that young people designate certain acts as "play" and therefore exempt from the requirements of everyday morality. In contrast to breathless journalistic accounts of contemporary Shanghai, which generally mention the past only as a foil for a globalized present, Farrer notes "a layering of multiple historical 'modernities'" (2002: 10) in Shanghai, encompassing the colonial and socialist pasts as well as the current moment. He argues that Shanghai's emergent sexual culture must be understood in the context of the market economy, in which the stories Shanghai residents tell about sexual choices, the role of money, inequality, and leisure-time activities are used (much as they were in the 1920s and 1930s; see Hershatter 1997) "to mark moral and social boundaries in a newly forming market society" (2002: 12).

Domestic and Undomesticated Femininity

During the Mao years, state pronouncements on the question of women emphasized the obligation of and opportunity for all women to contribute to society. The quintessential slogans were "women hold up half the sky" and Mao's pronouncement, "Times have changed. Whatever men comrades can do, women comrades can do." Much scholarship about the collective era has suggested that serious problems were elided by these formulations. The norm for achievement in work and politics was the unmarked male (Honig and Hershatter 1988; Dai 1995). The norm in urban dress was the cadre suit, except during the clothing reform campaign of 1955–56, which differentiated appropriate clothing by gender and urban/rural location (Finnane 2003). Accounts describing the years between 1949 and 1976 focus on the state's promotion of gender similarity, with some subtle differences in dress (T. Chen 2003b). Croll (1995) argues that the Mao-era approach to gender neglected the specificities of women's bodies and their social experiences as daughters and wives, denying women the very language in which to express the gender inequality in their daily lives. The emphasis was on men as the norm in revolutionary models, while women were capable of attaining modelhood if they exhibited sufficient revolutionary zeal (see also Chen 2003a). This argument, however, is necessarily limited by its sources, juxtaposing government rhetoric from the Mao years extolling gender equality with 1980s memoirs and fiction in which women turn a critical eye on the Maoist past.

Women's domestic labor was rendered invisible, and time spent performing it made women less able to rise to supervisory positions in the cities or earn equal workpoints in the countryside. This gender gap was informally acknowledged but not articulated as a social or political problem (Diamond 1975; Davin 1976; Parish and Whyte 1978; Andors 1983; M. Wolf 1985; Hershatter 2002). At the same time, women were clearly expected to take primary responsibility for maintaining a thrifty household, raising children, helping others, promoting public health, and studying—goals recognized by the "Five Good" campaigns in Women's Federation documents during the 1950s and 1960s (Hemmel and Sindbjerg 1984).

Except for a brief period in the mid-1950s (Davin 1975a, 1976), to be a housewife was not a glorified revolutionary role. Wang Zheng recalls the distaste she and her student friends felt in 1978 when they were given special movie tickets for International Women's Day. To be categorized—or, as we might say, interpellated—as a woman was associated with being a "house woman," or housewife. To young urban women raised in the PRC, this was a far less acceptable identity than that of youth, woman student, woman worker, or woman scientist, all of whom could participate fully in socialist construction (Z. Wang 2001). Many young women recall these images as enabling the transgression of gender boundaries, and regard them as a positive legacy of their childhood under Mao (Z. Wang 2001; Zhong, Wang, and Bai 2001). Housewife was a residual category, named as a mobilization target by the state but carrying no revolutionary cachet.

Sexuality and sexual behavior were no longer discussed as practices in need of modernization, as they had been during the Republican period; modernity was to be measured in the realms of production rather than reproduction (Hershatter 1996). Sexual difference in official discourse was narrowly construed, confined to scientific writing and marriage manuals that emphasized the male as initiator of sexual activity and the female as passive respondent (Evans 1997), a formulation entirely compatible with older notions of male-female complementarity. Therein lies a paradox: women performed many tasks that had been the preserve of men, but in the sexual and domestic realms, gender difference continued to be a foundational assumption. Harriet Evans (1995, 1997, 2002) has argued persuasively that throughout the revolutionary and reform periods, female gender was portrayed as an effect of sexual difference, "defined by a series of innate and essential characteristics associated with certain responses, needs, and capacities that naturally make women wives and mothers" (2002: 336; see also Jankowiak 2002). Side by side with the repeated campaigns of the 1950s to raise the status of women, grant them equal rights in marriage, and mobilize them for socialist construction through labor outside the home, important assumptions about "woman's nature" remained unquestioned in a time of rapid social and economic change. The same might be said about the recent period of economic reforms. Indeed, such unquestioned assumptions may have facilitated change in both periods by reassuring Chinese people that the world was not, in important respects, being turned upside down.

The explicit articulation of gender difference, never easily discussed in the lexicon of class, certainly lessened during the Cultural Revolution era. Little has been said, or written, about gender difference as perceived by those who lived it in the revolutionary era, although memoirs by former girl Red Guards, written years later from an expatriate vantage point, provide intriguing clues that their psychic lives, sexual desires, and sense of gender difference were far too complex to be contained by the strictures of public discourse (A. Min 1995; R. Yang 1997; Z. Wang 2001; see also Hershatter 1996; Honig 2000, 2003). Many women remember their years as "sent-down youth" in the countryside as a time of experimentation and adventure, albeit perilous and fraught with sexual vulnerability (M. Young 1989; Honig 2000, 2003; Lin 2003). Rae Yang's description (1997) of her dream life during her rural sojourn provides a rich account of inchoate (and not-so-inchoate) sexual yearnings. Wang Zheng's memories of secretly reading Victorian novels and identifying with the heroines, as well as her pleasure in covering her body with a gray plastic raincoat on her way to go swimming, suggest that physical modesty served as a form of gender identity and that "Victorian gender discourse . . . blended well with communist sexual mores" (Z. Wang 2001). Mores often diverged from practice, however, as substantial numbers of pregnancies, abortions, and out-of-wedlock births were recorded among sent-down youth in some locales (Honig 2003).

In the 1980s, one of the many charges leveled at Mao (often by party-state authorities) was that he had ignored "human nature," which was understood to be an irreducible set of behaviors knowable through scientific investigation. Popular and scholarly periodicals alike discussed the biology of sex difference, criticizing Maoist policies for having held women to male standards, ignoring women's particular characteristics and needs (Honig and Hershatter 1988). Work arrangements in factories and fields were criticized for taking insufficient account of women's menstrual cycles, bodily strength, and primary responsibility for domestic tasks, also assumed to be natural. The high-achieving "Iron Girls," with their manic work schedules and acrobatics on high-voltage power lines, became objects of national satire (Honig and Hershatter 1988; Honig 2000). Protective labor regulations were issued in 1988, calling attention to the special needs of women during menstruation, pregnancy, and lactation, and mandating that units with large numbers of women workers provide for these needs and for childcare (Croll 1995). Although such benefits were not implemented by autonomous employers, this "biologization" of women workers contributed to the growing unwillingness of work units to hire or retain married women during the reform period (Woo 1994).

Emerging notions of femininity emphasized gender difference, sexual appeal to men, and motherhood. Many factors contributed to this shift: commodification and shifting labor markets (J. Zang 2005), popular reaction to the state-sponsored feminism of the Mao era, and the state's withdrawal from regulation of both family relations and work, even as it has intensified its regulation of birth planning. Lisa Rofel (1999b) suggests that the intense attention to marking and marketing gender difference was both a critique of a failed Maoism and an assertion that "natural" gender roles had to be recognized in order for China to reach modernity. Among ethnicized minorities as well as among the Han, consumption and the commodification of bodies themselves came to signify the modern (Gillette 2000a, 2000b; Makley 2002; Walsh 2005).

In the reform era, adornment was presented as a natural female desire, with its necessary commodities to be supplied by an expanding consumer market (Honig and Hershatter 1988; Xiaoping Li 1998; Hooper 1999; Gillette 2000a, 2000b; Evans 2001; Farquhar 2002; Finnane 2005a; Friedman 2006). Over more than two decades of reform, the female body was reconfigured as alluring, vulnerable, dependent, and inferior (Hooper 1984; Honig and Hershatter 1988; M. Young 1989; Jankowiak 1993; Croll 1995; Xiaoping Li 1998; M. Yang 1999a; Z. Wang 2001; Evans 2000, 2002), characterizations that echo Republican-era sexual discourse (Dikötter 1995). For young women born and brought up in the reform era, fashion and beauty (including, by the 1990s, variable hair color) became arenas for newly permitted self-expression and experimentation with fantasies of self. To be fashionable, Evans suggests, meant to be "Western" (2001; see also Xiaoping Li 1998; Finnane 2005a), although localized fashions such as exposed short nylon stockings (Chew 2003), fashions adapted from other Asian locations, and reinvented Chinese traditions were also prominent. White skin and large breasts were featured as desirable attributes in product advertising, the former associated with modesty and self-protection from the sun and coarsening influences more generally, the latter explicitly linked both to nature and to "prosperity and civilization" (Johansson 1998–99: 75).

It is important not to overstate the break between Maoist and reform-era representations of femininity. In both periods, women were regarded as responsive and dependent in their sexuality (Evans 1997, 2000), and sexuality was discussed in a variety of contexts—mostly unofficial during the Cultural Revolution, but nonetheless important (Honig 2003). The topics and range of representations are far more diverse in the market reform period than in socialism's early years. Yet writings from both periods assume that gender is an effect of sexual difference, and since sexual difference is seen to be determined by immutable scientific verities, gender characteristics and the sexual behavior associated with them are not candidates for social change. In both periods, the experience of marriage and motherhood has been near universal, and even with the proliferation of erotic images and venues for sexual activity, reproduction remains central to most discussions of women's sexuality in the press, advertisements, medicine, and educational materials, as well as in what we know about rural conversations (Friedman 2000). In both periods, domestic labor and the maintenance of family have been women's responsibility, defined not as work but rather as a burden (Jacka 1997). Prescriptive writings of the Maoist period assigned wives responsibility for conjugal and family harmony and for supporting their husbands, even as they themselves were exhorted to enter a wider work and political arena. Women were assumed to have a particular affinity for the domestic and emotional labor of maintaining a household. Although state propaganda anticipated a future in which housework would be socialized, and experimental gestures were made in that direction during the Great Leap Forward, until the revolution came to fruition, housework was to be primarily women's responsibility (Evans 2002; Manning 2005).

But while women under Mao were supposed to do all this while also maintaining their concern with the world beyond the home, in the reform era, both "housewife" and "mother" were reconfigured as central roles for women. The increased availability of domestic consumer goods such as washing machines and processed foods was presented as a benefit to women in individual family units (Robinson 1985; Davin 1989; Hooper 1999); collectivized or community facilities to lighten the domestic workload were not even marginally on the public agenda, although local investment in childcare centers may have increased somewhat (Robinson 1985; Croll 1985c). Domestic space was represented in advertising, fiction, television, and the press as an enhanced rather than residual realm coordinated by a discerning female consumer (Yang 1999b). The history of the bourgeois Shanghai family of the Republican period was rediscovered and partially valorized (W. Yeh 2005). The phrase "virtuous wife and good mother," which had circulated in the early twentieth century (Borthwick 1985), enjoyed a resurgence (M. Wolf 1985; Honig and Hershatter 1988; Beaver, Hou, and Wang 1995; Milwertz 1997), as did the notion that women were primarily responsible for the healthy development and moral education of children (Robinson 1985; Croll 1985c; Davin 1989; Jacka 1990, 1997; Greenhalgh and Winckler 2005).

In the late 1980s, the northern village of Daqiuzhuang briefly gained notoriety when it made women's return to full-time housework a linchpin of village economic development strategy (Jacka 1990; Beaver, Hou, and Wang 1995). A popular TV soap opera aired in 1991, "Yearnings," featured a character who gained a serious national following because of her selfless attempts to sacrifice for an uncaring husband and a disabled adoptive child (Rofel 1994b; Evans 2002). Milwertz (1997: 122) points out that urban women have responded to the one-child policy by pursuing the "cultivation of the perfect only child," one who is given every possible educational, extracurricular, and material advantage, guided and supervised by a dedicated and anxious mother. In this context, she suggests, urban women continued to build a "uterine family," this time to secure care in old age rather than an improved position with husbands and in-laws. Suzanne Gottschang (2001: 90) points to "conflicting ideals of motherhood" wherein companies market infant formula to new mothers by appealing to their desire to be sexually attractive, "scientific," and modern, while a state campaign for infant health uses similar images to encourage women to breastfeed.

In the early 1980s, the Chinese press began to report cases of violence against women. Public discussion of such violence should to be understood in the context of the commodification of social relationships, on the one hand, and the strengthening of normative domestic roles for women on the other. Whether the actual incidence of violence was on the rise or whether it was being more fully reported and recognized as a problem is not clear (Whyte 2000). Violence has been directed at married women fulfilling normative gender roles as wives (M. Liu 2002; X. Wang 2004; McDougall 2005), particularly if they have married far from home (Davin 1997, 1999) or failed to produce male children (Honig and Hershatter 1988; Gilmartin 1990). Sometimes, as mentioned earlier, such incidents were categorized (or misrecognized) as feudal remnants which caused families to abuse women who gave birth to girls (Anagnost 1988). Alternatively, they were framed as illustrations of women's legal rights, in which wife beating, interference with women's marriage choice, female infanticide, and rape were condemned (Honig and Hershatter 1988; Gilmartin 1990; Croll 1994; Hershatter 1997). Self-directed violence of the most extreme sort—suicide—has emerged in recent mental-health studies as a profoundly gendered phenomenon. In contrast to international patterns, suicides in China among women far outnumber those of men (Phillips, Li, and Zhang 2002a; Pearson and Liu 2002; M. Liu 2002), and the suicide rate among young rural women in the 1990s was 66 percent higher than that of their rural male counterparts. Researchers attribute many of the suicides and attempted suicides not to mental illness or economic difficulties but rather to impulsive decisions made in the aftermath of spousal or family conflicts, often involving a physically abusive husband, with the added factor of readily available lethal pesticides (Phillips, Li, and Zhang 2002a, 2002b; Pearson and Liu 2002; M. Liu 2002; Pearson et al. 2002). As in earlier periods, anger, the desire for revenge on family members, and the ability to assert a powerful demand for justice, albeit posthumously, appear to remain potent motivations for suicide among rural women (Pearson and Liu 2002; M. Liu 2002).

In spite of such abundant evidence that home was not always a haven from danger, another theme in reporting on violence against women was the dictum not to stray too far from the protection of domestic life. Cautionary tales warned women to beware of abduction, stay out of prostitution, and protect themselves against rape, illustrating these points by recounting the gruesome misfortunes of victims. In Lijiang during the late 1990s, women taxi drivers (unusual elsewhere in China) became the subject of stories about death and dismemberment, and more generally about danger, immorality, and ambiguously sexed or intractably smelly bodies. Emily Chao (2003) suggests that these tales, which incorporated older notions of female pollution, fox spirits, and witchcraft, expressed anxiety about "women out of place," reinforcing through talk the boundaries between respectable and licentious women, between rural migrants (the drivers) and urban dwellers, and between unregulated entrepreneurs and the more constrained and indignant state sector employees. Evans (1997) points out that public discussions of trafficking, prostitution, pornography, rape, adultery, and homosexuality all portray women who engage in unapproved and undomesticated behavior as victims or as depraved, reinforcing the narrow range of subject positions that constitute normative female sexuality.

The valorization of gender difference in the reform era underscores the ongoing romance with science that has been an enduring feature of efforts to define a Chinese modernity in the twentieth century. Yet outside China, scientific theorizing about gender has shifted dramatically in recent decades, while the questioning of foundational scientific truths has become a quintessential sign of the postmodern. It remains to be seen how or whether these developments will inflect Chinese discourses on gender and sexuality, which are increasingly engaged in transnational conversations.

2. Labor

As an ensemble, the scholarship on women and labor in twentieth-century China follows a familiar trajectory of feminist scholarship. It begins by establishing that "women were there, too," working in factories, fields, and homes and contributing to household income and working-class formation. It proceeds to an examination of how the presence of women changes the overall historical narrative, establishing key moments when women's mobilization shaped the outcome of revolutionary organizing or state initiatives. Finally, it attends to the ways in which the categories "women" and "gender" themselves have been produced under specific historical circumstances, and how they in turn have become important components in visions of Chinese modernity.

This literature calls attention to the gendered division of labor as a fundamental framing device, even as its specific contents shift over time. The division of labor remains crucial in reflecting and producing normative forms of work for women and men, linked to larger notions of gendered personhood. Well into the twentieth century, women and woman's proper place have remained associated with the "inner" realm of the family and the household, while the proper place of men has been linked to the "outer" world of labor and public affairs (Jacka 1997; Rofel 1999b; B. Goodman and Larson 2005b; Dong 2005). Women have performed labor—often crucial income-producing labor—in both urban and rural households, for the benefit of families both wealthy and poor. Nevertheless, those women whose paid labor has taken them outside their family's domestic space, however capaciously and flexibly that space is defined, have felt themselves and have been seen by others to be vulnerable to kidnapping, trafficking, sexual violation, and potential disgrace (Pruitt 1967; M. Wolf 1985; Rogaski 1997; Rofel 1999b; Pomeranz 2005). As Lisa Rofel puts it, "Transgressing the historically variable border of inside/outside, then, meant the loss of full female personhood within one's kinship world, which is to say within one's social world" (1999b: 65). Important as this normative inner/outer boundary is, however, attention to the specificities of women's work redefines and often collapses the boundary between workplace and household, as well as that between paid and unpaid labor.

Studies of women and industrial labor in the twentieth century are addressed both to "the China field" and to scholars working on gender and labor questions in other regions. Research on women workers in urban China has paralleled and reinforced broader themes in Chinese history both before and after 1949, establishing that women were an important component of the industrial workforce; that they were present at moments of collective protest and revolutionary agitation, but had mixed political affiliations and long moments of quiescence; that their workplace loyalties and patterns of collective action were importantly shaped by native-place ties; that the lives of many of them were punctuated by return to rural places of origin; and that mobilization of women's labor was a key component of party-state policy under Mao. Studies of women workers have also paid attention to gendered themes salient to women's studies scholarship outside the China field: daily survival strategies, sexual vulnerability, operative notions of womanly virtue, a gendered division of labor in which women consistently have been undervalued, work histories prominently shaped by marriage and childrearing, and state policies directed at women.

URBAN WOMEN'S WORK IN REPUBLICAN CHINA

Studies of women in Republican-era factories first sought to show that "women were there, too" at one site where modernity was defined and Communist organizing flourished. In Shanghai, the most thoroughly studied of China's industrial centers, women comprised close to two-thirds of the factory workforce; by the early 1930s, almost three-quarters of Shanghai cotton mill-hands were women (Honig 1986). Regional differences and the timing of economic development were important: in Tianjin, until the Japanese occupation, only about 10 percent of cotton mill-hands were women, although the number rose rapidly thereafter (Hershatter 1986). In both cities, women cotton mill workers were tracked into less-skilled jobs for which they were generally paid piece rates. Until the late 1940s, mill management showed a marked preference for young unmarried women workers; marriage and pregnancy were cause for firing in many mills (Honig 1986; Hershatter 1986). Women were also important participants in silk textile production. In Shanghai and Hangzhou, women and children predominated in the unskilled tasks of silk spinning (Perry 1993; Rofel 1999b), while in Shanghai both men and women performed the skilled labor of silk weaving (Perry 1993). About women in other Republican-period industries—flour mills, match factories, cigarette production, and carpet weaving—or in other large textile-producing centers such as Wuhan and Qingdao, we know very little. Women and children also formed significant proportions of outworkers and casual laborers in urban settings, although precise numbers are difficult to come by. They processed foods and wool for export, glued matchboxes, wove mats, and sewed uniforms in homes and in small workshops (Hershatter 1986; Honig 1986). In Hangzhou, they worked in family workshops preparing silk yarn for weaving by men (Rofel 1999b).

Although the vocabulary of "inner" and "outer" realms is not often used explicitly in sources on urban women workers, women's venture into the exposed space of the factory merited notice and some anxiety. Some of the attention was positive: reformers in the late Qing and the first years of the Republic saw women's employment in factories as a way to expand modern industry and build an economically strong state while simultaneously raising women's status (Orliski 2003). Most Republican-era writings, as well as oral narratives collected more recently, characterize the factory floor as a dangerous place for respectable women. In reform-era interviews about the period before 1949, former workers recall their worry about the sexual vulnerability of young women in the workforce, as well as harassment of men and women who engaged in public social contact. Women mill workers, vulnerable to sexual assault by foremen and harassed or seduced by male workers, may have been regarded by the wider community as deficient in virtue (Hershatter 1986; Honig 1986; Rofel 1999b). It was not work per se but the location in which work was performed that exposed women to both danger and opprobrium (Rofel 1999b). What is not so clear, and is probably impossible to clarify at this distance, is this: Did women and their families in the Republican period feel that factory work was shameful for a woman, or is this sense of past shame itself an artifact of a post-1949 story about feudal oppression and socialist liberation?

Workers become most visible in the historical record at moments of collective action, and for twentieth-century China it is also there that their story intersects with the much-investigated course of revolutionary organizing. But just as scholars of the labor movement more generally have discovered a mixed history of militance and quietism, conflicting political loyalties, alliances with management, defensive or conservative organizing goals, and nonlinear activity of various sorts, so too with women's participation in collective action. Elizabeth Perry (1993) finds important gender differences in the timing of strikes: in the early twentieth century, many were initiated by unskilled women workers, whereas later, men were more active. She also points to differences among women across industries, with women tobacco workers more militant than those in cotton mills. Prominent women militants do not always conform to the heroic prototypes publicized in post-1949 China: one 1920s strike leader was gang-affiliated (Honig 1986; Perry 1993), while many 1930s activists were mobilized by the YWCA (Honig 1986). Within industries, skill was an important variable in shaping patterns of labor activity. Unskilled women silk spinners in the late 1920s were both volatile and resistant to Communist union organizing, while skilled women silk weavers became active later, emerging as key players in worker unrest in the 1930s and 1940s (Perry 1993). Hiring women in the cotton mills during the 1920s was prompted in part by the desire of mill owners to replace militant male workers with more tractable women (Honig 1986). During the Nanjing Decade (1928–37), women in Tianjin cotton mills and Shanghai silk filatures joined in defensive strikes to prevent factory closings and protect welfare provisions (Hershatter 1986; Perry 1993). Only after World War II did women workers emerge in substantial numbers as activists in an organized CCP-influenced labor movement (Honig 1986; Hershatter 1986; Perry 1993). The variety and unevenness of women's participation in collective action defy categorization and suggest that labor activity more generally may be equally resistant to easy narration.

Scholarship on women in factory regimes, even as it places women squarely within the narrative of this politically volatile and modern sector, suggests that a class-based narrative is inadequate, because gender tended to complicate both occupational tracking and class relations. Within a single textile factory, women in less-skilled occupations and men in artisanal jobs did not always have unified goals (Perry 1993). But just as attention to gender shows the inadequacies of class as a determinative unit of analysis, gender is undermined by crosscutting ties of kinship and native place. Like male factory workers in the Republican era and indeed like urban dwellers more generally, many women mill-hands came from the countryside, maintained ongoing ties there, and moved across the urban-rural divide multiple times in their working lives (Honig 1986; Hershatter 1986). Many were contract laborers, recruited by the powerful underworld organization known as the Green Gang, and had little control over their living conditions or the disposition of their income. In the city, they were enmeshed in native-place networks that included supervisors as well as other workers and often divided workers from each other by dialect, dress style, and political loyalties (Honig 1983, 1986, 1992).

Emily Honig's work on Subei people in Shanghai (1986, 1992) explores the interaction of gendering with native-place identity. Women from Subei were consistently tracked into the least desirable jobs, in silk filatures and brothels as well as cotton mills (Honig 1986). Honig found that imperialism, and specifically foreign ownership of cotton mills, exacerbated divisions among the workers. Some Subei women preferred to work in Japaneseowned mills, rather than endure the localistic prejudices of Chinese mill managers (Honig 1986). Subei people become the "Other" against which Shanghai people, many themselves recently arrived from Jiangnan, came to define themselves as sophisticated urbanites. Subei women were denigrated as coarse, loud, vulgar, and incapable of assimilation into an emerging urban modernity. This othering process survived the socialist years, even as rural-to-urban migration was closed off in the late 1950s, and remained intact into the 1980s (Honig 1992). A recent study of contemporary women migrant workers from Subei in Jiangnan silk factories indicates the continuing salience of this particular native-place division among women (F. Xu 2000). Yet the effect of native place on the shaping of gendered identity remains as yet largely unexplored in the literature on women workers.

Fragmentation can facilitate political activity, with or without class consciousness (Perry 1993). Native-place networks were a powerful basis for collective action, particularly when mediated through the process of pledging sisterhood (Honig 1985, 1986; Perry 1993). This practice was widely encouraged by Communist organizers in the 1940s, during and after the Japanese occupation. In less visible ways as well, native-place ties helped structure everyday forms of coping with factory regimes, from taking long bathroom breaks and napping on the job to stealing cotton yarn (Honig 1986; Hershatter 1986).

Women's nonmarital household labor—as concubines, servants, or slaves—remains understudied in scholarship on the Republican period. Ida Pruitt's classic *A Daughter of Han* (1967) is still the best account of paid domestic labor, with all the attractions and limitations that first-person accounts entail. Rubie Watson (1991) has explored inequality among wives, concubines, and maids in large Hong Kong-area households, arguing that although marked differences in status existed between the three groups, the boundary between free and servile women was less rigid than that between free and servile men. Literature on Hong Kong suggests that young female bond servants *(mooi-jai* or *mui tsai)* played an important role in households well into the twentieth century. Their situations were often ones of outright bondage (Miers 1994), but their treatment was also shaped by customary rights, kinship practices, colonial regulation, and a variety of reform movements (Jaschok 1988; R. Watson 1991; Jaschok and Miers 1994b; Sinn 1994; Chin 2002; Chin 2006). To date, we know little about their counterparts within Chinese national boundaries.

From the late Qing period on, women's magazines included stories about women in Western nations who worked in professions such as law, government, and banking. Writers for women's journals recommended that women of the emergent middle classes work as nurses and teachers, extending their familial roles into the public realm. Middle-class women were also encouraged to engage in sericulture and handicraft production of fine embroidery in order to enhance family income and "contribute to the nation-state from within the home" (Orliski 2003: 55). Shen Shou, a celebrated embroiderer who held a government post in the late Qing, exhibited her embroidered portraits abroad in the last years of the Qing and the early Republic. Her 1919 manual on embroidery, written with the male reformer and industrialist Zhang Jian, promoted fine needlework, no longer as a sign of womanly virtue, but rather as a means by which women could support themselves while helping to decrease China's dependence on foreign goods (Fong 2004). We still have remarkably few studies about the daily working lives of middle-class housewives in urban Republican China. Professional women are also seldom discussed, with the exception of Wang Zheng's 1999 book (see Chapter 3).

Another realm of Republican women's work that has begun to attract scholarly attention is the entertainment industry. Actresses in Beijing, Tianjin, and Shanghai performed folk songs, clapper operas (a form of rhythmic storytelling), drum songs, and Beijing opera in theaters and teahouses (Cheng 1996; Y. Huang 2004; S. Luo 2005). Taxi dancers and cabaret girls accompanied male patrons in Shanghai's dance halls, while hostesses replaced male waiters in teahouses (Henriot 1997; Hershatter 1997; Field 1999; Di Wang 2004). Prostitution, discussed in Chapter 1, employed substantial numbers of women. The boundaries between sex work and entertainment work were not firmly fixed, either in public discussion about appropriate female behavior (Cheng 1996) or in the working lives of individual women.

RURAL WOMEN'S WORK IN REPUBLICAN CHINA

We still know regrettably little about rural women's work during the Republican era. John Lossing Buck's 1937 study *Land Utilization in China* estimated that women performed only about 13 percent of all farm labor, with participation running higher in rice-growing regions than in those that grew wheat, and that they performed about 16 percent of all subsidiary work, again with regional variations (Davin 1975b; Croll 1985c). His surveys did not include activities that were generally performed by women, such as food processing and making clothing (Croll 1985c). Fei Xiaotong's 1938 fieldwork in Lu Village, Yunnan, found that women performed more days of field labor than men, suggesting that Buck underreported women's contributions to farming in rice-growing regions, if not elsewhere as well (Bossen 1994, 2002). In coastal Fujian, Sara Friedman finds, women had significant responsibility for agriculture (2006). Philip Huang (1990), drawing on Japanese surveys from the 1940s, finds that women contributed very little to sorghum and millet farming in north China but helped harvest winter wheat and barley, cultivate sweet potatoes, and pick cotton for the market. In the Yangzi delta, women threshed rice, raised silkworms, and cultivated cotton. In general, Huang finds that poorer women did more farmwork than those from well-off families, and that commercialization brought what he calls the "familization of production," with greater labor participation by women. Oral history interviews suggest that women in poorer farming households routinely did fieldwork, norms to the contrary notwithstanding (Judd 1994; Hershatter 2000). Women's labor may have been understood not as a distinct category, but as an integral part of a larger family strategy from which it could not be separated (Pomeranz 2005).

Local studies suggest interesting but by no means consistent variations in women's work by class and local political economy. Susan Mann's research on women's work in the Ningbo area (1992) points to class distinctions in the work that women did: embroidery and other home work for better-off women, hat weaving and factory work for the more vulnerable poor. Bridal laments and religious practices dating from the Republican period point to women's roles in spinning, weaving, cooking, and manure collection (McLaren 2004b). Rural girls and women routinely worked in the fields, but such labor was associated with sexual vulnerability, poverty, and violation of the social imperative that unmarried girls stay out of sight (Hershatter 2000; Pomeranz 2005). Although Buck hypothesized that low female labor rates were correlated with footbinding, the connection of footbinding practices and women's productive labor remains poorly understood (Hershatter 1986; Gates 1996b, 2001). In many regions, footbinding appears to have been quite compatible with women's participation in agricultural labor (Bossen 2002). Women and girls with bound feet worked at home to produce both goods for family use and luxury commodities for the market. Regional footbinding variations in age, tightness, and prevalence should be understood in relationship to labor possibilities for women and girls (Gates 1996b, 2001).

Recent scholarship posits connections between the growing industrial sector, particularly in textiles, and changing patterns of rural women's work inside and outside their households. In the Republican period, rural footbinding rates may have declined when imports hurt home textile production and made it less feasible for families to keep their wives and daughters confined to "inside" labor (Gates 2001; Bossen 2002). Lynda Bell (1994, 1999) examines the raising of silkworms and silk cocoons in Wuxi farming households as silk filatures proliferated from the 1860s to the 1930s. She argues that Wuxi farms were so small and rent demands so high that women had to supplement household farming earnings. Cocoon production, an "inside" task that did not contravene expectations about what women should do, was the best available alternative, even though the returns to female labor were low and the risks of cocoon damage and market fluctuations were high. Bell points out that the minimal income women brought in was unlikely to result in higher status. Rather, women were likely to be blamed if the silkworms failed, on the grounds that one or another polluting female bodily fluid had contributed to the failure. Worst off were those women remote from urban centers whose husbands went elsewhere to seek nonfarm work, leaving a feminized agricultural sector to fend for itself with few urban remittances, a cautionary tale for the current reform-era situation in many rural areas. In an intriguing aside, Bell points out that by the 1930s most sericulture agricultural extension workers who went out to educate peasant women about better cocoon raising were themselves young women; this is a group of educated women about whom very little is known.

Kathy Walker's study of the northern Yangzi delta (1993, 1999) traces the role of peasant women in cotton textile production. With the founding of treaty ports, Chinese merchants became the agents linking rural peasant labor, imported yarn, and market outlets in Manchuria and elsewhere. Commercial managerial farming and landlordism expanded, accompanied by what Walker calls the "subproletarianization" of most peasants, in which "large numbers of poor, destabilized peasants" were reconstituted "as a cheap and partially unfree labor force" (1999: 203). In this context, men joined the off-farm casual labor force, while the demand for ever-cheaper peasant labor drew women into the cotton fields as weeders and pickers. Walker suggests, in contrast to Buck, that both north and south China developed a market for women's farm labor in the early twentieth century, one in which the commoditization of women accompanied the growth of commercial agriculture. Walker sees in these developments an early instance of the feminization of agriculture in which women played important roles in both family and commercial farming (1993, 1999). Women fieldworkers included not only waged laborers, but "disguised" labor in the form of concubines, daughters-in-law, and the use of daughters as working collateral on usurious loans.

In a more optimistic analysis of farm surveys conducted throughout China around 1930, Marshall Johnson, William Parish, and Elizabeth Lin find that 28 percent of all farm products were marketed (1987: 260), and that market contact "appears to have generated more jobs for women and potentially given them a more significant economic role in the family" (268). Contact with the market did not appear to damage women's overall capacity to make money from sidelines, although in some areas home spinning was displaced by factory-made goods. Women participated in field agriculture under a number of regionally variable conditions: in the Yangzi delta where market involvement was high (and feminization of agriculture may have begun early), but also in southwestern rice-growing regions and northwestern areas where animal husbandry was dominant. With women's increasing capacity to earn money, they note, marriage age and marriage payments both increased.

In its rural base areas, the Chinese Communist Party mobilized women to do farm work and produce clothing while the men joined the army (Croll 1980, 1985c; Davin 1973). From the late 1930s on, the party's main goal for women was to provide aid in the war effort against Japan (Jackal 1981; Stranahan 1983b). During this period, the party began to stress the participation of women in social production, particularly of textiles, as the key to their emancipation, downplaying themes of family revolution (Davin 1973, 1976; K. Johnson 1983; Jackal 1981; Stranahan 1983b; Croll 1985c). In party publications from Yan'an in the early 1940s, the quintessential female figure was the labor heroine, who showed her perseverance and patriotism by working in agriculture or in spinning and weaving cooperatives that supplied soldiers and residents of the base area with clothing and shoes under conditions of blockade by the Guomindang. Such women, like their male counterparts, were an important part of the party's campaign to develop local leadership and link the party to the masses (Jackal 1981; Stranahan 1983a, 1983b).

WOMEN'S WORK IN THE PEOPLE'S REPUBLIC

During the early years of the PRC the party continued to insist, as it had in Yan'an and other base areas, that women would achieve liberation by participating in movements to benefit the nation, specifically those to raise production (Davin 1973, 1975b, 1976; Salaff and Merkle 1973; Croll 1979, 1985c; M. Young 1989; Evans 1999). Women's labor was regarded as an integral part of state development strategy. Campaigns to publicize women labor models in the 1950s emphasized women's enthusiasm for labor, their farming skills, and their strong bodies (Davin 1975b, 1976; Sheridan 1976; Hershatter 2000, 2002; T. Chen 2003a, 2003b). In periods of labor shortage, particularly during the Great Leap Forward of the late 1950s, women were mobilized in great numbers to join in paid urban and rural labor, in many cases freeing men for more highly skilled work (Andors 1983; Manning 2005). During periods of economic slowdown, such as the mid-1950s and early 1960s, however, state exhortations emphasized the importance of women's domestic roles: wife, mother, and housekeeper (Davin 1976; Croll 1980; Andors 1983; Hooper 1984). Kimberley Manning (2005) calls the official Maoist approach to mobilizing women "Marxist maternalist," because it sought to achieve gender equality by drawing women into remunerated labor, while continuing to attend to their reproductive health and unquestioned role in maintaining the family.

Overall, during the Mao years (1949–76), paid employment became a standard feature of urban women's lives (Z. Wang 2003). Studies of urban women's work during that period have focused on state policies that simultaneously called for gender equity and downplayed gender distinctions in favor of class, with mixed results for women's status, pay levels, and political activity. Men and women maintained rough wage equity for the same kind of work, but a gendered division of labor tracked men into the higher-paying state sector and into more skilled, prestigious jobs across sectors (Davin 1976; Andors 1983; Bauer et al. 1992; Y. Jiang 2004). These trends have continued and by some accounts intensified during the reform period (Broaded and Liu 1996; Riley 1997). In times of economic retrenchment women were treated as a source of surplus labor rather than an integral component of socialist construction (Andors 1983; Bauer et al. 1992). The state-mandated retirement age for men (sixty) was higher than that for women (fifty-five; Bauer et al. 1992). Within sectors, men tended to be more politically active and held a greater proportion of leadership positions (Andors 1983). Scholars have explained this as the result of negative social attitudes about women in leadership, as well as women's greater responsibility for household tasks, which drew them away from political meetings outside of working hours (Z. Wang 2003). In urban neighborhoods, however, formerly unemployed women took on new social welfare and surveillance tasks, becoming unpaid but locally powerful adjuncts of the state (Z. Wang 2005a, 2005b).

In the countryside, women received equal rights to land during the land reform, although in practice land was cultivated by the household (Davin 1973). The most important changes for women, however, came with the advent of collective agriculture and the Great Leap Forward (Davin 1975b, 1976; P. Huang 1990; Gao 1994; Hershatter 2002; Manning 2005; Friedman 2006). If one were to take Joan Kelly's (1984) question, "Did women have a Renaissance?" and adapt it to China by asking, "Did rural women have a Chinese revolution?" the Great Leap and collectivization periods would loom much larger than either 1949 or the Cultural Revolution. As collectivization progressed through mutual aid teams, lower and higher producers' cooperatives, and people's communes, women were expected to join in collective labor and were remunerated in work points. The mobilization of their labor was an important component in the state's rural development strategy, which focused initially on intensive cultivation and the diversification of economic activities, then began to encompass the improvement of agricultural techniques. Officially reported rates of women's participation in agricultural production reached 60 to 70 percent in 1957, and 90 percent by 1958, dropping again thereafter. Overall, the regional differences in women's agricultural participation reported by Buck appear to have persisted, with the highest rates in the south (Croll 1979, 1985c). During the Great Leap Forward, as many men were sent to work on steel-smelting or water-control projects, women took over much of the fieldwork and staffed nascent communal welfare facilities (Croll 1985c; Pasternak and Salaff 1993; Hershatter 2002; Manning 2005). In the post-Leap period, men began to move into small-scale rural industries, leaving women to work the land (Andors 1983) in another case of the feminization of agriculture.

Croll notes that state policies on women's labor were founded on contradictory assumptions: Mao's statement that "anything a man can do a woman can also do," and the widely shared belief that women's physical strength and characteristics suited them for lighter and less-skilled tasks (Croll 1985c). Work relationships enlarged women's social networks beyond their natal and marital families (Davin 1988; Hershatter 2000). At the same time, however, women routinely earned fewer work points than men for a full day's labor. Their lesser earning capacity engendered a variety of responses, including low morale, limited workforce participation, acceptance of their lower remuneration as "natural," and spirited back talk (Davin 1975b, 1976; Parish and Whyte 1978; Andors 1983; Hemmel and Sindbjerg 1984; Croll 1985c; M. Wolf 1985; Potter and Potter 1990; Pasternak and Salaff 1993; Unger 2002). Despite the lower rate of women's daily work points, their earnings were essential both to the collective and to their households (Pasternak and Salaff 1993; Hershatter 2003). Work points earned by household members were generally distributed to the head of household, not to individuals. Throughout the collective period, rural households remained units of production to a limited degree, with women chiefly responsible for the sidelines that brought in extra income (when they were permitted) and for the cultivation of the family's private plot (Croll 1981, 1985c, 1994; Hemmel and Sindbjerg 1984; P. Huang 1990; Jacka 1997; Mueggler 1998; H. Zhang 1999b).

Women also performed uncompensated domestic labor such as food processing and preparation, sewing and shoemaking, and child care (Davin 1975b, 1976; Andors 1983; M. Wolf 1985; Croll 1994; Hershatter 2003; H. Yan 2003). Collective facilities for all of these were limited to nonexistent, with the exception of a brief and disastrously managed series of experiments with collective dining halls during the Great Leap Forward (Davin 1975b, 1976, 1979; Croll 1985c; M. Wolf 1985; Gao 1994; Jacka 1997). In a common pattern, the older generation relied upon work points earned by younger adults, while the younger adults depended on their elders to provide housing and unpaid domestic labor (Davin 1975b, 1976; Croll 1981, 1983; Hemmel and Sindbjerg 1984; Manning 2005). Domestic work remained the purview of women, socially invisible (Hershatter 2003) and confined inside the household, which was categorized by the state as a sphere of decreasing economic importance (Jacka 1997) and a source of potentially bourgeois or feudal thinking (Rofel 1999b).

Croll (1985c) suggests that in the 1960s, the official women's movement changed its emphasis. Rather than regarding women's participation in social production as the key to emancipation, official campaigns began to target persistent attitudes about women's inferiority, especially such attitudes among women themselves. The focus on ideological change rather than production or social arrangements persisted during the Cultural Revolution and its aftermath. The 1973 campaign to criticize Lin Biao and Confucius, whatever its other entanglements in inner-party politics, provided a rare moment when gender inequality was openly addressed in the context of a political campaign, as Confucius was excoriated for regarding women as inferior and Lin Biao for acting as his covert disciple (Andors 1983; K. Johnson 1983; Croll 1980, 1985c).

Writing in the early years of the reform period, European and American feminist scholars offered a mixed assessment of the PRC's success in moving toward gender equality. An important piece of their critique focused on the gendered division of labor. The party-state, they said, had made important steps in legislating gender equality, mobilizing women for production, and promulgating the notion that women were equal to men. But scholars found inadequate the official explanation for persistent inequality—that remnants of feudal thinking persisted, particularly among the peasantry. Instead, they emphasized that although women had been mobilized to join in productive labor, they continued to be tracked into less-skilled, lower-paying jobs. In the industrial sector, women were concentrated in collective neighborhood workshops, where pay and working conditions were worse than in the state-owned sector (M. Wolf 1985). In the agricultural sector, more work points were allocated to "heavy" work performed by men, but "heavy" often denoted tasks involving large draft animals or the use of machinery presumed to require a skill; women's jobs paid less even when they involved more physical labor or brought in more income to the collective (M. Wolf 1985; Jacka 1997). Ever flexible in its content, the gendered division of labor consistently privileged men. As small-scale industries developed in the countryside, men moved into nonagricultural or supervisory positions, leaving women to perform the bulk of the less-skilled farm labor (Andors 1983; Croll 1983, 1985c; M. Wolf 1985; Jacka 1992; Judd 1994). Even as urban and rural women entered the paid labor force, within the household the bulk of domestic tasks and childcare continued to be the purview of women, intensifying their workload, especially after marriage, and affecting their ability to earn wages or work points and participate in political or leadership activities (Andors 1983; M. Wolf 1985; Pasternak and Salaff 1993; Parish and Busse 2000; Hershatter 2003, 2005a). The domestic workload remained heavy partly because the state's accumulation strategy called for investment in heavy industry rather than in producing consumer goods (clothing, shoes, washing machines) that might have lessened women's reproductive labor. In Elisabeth Croll's formulation, "the government had to a certain extent come to rely upon female unpaid labour to subsidize economic development programmes" (1983: 9).

In the countryside, collectivization not only undermined sidelines, an important sphere of women's economic activity, but also devalued domestic work of all types (Jacka 1992, 1997; Hershatter 2003). Furthermore, peasant households in the collective prospered according to the number of laborers they had. Thus parents had an incentive to increase household size; value permanent sons over daughters, who married out; and control the procurement of daughters-in-law who could give birth to a replacement generation of laborers. The persistence of patrilocal marriage made it impossible for farming households or the larger collectives based on networks of male kin to regard daughters as equal to sons (K. Johnson 1983).

In short, feminist scholars charged, the Maoist party-state had subscribed to a reductionist theory of women's liberation, focusing almost exclusively on bringing women into social production. It had assumed that economic development would lead to women's equality, rather than using the criterion of women's equality as a means to evaluate development policies (Andors 1983). It had been inconsistent in its pursuit of gender equality, always willing to give gender equality a lower priority than class conflict, patriarchal allegiances, or production goals (K. Johnson 1983; M. Wolf 1985). It had neglected the complex connections between women's economic role and cultural practices, contenting itself with a conservative approach to family relations and other social relations in which women were enmeshed (K. Johnson 1983; Jacka 1997). Paradoxically, the materialist approach of the party-state emphasized residual ideological sources of gender inequality to the neglect of material factors, including those factors newly created by state development policies themselves. The result, as Margery Wolf (1985; see also H. Yan 2003) puts it, was a "revolution postponed."

WOMEN'S WORK IN THE REFORM ERA

The feminist critique that attempts to achieve gender equality had over-emphasized ideology and neglected material factors mirrored the assessment that Deng Xiaoping and his comrades made of the Maoist period as a whole. For the Chinese reform leadership, however, addressing material factors meant permitting, even encouraging, inequalities in order to allow more advanced areas, sectors, and households to jump-start economic development. The result of a quarter-century of reform has been the proliferation and widening of inequalities—including those of gender—in the labor market. The same period has seen intensified attention to difference, including gender difference, across discursive realms.

At the outset of the reform period, the state announced a shift in priority from heavy to light and service industries, and promised increased resources to agriculture. For rural women, more than 80 percent of whom worked in collective agriculture, the biggest changes were the production responsibility system (in which households contracted out land from the collective) and the expansion of sidelines, both of which strengthened the peasant household as the unit of production (Croll 1983, 1985c). Many major features of the reforms have entailed shifts in or intensifications of a gendered division of labor. Women's previous roles in heavy industry and their participation in risky or dangerous labor were criticized as yet another instance of Maoist disregard for "natural" sex differences (Honig and Hershatter 1988; Jacka 1997; Y. Jiang 2004). For the reform period, scholars have tracked new urban and rural employment opportunities for women; their vulnerability to discrimination, harsh working conditions, and sexual harassment; and their role in the emergent floating population (M. Zhao and West 1999). Whyte (2000) offers a cogent warning about how difficult it is to assess overall trends in gender inequality during the reform era.

One important determinant of women's work opportunities is girls' differential access to education, itself a product of gender typing and the preferential allocation of resources to sons (Hooper 1984; Bauer et al. 1992; Bian, Logan, and Shu 2000; D. Li and Tsang 2003; D. Li 2004; W. Ma 2004). From 1949 to 1987, the gender gap in urban school enrollment and educational attainment narrowed, although it remained more pronounced in tertiary education (Bauer et al. 1992). In the early 1980s, both scientific and popular writings talked about how girls' intellectual abilities declined at puberty (M. Wolf 1985; Honig and Hershatter 1988); Beverley Hooper (1984) notes that some sources mention a decline in young women's mental abilities in college and beyond. One study of Wuhan students suggests that gendered stratification in the urban labor force is reflected and produced anew when students move from junior high into academic or vocational high schools. Girls with aspirations for higher education face gender-specific possibilities of becoming a less attractive marriage partner or failing to find a job, while boys expect to benefit more from additional academic achievement. Regardless of parental background, girls opt for keypoint academic programs (which receive the most resources and impose the highest entrance requirements) in far fewer numbers than boys, perpetuating a cycle in which more boys receive more education and enter technical and professional jobs at higher rates (Broaded and Liu 1996).

This reflects broader national trends in which girls in 1982 were 43.7 percent of primary school students and 39.2 percent of high school students (Hooper 1984: 321). In the early 1990s women were 70 percent of all illiterates, about one-third of vocational and technical students, one-third of university undergraduates, and a quarter of graduate students (Croll 1995: 134–35). An analysis of nationwide data from the 1980s and 1990s, however, suggests that in urban areas the percentage of female students enrolled in both high school and college is rising (Tang and Parish 2000; see also Z. Wang 2003), a finding that points to the contradictory and complex effects of reform-era policies on the status of women. And a Wuhan study of eighth graders in 1998–99 suggests that one effect of the one-child policy is to increase family investment in and expectations for urban girls, and thus to improve their performance in school (Tsui and Rich 2002).

Margery Wolf (1985) argues that the largest differential in access to education is not a gender gap, but an urban-rural one. In the countryside, she found, girls learned rudimentary literacy skills and then were often kept at home to do domestic labor. Among rural primary school students, nonattendance and dropout rates appear to be consistently higher among girls (Croll 1995; Riley 1997; D. Li and Tsang 2003). In the mid-1980s, rural surveys indicated that as school fees went up, parents began keeping their girl children at home to do domestic and agricultural work, saving their educational investment for the male children, who would not marry out (Hooper 1984; Davin 1988; Jacka 1997; D. Li and Tsang 2003; D. Li 2004).

Urban Labor in the Reform Era

In the early years of the reforms, absolute numbers of women employed in state and collective enterprises increased, with women comprising slightly more than one-third of the non-agricultural workforce (Robinson 1985: 35). At the same time, official periodicals noted a tendency for urban woman workers with small children to be furloughed at partial pay—sent, as Tamara Jacka (1990) puts it, "back to the wok." Through the mid-1990s, clerical, service, and sales jobs for women increased (Parish and Busse 2000). Data drawn from the 1990 and 1995 censuses, however, showed a 7 percent decline in paid labor among young women in cities and towns, some of it linked to women remaining at home to care for children (Parish and Busse 2000).

Studies of numerous sectors have documented job discrimination against women during the reform era, associated with perceptions that women's household and childrearing duties incur extra costs for the work unit and make women less productive workers or even that women properly belong in the domestic domain (Hooper 1984; Robinson 1985; Honig and Hershatter 1988; Jacka 1990; Woo 1994; Brownell 1995; Croll 1995; Gates 1996a; Riley 1997; Evans 2000; Parish and Busse 2000; J. Zang 2005). As they were in the Mao years, women continued to be clustered in collective rather than state-owned enterprises and in lower-paying sectors that could be regarded as an extension of the gendered domestic division of labor: catering, textiles, health, and early childhood education (Robinson 1985; Bian, Logan, and Shu 2000). Women appear to have less job mobility than men (Bian, Logan, and Shu 2000). A study based on the 1987 One Percent Population Survey found that urban women were underrepresented in more powerful positions, even when their education and experience were similar to those of men (Bauer et al. 1992).

Gendered disparities in urban waged work have remained stable (Bian, Logan, and Shu 2000) or intensified (Maurer-Fazio, Rawski, and Zhang

1999) in the period of economic reform. A study based on annual year-books of labor and wage statistics found that the ratio of women's to men's wages among 150 million regular urban employees declined between 1988 and 1994. Overall, women's earnings compared to those of men showed an overall decline from 55 percent in 1988 to 42 percent in 1994. Adjusted for location and type of ownership (state, collective, private), the ratio improved somewhat but still got sharply worse over time, from 66 percent in 1988 to 46 percent in 1994. Adjusted for economic sector and location, it stood at 86 percent in 1988, rose to 94 percent in 1991, then declined significantly to 75 percent in 1994. Surprisingly, the gender pay gap was smallest in some parts of the urban collective sector—where women sometimes earned more than men—grew larger in the state sector, and was largest of all in foreign and privately owned enterprises. The study concludes that gendered wage differences are substantially the result of the concentration of women workers in low-wage industries, and that growing wage variability in the Chinese economy is apt to make the gap increase (Maurer-Fazio, Rawski, and Zhang 1999).

Furthermore, in the 1990s and beyond, in response to management pressure, women retired at earlier ages and higher rates than men. They were also were laid off *(xiagang)* in higher numbers, comprising almost 40 percent of the urban work force but more than 60 percent of laid-off urban workers (Maurer-Fazio, Rawski, and Zhang 1999; Bian, Logan, and Shu 2000; Z. Wang 2003). Since laid-off women are still considered employees, but receive dramatically reduced wages, this too accentuates the wage gap (Maurer-Fazio, Rawski, and Zhang 1999; see also Bian, Logan, and Shu 2000). This study is partially disputed by William Parish and Sarah Busse (2000), who draw generally more optimistic conclusions, but others (see, for example, X. Huang 1999; Milwertz 1997; Jacka 1990; Y. Jiang 2004) point to increased labor market stratification, both between men and women and among women (married vs. unmarried, migrant vs. local).

The status and security associated with work in a state-owned factory has diminished under the reforms, leading to increased stress upon women workers (M. Zhao 1999; Z. Wang 2003). Writing of Hangzhou silk workers in the 1980s and 1990s, Rofel (1989, 1994a, 1999b) suggests that generational difference inflects women's understandings of the Maoist past, of gender, and of modernity. Women who worked in the pre-1949 silk industry experienced "Liberation nostalgia." For them, the revolution removed the stigma attached to women who worked in the "outside" space of the factory, affording them opportunities to refashion themselves as honorable laborers and perform tasks that formerly had been the preserve of men. This labor, and the transgression of gender boundaries it entailed, became and remained central to their identities as women. For the Cultural Revolution generation of women workers, their formative experience in the mills entailed resisting authority. In the reform period, they continued this practice in oblique form. They resisted management practices designed to increase their productivity, as well as official and semiofficial representations of them as obstacles to modernity, lazy individuals inured to responsibility by years of "eating out of one big pot." Although men as well as women have been subject to new disciplinary regimes, the jobs affected primarily have been women's work. Some of these practices, particularly the position-wage system introduced in the mid-1980s, have privileged younger workers (Rofel 1989, 1999b). But members of this younger cohort, unlike their seniors, have not identified themselves primarily as women factory workers. Instead they have located their self-understanding in discourses of femininity and motherhood, relegating worker identity to a peripheral status (Rofel 1994a, 1999b).

Each of these generational positionings reflects, but cannot be reduced to, the distinct state visions of modernity that affected the three cohorts. For all three cohorts, however, "gender serves as one of the central modalities through which modernity is imagined and desired" (Rofel 1999b: 19). Rofel's work opens up a productive set of questions about how different temporal points of entry have produced different notions of "woman" and "worker," even within a single factory in a specific industry. Furthermore, her work suggests that local meanings of gender, reform, or modernity cannot be adduced completely from state pronunciamentos. They are, rather, worked out in part on the shop floor (and on work breaks, and after hours) by women who are the intended objects of party-state policy (1992, 1999b).

Rofel's study concludes before the large-scale layoffs of the 1990s in state-owned industries, but it is clear that middle-aged and older women, regarded as unskilled and perhaps untrainable, have been treated as the most superfluous of all workers (Gates 1999; Evans 2002), often encountering downward mobility into paid domestic labor (Z. Wang 2003). Young women, in contrast, are valorized in both state-owned and private factories for their productivity (Rofel 1989, 1999b), docility, nimbleness, and low wage cost (Croll 1995).

Little has been written as yet about several groups of women in emergent areas of the privatizing economy. One such group is the wives of "new rich" entrepreneurs, many of whom run family-based businesses. David Goodman's study of such enterprises in Shanxi finds that in both urban and rural enterprises, wives have taken on the role of business manager.

He dismisses "the notion that the wives of the new rich were 'nonwork-ing'" (2004: 30). Another group is women managers in the private sector. A recent survey of such women in Shanghai and Beijing finds that they regard networking and establishing relationships *(guanxi)* with male busi-ness associates as integral to their success, that they remain preoccupied with balancing family and work demands, and that they draw support from Web sites for professional and business women (Wylie 2004).

Migrant Labor in the Reform Era

During the Mao era, small numbers of married women had migrated to urban areas to work as domestics (H. Yan 2003), but the residence regis-tration *(hukou)* system ensured that most rural people remained in the countryside. In the reform era, restrictions on population movement were lifted, although many barriers to taking up full legal residence in a new place remained (Solinger 1999; Davin 1999). In addition to migrating for marriage (C. Fan and Huang 1998; C. Fan and Li 2002) and in some cases being trafficked from poor to rich regions for the same purpose, many rural women migrated to cities in search of work. Known as *dagong mei*, work-ing sisters or working girls, they comprised 30 to 40 percent of the floating population, whose total size was estimated in the late 1990s at 100 million. In regions such as the Special Economic Zones of south China, however, women may have comprised three-quarters or more of the total migrant population (Pun 1999; Solinger 1999; Jacka 1998, 2000; Woon 2000; Jacka and Gaetano 2004). Four million *dagong mei* were concentrated in the Pearl River delta in the mid-1990s (S. Tan 2000). Migrant women are the major-ity of workers in toy and electronic manufacture, textiles, domestic work, and prostitution (Jacka 2005).

Women are less likely than men to leave rural areas (Davin 1999; X.Yang 2000; C. Fan 2003), have fewer and lower-paying job options (H. Zhang 1999a; S. Tan 2000, 2004; S. Goldstein, Liang, and Goldstein 2000; F. Wang 2000; F. Xu 2000; C. Fan 2003; Liang and Chen 2004; Jacka and Gaetano 2004; Jacka 2005), do not migrate as far from home (Jacka 1997; Riley 1997; Davin 1999; X. Yang 2000; S. Goldstein, Liang, and Goldstein 2000), and tend unlike men to migrate primarily when unmarried (Davin 1997, 1999; Jacka 1997, 2005; X. Yang and Guo 1999; F. Wang 2000; C. Fan 2003; Liang and Chen 2004; Jacka and Gaetano 2004).* Women who decide to migrate

---

*For recent countervailing data about the increasing migration of married women, see Lou et al. 2004; and K. Roberts et al. 2004. On married women migrants in Beijing, see Jacka 2005.

are apt to exhibit particular individual and household circumstances (higher educational level, not yet married), whereas migrant men, regardless of individual factors, appear to be motivated primarily by economic conditions in their home villages (X. Yang and Guo 1999). Women who do make the move tend to stay in the city longer than men do (Song 1999). The majority move to urban areas for economic reasons, often doing so without other family members (F. Wang 2000). But even when they migrate alone, women, like men, tend to be sent to the cities as part of a rural household strategy. Their remittances home are an important family resource, helping fund wedding expenses, home building, and small rural enterprises (Davin 1997, 1999; H. Zhang 1999a; Jacka 2005; F. Xu 2000, however, sees such remittances as less important).

As urban women have increasingly moved out of urban textile work, which they regard as dirty, tiring, and low paying, young rural women have replaced them (Rofel 1999b; Solinger 1999). In the Special Economic Zones (SEZs) of the Pearl River delta, women work in foreign-owned factories assembling electronic goods, toys, clothing, and shoes (Davin 1999). The SEZs, which have attracted a great deal of Hong Kong capital, have become a space in which international capital and migrant women laborers interact uneasily with each other and with local governments, who have little incentive to enforce national and provincial regulations protecting migrants because they fear the loss of international capital investment (S. Tan 2000).

Prevalent urban discourses on the floating population are overwhelmingly negative (Solinger 1999; Jacka 1998, 2000, 2005; S. Tan 2000; F. Xu 2000; Sun 2004a; Hanser 2005; Pun 2005), with minor notes of ambivalence and exhortations to sympathy (Jacka 2005). Rural migrants are held responsible for urban crowding, crime, and health problems, and have also become the target of urban dwellers' displaced anxieties as the state dismantles the regime of guaranteed jobs, subsidized housing, health care, and other public goods that they enjoyed for more than forty years (Solinger 1999; also see Chao 2003). Migrants themselves have no access to such services and are subject to regulation, surveillance, discrimination, and abuses of power (Solinger 1999; Jacka 2005). If migrants stand in for the depredations of the market in the minds of permanent urbanites, women migrants are often portrayed in the press as victims of that same market, easily tricked and subject to abuse and sexual harassment, in ways that heighten the distance between their purported naïveté and the putatively more sophisticated urban population (Jacka 1998, 2000, 2005; S. Tan 2000, 2004; Sun 2004a). They are also blamed for engaging in prostitution (V. Ho 1998–99; F. Xu

2000; Chao 2003; Sun 2004a), conducting extramarital affairs with local men, and destabilizing marriages (S. Tan 2000). Additionally, they have drawn the attention of population researchers when they become sexually active (often without using contraception) and cohabit with men from the migrant population, resulting in unwanted pregnancies and abortions (Z. Zheng et al. 2001).

In 1992–93, Ching Kwan Lee conducted fieldwork in two plants operated by the Hong Kong-based Liton Electronics Ltd., one in Hong Kong and the other in Shenzhen. Lee describes "two worlds of factory women": in the Shenzhen plant, young unmarried women from the countryside labored under a minutely calibrated and closely supervised disciplinary regime, while in the Hong Kong factory, middle-aged women performed identical tasks on a much more flexible schedule (Lee 1998). Many aspects of the Shenzhen arrangement—young workers separated from their places of origin, overlapping family and localistic ties among workers and between workers and supervisors, fines for infractions, and housing provided by the work unit—would be familiar to veterans of Republican factory regimes (both Chinese- and foreign-owned). In contrast, the Hong Kong workforce of what Lee calls "matron workers" appears to have evolved from the "working daughters of Hong Kong" in the early 1970s described by Janet Salaff (1981). In effect, the Hong Kong factory workforce has aged, while young Hong Kong women now seek work outside the declining manufacturing sector. What has remained constant for these Hong Kong workers is "familial hegemony," in Lee's term. As daughters, Salaff found, their labor power was controlled by their parents; as mothers, Lee tells us, they remain in factory work partly because they can combine it with domestic responsibilities. Lee attributes the differences between the "two worlds" of Shenzhen and Hong Kong to the differing social organization of the two labor markets, which she says mandates different management strategies and results in "two gendered regimes of production." Her work suggests areas for further exploration about factory regimes and gendered labor markets: Does the origin of investment capital make a difference? Does urban location? Does distance of the workers from their places of origin?

Pun Ngai (1999, 2005) describes how Shenzhen managers in the mid-1990s used rural origin, finely calibrated regional and dialect differences, and gender to create social hierarchies with *dagong mei* at the bottom. This attempt to impose labor control depends on inducing a sense of inferiority in *dagong mei* while inciting a simultaneous desire among them to overcome rural origins by becoming modern, disciplined workers. Pun points out that whereas *gongren* (worker) in Maoist discourse was a gender-neutral term, *dagong mei* are obviously female, young, and expected to perform gender-specific roles in the factory. Yet managers constantly berate *dagong mei* for failing to act like proper women, suggesting that the attempt to furnish young women workers with a prefabricated identity is not completely successful. In a study of *dagong mei* in an electronics factory in Shenzhen, Pun (2000, 2005; see also Unger 2000; S. Tan 2000; Woon 2000) describes a work environment that, except for the specifics of production, differs little from that of Republican-era cotton mills: twelve-hour work days, crowded dormitories, factories with the temperature controlled for the convenience of the product rather than the worker, required use of irritating and dangerous substances, and workers in chronic bodily pain. Pun understands the pain as "an index of social alienation and domination in the workplace" (2000: 542), but also, somewhat less convincingly, as a form of resistance to the work itself. She also speculates (2000, 2005) about the psychic trauma such women experience when they realize that they are caught between an unacceptable past (their poor hometowns), a difficult present (the work and their sense that they have been commodified), and a rapidly approaching and unpredictable future (twenty-four is considered old among the workers in such factories). Women have been known to respond to bad working conditions by slowing down production lines, returning home, or striking (Jacka 1997; H. Zhang 1999a; Pun 2005), and employers have responded by requiring women to pay a deposit, withholding payment, or impounding their identification cards (S. Tan 2000).

Beyond the special economic zones of Shenzhen, Feng Xu (2000) examines the lives of migrant women working in silk factories in a small Jiangnan town in 1995–96. She finds that when unmarried rural women from Subei leave home to become factory workers, they "cross gender, class and place of origin boundaries" (F. Xu 2000: 30). As with earlier generations of rural migrant factory women, this transgression of boundaries makes them vulnerable, cheap, highly controlled labor and denigrated natives of a "backward" region. It also, women migrants report, provides opportunities to escape from household obligations, evade parental control, experience town life, and acquire a degree of independence.

Lisa Rofel (1994a, 1999b) describes older Hangzhou urban factory workers as speaking bitterness in a nostalgic register. By this she means that they feel the state is no longer listening or endorsing their past heroism at work. In speaking bitterness they are talking back to contemporary state discourses that marginalize them, addressing a state that initially provided them with the language and the venues to speak bitterness in the 1950s (Hershatter 1993). Jacka (1998; also see Jacka and Petkovic 1998) finds that the Maoist discourse of speaking bitterness endures in the language that *dagong mei* use to describe unjust treatment by urban people, although theirs is not a grievance endorsed by the state, and they are too young to have lived with Maoist terminology or political practice firsthand.

Jacka (1998, 2005) explores the stories that *dagong mei* tell about themselves in Hangzhou and Beijing as a form of "answering back" the urbanites who denigrate them. Rural women working in silk and cotton textile factories, clothing manufacture, and service industries describe how they conduct themselves honorably and resourcefully in a world of exploitative and uncaring urban people who discriminate against them. Their narrative predilection for self-dramatization and hopeful endings, Jacka suggests, may draw upon the conventions of television drama and post-1949 political discourse. At the same time, Jacka observes, their own depictions of rural life as dull and migration as a way out of family and village oppression reinforce urban tales about the "backwardness" of rural China and its inhabitants (Jacka 1998, 2000, 2005; Jacka and Petkovic 1998). In her most recent study of Beijing migrant women (2005), Jacka asks, "What histories of experience constitute the rural migrant woman, and what discourses enable and constrain those histories?" In the process of migration from rural locations (regarded as marginal to national modernity) to urban areas, women generate and encounter changing expectations about self and behavior, understand themselves to be moving away from established norms, and frequently describe themselves as caught painfully between rural and urban identities. Jacka finds that gender does not loom nearly as large as rural origin in their narrations of identity and experience.

In what Hairong Yan (following Gayatri Spivak [2000]) calls a "spectralization of the rural," post-Mao economic changes have "robbed the countryside of its ability to serve as a locus for rural youth to construct a meaningful identity." Women migrants, Yan argues, have come to regard the countryside as a "field of death" that they must flee in order to become modern subjects (2003: 579; see also Pun 2005; Jacka 2005). First-person accounts of migrant women's working lives, while detailing difficult working conditions, harassment, and uncertainty about the future, routinely portray migration as an important rite of passage that transforms the women, rendering them wiser and more mature and altering their aspirations (H. Zhang 1999a; Jacka 2000, 2004, 2005; H. Yan 2003; Jacka and Song 2004; Beynon 2004). Migrant women may feel torn "between the desire for personal autonomy and the sense of moral obligation to the family of origin" (Woon 2000: 148; see also Jacka 2005), but they also articulate explicit desires to see the world, earn their own income, and enhance or postpone their marriage choices (H. Zhang 1999a; H. Yan 2003; Jacka 2005).

Whereas most studies of women migrant laborers to date have focused on factory workers, Li Zhang (2000, 2001) reminds us that women migrants are a diverse and stratified group. Her ethnographic research on 1990s Wenzhou migrants in Beijing's Zhejiang village traces three types of situations. In wealthy migrant families that have moved from garment production to marketing clothing and real estate development, women have left household-based production, often at the behest of their husbands, for a newly created "inner" realm where they supervise domestic consumption, finding themselves increasingly excluded from male-dominated business transactions and social spaces. Zhang finds that women often see this new role as confining and resist it in a variety of ways. In less prosperous migrant households in the same community, women engage in garment production at home or cook for and supervise waged laborers, specializing in "inside" production tasks rather than the "outside" procurement of materials or marketing, which are handled by men. As in other labor situations (Jacka 1997; Rofel 1999b), "inside" and "outside" are flexible and often redefined; selling garments at a fixed counter or stall in the market, for instance, is "inside" work suitable for women, while traveling to arrange new sale sites is an "outside" male task. Finally, young woman workers, often from other areas, are hired to make garments in Wenzhou household workshops. Unlike the first two groups, they do not migrate with families and tend to have little control over their working conditions or their own time and space. Zhang's analysis shows that differential access to social spaces helps to configure gender relations; women's ability to engage in productive labor and earn wages does not guarantee gender equality in the reform period any more than it did under Mao.

Young rural women have also found employment in township and village enterprises (TVEs), which may or may not be near their home villages (Croll 1983, 1995; Gao 1994; Zhou 1996; Jacka 1997; H. Zhang 1999b; Jin 2004; Yuen, Law, and Ho 2004; Friedman 2006). In 1979, about 28 million workers, one-third of them women, worked in such enterprises (Croll 1983: 39); by 1992 the number had grown to 100 million, more than 40 percent of them women (Croll 1995: 129). In 1993, the absolute number employed rose to 123.5 million, with women comprising 30 to 40 percent. Here as in other enterprises, women were found in the lower income ranges, but gendered income differences were small (Jacka 1997).

At the same time that various factory regimes, in urban and rural venues, sought out young women workers, the rapid proliferation of venues for sex work, hostessing, and secretarial jobs has placed a premium on youthful and attractive female labor (Z. Wang 2003; Zheng 2004; Yuen, Law, and Ho 2004; Hanser 2005). No longer "eating out of one big pot" side by side with their male counterparts, wage-earning women from both urban and rural areas often traded on their youth and beauty by "eating spring rice" instead—a phrase used to refer exclusively to women. Hanser (2005) argues that class distinctions in urban China were often conveyed through gendered images; department stores serving elite consumers, for instance, differentiated themselves from state-owned or low-class retailers by featuring tastefully dressed, attractive young female attendants. Among prostitutes in some Chinese cities, rural women predominated (Solinger 1999), particularly in the lower-paying echelons. But segmentation in the sex-work labor market was evident, with reports of university graduates and attractive young urban women choosing prostitution as a lucrative enterprise that also gave them access to socially powerful men (Hershatter 1997; V. Ho 1998–99).

Rural women of various ages have also moved into urban domestic work, which is generally not an occupation urban people fill themselves (Gao 1994; Croll 1995; Davin 1997, 1999; Jacka 1997; H. Zhang 1999a; Solinger 1999; Jacka 2000, 2005; Z. Wang 2003; H. Yan 2003; Gaetano 2004; Sun 2004b). Native-place connections are important here; many nursemaids are from poorer areas in Anhui and Sichuan. Nursemaiding in Beijing has become a transitional occupation for women who then move on to private business or other service work (Croll 1995; Jacka 1997; Solinger 1999). Davin (1999) suggests that of all migrant laborers, young women working as maids observe at closest range urban standards of living and social practices. For all young women migrants who eventually return to their villages, the move back home may be fraught with the attempt to integrate aspects of the urban life they have seen into a rural environment (Davin 1999; Jacka 2005). Those who return to the countryside after some years away may have problems readjusting to rural life and marriage (S. Tan 2004; Beynon 2004; Fan 2004; Murphy 2004).

Rural Labor in the Reform Era

Perhaps the most important feature of the rural reforms was the reemergence of the household as the primary unit of "production, consumption, and welfare" (Croll 1994: xii). In the early years of the reforms, land was reallocated to households, although in many places men were issued more than women were (Judd 1994). Feminist scholars worried that the return to household farming would mean the confinement of women to isolated labor under patriarchal authority (Andors 1983; Croll 1983; Dalsimer and Nisonoff 1987; Davin 1988, 1989), and some researchers do report that women's status has fallen (H. Yan 2003). As Ellen Judd dryly notes, however, "Advantages that Western feminists see for Chinese women in all-women work groups in a collective economy do not seem to be valued by rural Chinese women, who did not experience these work groups as necessarily supportive or enhancing" (1994: 233). Rather than a restoration of prerevolutionary arrangements, since the mid-1980s a rather different pattern of gender stratification has emerged. Women have been actively involved in household-based enterprises (Judd 1994; Y. Jin 2004), peddling farm goods at periodic markets, opening small-scale stores, and running restaurants (Zhou 1996). Jacka (1997) argues that three dichotomies, none of them new, shaped the gendered division of labor in rural reform China: outside/inside, heavy/light, and sometimes skilled/unskilled, with the first and more highly valued term in each binary associated with men. These binaries, which she calls stereotypes rather than categories of fixed content, are reproduced through education, recruitment, and individual careers. As in earlier periods, "inside" did not imply literal confinement in domestic space, and could involve work in the fields and in the village, while "outside" increasingly came to imply work beyond the village.

As men of all ages and younger women have left in increasing numbers for work in cities and towns, agriculture has become even more feminized than it was under Mao. In many areas it is almost exclusively the responsibility of married and older women (Croll 1983, 1995; Zhou 1996; Davin 1997, 1999; Riley 1997; Jacka 1992, 1997; H. Zhang 1999b; Judd 1994; Bossen 1994, 2000, 2002; Michelson and Parish 2000; X. Yang 2000; C. Fan and Li 2002; C. Fan 2003; Murphy 2004). In some areas, women have become agricultural contractors responsible for relatively large tracts of land (Croll 1994). Yet agriculture's place in the gendered division of labor is flexible: "where demand for agricultural employment cannot be fully satisfied, women's domestic responsibilities are used as a legitimation for keeping women off the land. Where, on the other hand, a maintenance of labour in agriculture is of more concern, women's domestic responsibilities are used as a legitimation for keeping women on the land" (Jacka 1997: 136).

Where men left for distant venues, returning home only occasionally, women become the effective heads of household; Croll (1995: 127) found this to be the case for 23 percent of all Guangxi households and 61 percent of the poorer households. Women began to engage in the production of delicate needlework goods, and were paid on a piecework basis, often by local levels of government that contracted sales with foreign companies (Croll

1994). Domestic sideline production, historically the province of women (Croll 1983), by the late 1980s burgeoned into a "courtyard economy" that drew on two potential resources: women's underused labor and courtyard space (Judd 2002). In the 1980s this formed the centerpiece of rural development plans encouraged by the Women's Federation and other agencies (Jacka 1992, 1997; Judd 2002). Participation in the courtyard economy, whose development varied by region and proximity to urban markets, gave women increased flexibility and income as well as an increasingly heavy workload (Croll 1995; Jacka 1997; Judd 2002). In poorer interior areas, county development strategies often neglected projects that would provide for the basic needs of rural women, including water, electricity, education, and microloans (Han 2004). Domestic labor, as before, was mainly the purview of women, among minority groups as well as the Han (Pasternak and Salaff 1993; M. Zhang 1999). Women also became "managers and inventors of ritual occasions" including festivals, celebrations, and local theatrical performances (McLaren 2004b).

Among the occupations that have reopened to women in the reform era is entrepreneurship (Gates 1999; H. Zhang 1999b; Z. Wang 2003). Yet the movement of women into petty commerce has been constricted by lingering—or perhaps constantly reconfigured—notions of inner/outer social locations. Women in the market have been seen as "too brazen" (Rofel 1999b: 103) or have worried that the social requirements of doing business— traveling alone, smoking, talking to non-kin men—might damage their reputations (Honig and Hershatter 1988; Judd 1990; F. Xu 2000). Mayfair Yang (1994b) notes that many men thought that women who wanted to develop the network of social connections *(guanxi)* required in business would invariably be asked for sexual favors. At the same time, however, she finds that women are often deployed by their male relatives to make requests of other men, and women are very active in the "domestic" cultivation of *guanxi* among relatives, friends, and neighbors. And in Fujian and Zhejiang, women have been the central actors in rotating savings and credit associations *(hui)* that are used to fund small-scale enterprises. Tsai (2000) argues that women's lack of mobility relative to men in the reform era has made them a better credit risk and increased their opportunities to exercise economic agency, while the social costs for women of joining such associations are less than those for men.

In a study of gendered identities among the Naxi people of Yunnan during the reform era, Sydney White (1997) finds that Naxi men and women "reify the hardship, suffering, and sacrifice of Naxi women for their families" (317), a suffering epitomized by nonstop work in the fields and at home. White argues that in contrast to the ethos of suffering among Han women (which is ubiquitous in Han rural women's narrations of self; see Hershatter 2003, 2005a), the Naxi do not privatize such suffering, but valorize it within families and communities. Although Han and minority notions of female suffering may have more in common than White suggests (or, alternatively, may be even more varied if other minority groups are considered as well), this inquiry opens up a series of questions about how women's virtue in relationship to work is being reformulated under the new circumstances of the reforms.

3. National Modernity

Twentieth-century Chinese intellectuals and revolutionaries, and China scholars after them, have had a longstanding preoccupation with the failed Chinese state prior to 1949 and hence the need for revolution, and the expansive revolutionary state after 1949 and its degree of success. Women's status emerged early on in this analysis as a key symptom of a weak state and a key sign of a strong one. In twentieth-century China, women were figures through which national modernity was imagined, often articulated through a language of crisis: if the status of women is not raised, if the factors that drive women into prostitution are not ameliorated, the nation will perish. If Chinese women are liberated, the Chinese nation will be strong, leaving behind both feudalism and the precarious sovereignty of semicolonialism (R. Chow 1991b; Hershatter 1993, 1997; Greenhalgh 2001; Karl 2002). Long before the emergence of the PRC and its policies, "the woman question" focused on a critique of Chinese state forms that shaded over into a critique of Chinese civilization itself.

In the late nineteenth century, Liang Qichao famously declared that China was being decimated by an expansive West because it was a weak civilization, and that it was weak, in part, because its footbound, cloistered women were not productive citizens, but parasites. Factual accuracy is not important to this argument: Liang had to look away from the massive amounts of productive labor performed by both peasant and elite women, in the household (for all) and in the household's interaction with the market (for poorer families), in order to make this statement. Nevertheless, the linkage he made between women, the health of the civilization, and the viability of the state was taken up enthusiastically by others.

Eventually this linkage was elaborated into what Dorothy Ko (1994, 2005) has called the May Fourth story, told by intellectuals of the New

Culture movement and its political offshoots (including, eventually, the CCP): that Chinese civilization was in thrall to a disabling hierarchy, that women and their status in the family, under the weight of Confucian (later "feudal") thinking, were emblematic of that disability, that only by ending the hierarchy would the Chinese people, and their state formation, cast off disability and "stand up," as Mao put it in 1949. In this telling, Chinese women were simultaneously the victims of disabling ideologies and practices, and the site of disability, the backward and benighted object in need of reform. From the time of the New Culture/May Fourth moment of the late 1910s and early 1920s, depending on who was writing, this "woman and the nation" story marched forward more or less in step with the growth of the revolutionary movement. (In some accounts the May Fourth moment was preceded by a brief surge of heroic women's revolutionary activity in the immediate run-up to the 1911 Revolution.)

As many historians of women and the Chinese revolution have pointed out, this formulation led to powerful dual consequences. It put gender equality on the agenda of all revolutionary parties and many intellectuals in the twentieth century. Liberating women from oppression was an integral part of liberating the nation from weakness and therefore an important way in which revolutionaries justified their claim to power. For the revolutionary CCP and for its less effective adversary, the GMD, the status and treatment of women were taken as a signal of how well state-building was going. The Communist Party, in particular, drew much of its power from its promise to rescue the nation from feudalism, imperialism, Japanese invasion, and Guomindang oppression. At the same time, it subordinated the fate of women to that of the nation, and whenever raising the status of women was perceived to threaten the status of the nation, or its prospects for revolutionary transformation, gender equality was deferred.

Scholars, especially those attentive to feminism, took up this story, tracking the changing state policies of the PRC and asking: How have they affected women? How successful were their reforms? How willing to subordinate gender to class? With the onset of economic reform in the early 1980s, women's studies scholars continued to raise many of the same kinds of questions, although an attention to socialism's neglect of women was replaced by dismay that the state might be abandoning women altogether to the depredations of global capitalism.

QING CONVERSATIONS

Nineteenth-century Westerners in China, many of them missionaries, concentrated their critique of women's status and their reform efforts on abolishing footbinding and educating girls (Drucker 1981; Borthwick 1985; C. Tao 1994; Kwok 1996; H. Fan 1997; Mann 1998; W. Ye 1994, 2001; Ko 2005). Because most of their contact was with poor women and the wives of treaty-port merchants, early missionaries were not cognizant of a long tradition of women's learning among elite families (Mann 1998). By the turn of the century, however, some aimed at schooling girls from educated families in missionary institutions such as McTyeire School in Shanghai (Ross 1996) and St. Hilda's School in Wuchang (J. Liu and Kelly 1996). In the twentieth century, women missionaries became involved in projects devoted to the rescue of young prostitutes in Shanghai (Gronewold 1996) and domestic slave girls in Yunnan (Jaschok 1994); similar institutions had been established in the nineteenth century by treaty-port gentry opposed to the abuse and trafficking of young girls (Rogaski 1997). New community networks formed among Chinese Christian women in Protestant denominations, and some participated in health and social work campaigns (Jaschok 1994; Kwok 1992, 1996). These commitments to social welfare later led some Chinese Christian women, particularly those of the YWCA, into labor organizing and radical politics (Honig 1986, 1996; Kwok 1992).

At the turn of the twentieth century, in an atmosphere of national crisis, reformers expanded upon missionary arguments about women's low status. Kang Youwei petitioned the throne to ban footbinding, while Liang Qichao named women's education as the key to all reform efforts, including strengthening the economy, producing "sage mothers and good wives," and improving the race (Ono 1989; Borthwick 1985; Gipoulon 1989–90; Rong 1983; Levy 1992; C. Tao 1994; Z. Wang 1999; Bailey 2001; McElroy 2001; Judge 2002b; Zurndorfer 2005). Anti-footbinding societies became popular in coastal cities and then moved inland (Croll 1980; Ono 1989; Drucker 1981; Levy 1992; C. Tao 1994; Cheng 2000; Ko 2005). Qian Nanxiu (2003) has recently argued that women reformers in the 1890s pursued an agenda somewhat distinct from that of their male counterparts. Focusing less upon the oppression of "tradition" than on the organization of "worthy ladies" (xianyuan), Xue Shaohui and other women helped to found a girl's school, a journal, and a study society. Supported in their organizing efforts by some Western women in Shanghai but drawing their main inspiration from classical practices of Chinese women's learning, they celebrated women's erudition, seeking to nurture women's talent and knowledge for the revitalization of China.

After the failure of the 1898 reforms, this optimistic note faded. Women writers such as Chen Xiefen characterized women as enslaved in an unequal gender system, which in turn helped weaken China and expose it to the danger of enslavement by global colonizing forces (Karl

2002). Radical anti-Qing activists such as Jin Songcen, author of the 1903 *Women's Bell*, envisioned women who would study, work, own property, choose their own friends and husbands, and participate in politics (Rong 1983; Borthwick 1985; Z. Wang 1999; Bailey 2001). In Jin's vision, women would strengthen the nation by becoming more like men; women's rights were subordinated to this overriding nationalist project (Zarrow 1990; Edwards 1994). Many of these writings made explicit appeal to Western gender relations as a model (Borthwick 1985; Gilmartin 1999; Cheng 2000). Qing reformers and revolutionaries shared with the missionaries a representation of Chinese women as benighted and oppressed, albeit in need of saving by nationalistic reform rather than Christianity (Cheng 2000). As Dorothy Ko (1994), Hu Ying (1997, 2000), and others (see, for example, Judge 2002b, 2004; N. Qian 2003) have pointed out, this story of the Chinese woman and her identification with a nation mired in oppressive tradition entailed forgetting that elite women had been educated for centuries, or disregarding and trivializing their literary accomplishments. What we now conventionally call the "May Fourth" story of oppression/ tradition and liberation/modernity, Hu Ying argues, actually took shape in the late Qing.

This narrative also elides the role of non-elite women in antimodern rebellions against the Qing New Policies, far-ranging and expensive reforms inaugurated in the last years of dynastic rule. These rebels included Ninth Sister Liao in the 1902 Sichuan Red Lantern uprising, Ding Fei and her Jiangsu vegetarian sisterhood, and others (Prazniak 1986, 1999). The scant records of their activism are a reminder of how little we know of the daily lives of peasant women, but the record does offer intriguing hints that "involvement in the market economy and participation in lay Buddhist networks" (Prazniak 1999: 244) contributed to women's collective actions (on women in the Boxer Rebellion, see also Ono 1989).

Shanghai magazines and newspapers at the turn of the century portrayed "new women" in unprecedented spatial and social locations, establishing them as embodiments of the modern (Mittler 2003). In late Qing novels set in Shanghai, courtesans were represented as trend setters, experimenting with hybrid mixtures of Chinese and foreign clothing in a manner that destabilized social and national identities. This instability in turn occasioned anxious commentary about a turmoil-filled social world within the novels and in the wider society (Zamperini 2003). In other Qing novels and travelogues, Chinese woman travelers abroad became key figures through which boundaries between "inner" and "outer," Chinese and foreign, were redefined (Y. Hu 1997, 2000). At the same time, reworked and appropriated tales of imported woman figures such as *La Dame aux camélias,* Sophia Perovskaia, and Madame Roland acted "as a catalyst" for the emergent figure of the new Chinese woman (Y. Hu 2000).

Women students who traveled to Japan and the United States were also important agents in imagining China as a nation and reconfiguring the place of women in it. In the early twentieth century, Chinese students (both male and female) in Tokyo, many of them anarchists, denounced the oppression of women over thousands of years of Chinese history, calling for a revolution in beliefs and practice (Ono 1989; Borthwick 1985; H. Liu 2003; Xia 2004). Chinese woman students in Japan during the first decade of the century seldom numbered more than 100, but many of them became important in the revolutionary movement that overthrew the Qing (Judge 2001). Joan Judge points out that as the Chinese national subject was being invented in the late Qing period, male thinkers of every persuasion incorporated women into their vision of the nation: conservative monarchists promoted nationalist patriarchy (Judge 2001, 2002a; see also Duara 1998, 2003), constitutional monarchs emphasized "mothers of citizens" (see also Judge 1997), and radical nationalists and revolutionaries (including many women) called for women's full political participation in a modern nation. In several recent articles on Chinese women students in Japan, Judge (2001, 2002b, 2003, 2005) has explored the "paradoxes that arise when women use nationalism as their own authorizing discourse" (2001: 765), a process that enabled them to develop new subjectivities but also constrained them within the bounds of a patriotic femininity. Development of individual talent or collective feminist goals was secondary to rescuing China from its national crisis, a theme later continued by the Communist Party. Nevertheless, Judge (2002b, 2003, 2005) suggests, in Japan these women students helped shape the transformation of cultural meanings of gender, often in ways that brought them into conflict with Japanese educators. As they attended classes and political meetings, founding and writing for radical women's journals, their sense of themselves, gender, and the world shifted so that the nation became a matter of concern for them.

Tokyo was arguably the site of the first Chinese feminist movement to take shape separate from nationalist anti-Qing activism. Organized by anarchist He Zhen in 1907, the Women's Rights Recovery Association located the cause of women's oppression in an economic system that forced them to depend upon men, rather than in national weakness (Zarrow 1988, 1990). For anarchists, "state and family were related forms of authoritarianism" (1990: 130), although He Zhen remained the only prominent women figure to emerge in the anarchist movement over the quarter-century that followed (Müller 2005).

Unlike He Zhen, most late Qing feminists were deeply involved in the antidynastic project of nation building. Most famous among them is the activist Qiu Jin, a 1907 revolutionary martyr for the anti-Qing cause and one of the few women revolutionaries of that period to become the subject of biographical research (Rankin 1975; Croll 1980; Ono 1989; Borthwick 1985; Gipoulon 1989–90; G. Lee 1991; Hieronymus 2005). In a series of sympathetic biographical essays about Qiu Jin written soon after her execution, her friend Wu Zhiying portrayed her as an unconventional but admirable character, arguing that Qiu was a pillar of the nation—one who, sadly, had been broken as the national edifice began to crumble (Y. Hu 2004). Other women, in Japan and in China's treaty-port cities, formed associations to promote women's education, help the poor, prohibit opium, and support nationalist boycotts and rights recovery projects during the last decade of the Qing period (Beahan 1976, 1981). Popular prints of the early twentieth century, including a genre known as "Amended New Year Pictures," drew on older conventions of imagery while portraying women in new roles such as student and patriotic activist (McIntyre 1999). Some women participated in the uprisings leading up to the 1911 revolution (Croll 1980; Ono 1989; Rong 1983; Yu-ning Li 1984).

The number of women involved in modernizing and revolutionary projects was small (Croll 1980). Girls' schools established by the Qing government in the year of Qiu Jin's death reached only 0.1 percent of school-age girls (Borthwick 1985). Yet schooling for girls continued to expand in Beijing, where Manchu women took an active role (Cheng 2000), and in Tianjin (McElroy 2001) and Shanghai. In the last decade of the Qing and in the early Republic, the numbers of girl students increased, while many educators hewed to a conservative social agenda aimed at raising good wives and virtuous mothers (Borthwick 1985; Gipoulon 1989–90; W. Ye 2001; Bailey 2001, 2003, 2004; McElroy 2001; Mittler 2003; Du 2005; Zurndorfer 2005). "Conservative," however, did not mean "unchanging." Late Qing textbooks for women (largely written by men) cited both ancient Chinese women (the mother of Mencius, Ban Zhao, Hua Mulan) and foreign women (Joan of Arc, Charlotte Corday, Harriet Beecher Stowe, Florence Nightingale) as exemplars of virtue, but many of these books downplayed classical learning in favor of new forms of practical knowledge and expanded the notion of model mother to include "mothers of citizens" (Judge 1997, 2000, 2002a, 2002b, 2004). Xue Shaohui, the woman author of one such text, used stories about foreign women to enlarge older definitions of womanly virtue to include scholarly, literary, artistic, and scientific accomplishments, as well as the motherly nurturing of talent for the nation (N. Qian 2004). Judge, labeling such combinations of ancient models with Western figures "archaeomodern" (2004: 104), contends that these textbooks created a new, universal category of "women," and "provoked a radical questioning of existing gender arrangements and social meaning" (2000: 135). In the last decade of the imperial era, periodicals written for women introduced nationalist issues to an urban female readership, advocating education for women as a means to improve their maternal skills and thereby strengthen the nation (Beahan 1975, 1976; Croll 1980; Nivard 1986; Cheng 2000; McElroy 2001).

Chinese women also studied in the United States, although this group was generally not active in revolutionary movements after their return, unlike the Japan alumnae. Weili Ye (1994, 2001) divides Chinese women students in the U.S. into three generational cohorts: a very small group of mission-educated women in the late nineteenth century who attended medical school in the U.S. and returned to China to practice medicine in a tradition of feminine Christian service, a larger group in the first fifteen years of the twentieth century who strove to establish a domestic sphere directed by a modern version of the "virtuous wife and good mother," and a more iconoclastic group in the late 1910s and early 1920s whose career aspirations took them into male occupations and whose feminist ideals were sometimes in tension with their nationalism (W. Ye 2001). A renowned member of the first group of doctors was Ida Kahn (Kang Aide), who became a powerful symbol of various versions of the new Chinese woman. For Liang Qichao, her accomplishments proved that educated women could help to build a strong nation (Y. Hu 1997, 2000, 2001, 2002). For Western missionaries, her conversion to Christianity and ethic of feminine service provided a model for Chinese women. Kang herself, in a short story published after the 1911 revolution, decried revolutionary violence and the practice of women taking up arms, at the same time celebrating the community of women (Y. Hu 2001, 2002).

NEW CULTURE AND BEYOND

After the 1911 revolution, the Republican government denied women suffrage (Witke 1973b; Croll 1980; Ono 1989; Beahan 1981; Rong 1983; Borthwick 1985; Nivard 1986; Yu-ning Li 1988; Edwards 2000c; Dong 2005) and continued to issue awards to virtuous widows, wives, and mothers

(Borthwick 1985; Bailey 2001, 2004). In the first two decades of the twentieth century, many commentators worried that girls' schools would become hotbeds of illicit sexual activity, pursuit of frivolous fashion trends, and unapproved public political activities (Cheng 2000; Bailey 2001, 2003, 2004). The Republican government advocated education for women, however, and girls' schools became a significant location where young women, as teachers and students, could begin to explore social activism and separation from immediate family supervision (Z. Wang 1999; Hsieh 1986; McElroy 2001; Xie 2001; Du 2005; Zurndorfer 2005).

With the publication of *New Youth* and the New Culture movement, and the mass social movements of the May Fourth demonstrations and their aftermath, women's subordination was once again explicitly linked to weaknesses in Chinese culture and the Chinese state, and modernity to women's emancipation (Witke 1970; Croll 1980; Ono 1989; Borthwick 1985; Barlow 1989, 2004; Gilmartin 1999; Z. Wang 1999; M. Lu 2004). In writings of the 1920s and 1930s, the female body was represented in fiction and essays as the literal ground of the nation. Rape of a woman frequently stood for violation of the nation by imperialist powers (Duara 1994; L. Liu 1994; Brownell 2000). Women portrayed as victims of the Shanghai stock market, or as financially and sexually promiscuous and/or vulnerable, enabled discussion of China's economic instability (B. Goodman 2005a, 2005b, 2005c), whereas women as consumers of modern hygienic products and childbearers were key to eugenic improvement, scientific modernity, and thus the strengthening of the nation (Barlow 2004, 2005). A woman engaging in prostitution was both victim of a weakened society and symbolic embodiment of national weakness (Hershatter 1997; Yingjin Zhang 1999b). Modernity, of which women's emancipation was a central part, was counterposed to Confucianism (Gilmartin 1999). A modern new woman, in May Fourth writings, would be educated, employed, independent, concerned with public life, and attentive to the plight of women more oppressed than she (Z. Wang 1999; B. Goodman 2005a, 2005c). Concern that "Chinese Woman" was inadequate to the task of modernity pervaded the work of many writers (Bailey 2001, 2004; Barlow 2004). These ideas, even when they referred to the peasantry, were primarily urban and elite in their focus and circulation (M. Wolf 1985).

Just as late Qing writers had done before them, May Fourth writers presented their critique as something wholly new, effacing the importance of education for elite women in the imperial era as well as critical discussions of women's place that stretched back several centuries (Handlin 1975; Ropp 1976; Holmgren 1981; Rong 1983; Ko 1994; Mann 1997; Gilmartin 1999;

Judge 2004; Ping-chen Hsiung 2005). Magazines such as *Funü zazhi*, published from 1915 to 1932, began to address women's emancipation, sexuality, love, and marriage (Croll 1980; Nivard 1984, 1986; Borthwick 1985; Z. Wang 1999; Gilmartin 1999; Bailey 2001, 2004; Y. Ma 2003). Male feminist critics produced and possibly were the readership for most of these writings (Nivard 1984; Gilmartin 1995, 1999; Z. Wang 1999; Y. Ma 2003). They articulated their own disempowerment as young men in a Confucian family system by identifying with women (Schwarcz 1986), portraying them as suffering victims and martyrs to arranged marriages (Witke 1973a; Schwarcz 1986; Prazniak 1997; Gilmartin 1999). They embraced the behavior of Henrik Ibsen's character Nora in *A Doll's House*, who proclaimed that her sacred duty to herself outweighed her prescribed social role (Schwarcz 1986). Among these critics was Mao Zedong, whose articles criticized Chinese social practices that confined women's activity, from dress norms to arranged marriages (Prazniak 1997). In speaking for women, Wang Zheng (1999) points out, intellectuals continued their socially sanctioned practice of representing the less capable and fortunate even while they attacked the social arrangements that had conferred this privilege and responsibility upon them.

For (mostly male) urban reformist and revolutionary intellectuals from the mid-1920s to the mid-1930s, the state of women was inarguably linked to the state of the nation; they partially worked out the content of semi-colonial modernity in the course of discussions about the modern woman (Edwards 2000a). These ranged from anguished debates about the causes and significance of widespread prostitution (Hershatter 1992b, 1992c, 1997; Henriot 1997) to portrayals of women consumers (Edwards 2000a; Dal Lago 2000) to discussions about what sort of fashionable female garb and bodily posture would signify modernity (Finnane 1996; Dal Lago 2000; Wilson 2002; Carroll 2003; Bailey 2004). Women's fashion in the early years of the Republic was not only "a national problem" (Finnane 1996) and the subject of government-sponsored clothing reform (Carroll 2003; Laing 2003; Bailey 2004), it was also deadly serious business, as hair bobbing during the National Revolution became first a political statement and then a cause for torture and execution (Croll 1980; Gilmartin 1994; Edwards 2000a). Commitment to the Communist cause often meant the rejection of prevailing standards of female adornment. Women's beauty and self-adornment, whether mobilized for political purposes or attacked as signs of backwardness, remained objects of state attention throughout the history of the CCP before 1949, the Mao years, and the period of economic reform as well (Dal Lago 2000; Ip 2003; T. Chen 2001, 2003b; Wilson 2002; Friedman 2004, 2006; Finnane 2005a, 2005b).

By the 1930s, intellectuals were denouncing attention to dress and consumerism as pseudomodern practices without the substance of serious devotion to education or the national welfare (Edwards 2000a; Carroll 2003). By "policing the modern woman," intellectuals sought unsuccessfully to maintain their moral and political authority even as they were increasingly marginalized by GMD power holders. In China, Edwards (2000a: 125) argues, the modern woman was not a "feminist icon" but rather "a trope for intellectual class anxiety." Such anxieties were played out in films and the tabloid press, notably in the 1935 controversy over the film *New Women*, in which the on-screen suicide of the protagonist was followed a few weeks later by the actual suicide of the star Ruan Lingyu (Yingjin Zhang 1994, 1996; Harris 1995; M. Chang 1999). "New women," comments Yingjin Zhang, were "configured both as a new subject of potential social change and as a new object of modern knowledge" (1994: 605; see also Zurndorfer 2005). In many films they were symbolically and sometimes literally contained by men. Potential social change, in these films and in left-wing literature, often meant the emergence of women as militant patriotic workers (Yingjin Zhang 1994, 1996; Harris 1995; Field 1999).

Some recent scholarship traces the gendered hierarchy embedded in May Fourth discourse itself. May Fourth notions about individual fulfillment, as adumbrated in Republican-era writings, were implicitly addressed to the problems of male individuals, while women were expected to strengthen both the family and the state through their reproductive and domestic labor (Glosser 1995, 2003). Other scholarship has tracked the political activism of women students and suffragists during the May Fourth era and its immediate aftermath, from the founding of the Chinese Communist Party through the mass mobilizations of the mid-1920s (Croll 1980; Gilmartin 1989, 1993, 1995, 1999; Edwards 1999). Women's emancipation became a central feature of the programs of both the Communists and the Nationalists.

WOMEN AND THE CCP

Gilmartin (1989, 1993, 1994, 1995) suggests that early male Communists, products of the May Fourth environment, regarded Marxism and feminism as generally compatible. She catalogues the party's early efforts to recruit and train women leaders. In a partial revision of earlier treatments (such as Witke 1973b; Leith 1973), she shows that Xiang Jingyu, the party's most famous female organizer, supported a wide range of women's groups, while seeking to influence them in the direction of less elitist, more inclusive policies (see also Gipoulon 1984; McElderry 1986). For young women, Gilmartin argues, the party offered hope of new egalitarian arrangements between men and women, but ultimately it failed to deliver on that promise, instead confining women to informal positions of power (see also Beahan 1984) or posts that were dependent upon their relationships with Communist men (McElderry 1986). Gilmartin does not present this as a simple issue of male bad faith. She examines female complicity in these arrangements, exposing deeply held beliefs about the proper role of women that affected organizers of both sexes. Turning to women's participation in the nationwide military and political ferment of the National Revolution from 1925 to 1927, Gilmartin (1989, 1994, 1995) describes profound upheaval in the lives of women in Shanghai, Guangdong, Hubei, and Henan, as well as the centrality of gender reform to this massive but ultimately unsuccessful revolution (see also Leith 1973; Hsieh 1986; Xie 2001). But in the face of tensions over whether to stress nationalism or gender oppression in the mobilization of women, male Communists such as Peng Pai moved away from emphasis on women's emancipation in their attempts to organize peasants.

During the early 1930s in rural Jiangxi, and later in Shaanganning and other base areas, the CCP experimented with implementing pieces of the May Fourth agenda, notably freedom of marriage, in an environment very different from that of urban coastal China. The immediate problem of "woman work" (i.e., educating and mobilizing women for revolutionary purposes) in the fledgling base areas was how to mobilize peasant women while winning rural support more generally. As noted earlier in this volume, scholars have generally argued that when the interests of May Fourth reformers met the (supposed) conservatism of rural peasants, the result was a party decision to tone down marriage reform and instead emphasize mobilizing women for production, a hoary Engelsian goal as well as an immediate practical need.

Beyond that general consensus are differences in interpretative emphasis. Delia Davin (1976) argues that Jiangxi policies were driven primarily by expediency and the need to support the military. She points out that in both Jiangxi and the Northwest, it was quite reasonable for party authorities to link women's low status with lack of participation in social production, since women in these regions performed little farm labor and were demonstrably oppressed. Elisabeth Croll finds the long-term relationship of feminism and socialism in China before and after 1949 "inherently uneasy, complex and, at certain junctures, antagonistic" (1980: 5). Kay Ann Johnson (1983) and Judith Stacey (1983) see the move to mobilization as a critical compromise that weakened the revolution's commitment to gender equality. Johnson locates part of the problem in the inadequacy of Marxist theory and the writings of Friedrich Engels, which gave insufficient attention to kinship structures and patrilocality in particular. Kathy Walker (1978) takes a more sanguine view of the Jiangxi era, describing a mobilization of women for two purposes: the war effort and their own liberation from low status, constrained activities, and material oppression. Several authors call attention to the dissatisfaction of women intellectuals (particularly Ding Ling) with party policy toward women in Yan'an and the party's severely critical response (Davin 1976; Croll 1980; Jackal 1981; Stranahan 1983a; Barlow 1989, 2004). Patricia Stranahan (1983a) suggests that the party during the Yan'an period appealed to rural women by offering them and their families a better life rather than full equality. Roxann Prazniak marks 1936 as the year when Mao's views about the woman issue became "more routine" and clearly subordinated to other concerns (1997: 25). Stacey (1983) sees CCP activity both before and after 1949 as marked by an effort to preserve patriarchy, entailing a move from family patriarchy (which might be labeled "feudal") to public patriarchy (which could be called "socialist"). In contrast, Margery Wolf (1985) argues that the preservation of patriarchy through to the end of the Mao era was not a conscious intention but, rather, the result of "cultural blinders" under which a male leadership set revolutionary priorities without taking the gendered effects of their policies into account and set aside gender equality whenever the economy required it or the rural population resisted it. Louise Edwards (2004b) locates the problem even before the CCP's flight to the countryside, in a confinement of women's political engagement to "women's work," comprising the mobilization of women to build both the Nationalist and Communist parties.

Tani Barlow (1994b) points out that during the early twentieth century, Chinese intellectuals moved from kin-inflected gender, in which daughter, wife, and other kinswomen were primary identifications, to a gender binarism influenced by Victorian thought in which "woman" *(nüxing)* and "man," each with their own immutable physiology, were paired in social thinking. In Maoist thinking both before and after 1949, Barlow continues, "woman" *(funü)* became a statist category comparable to "youth," to be interpellated into the social order via party-sponsored mass organizations. In a more recent work, Barlow presents *funü* and *nüxing* as historical catechreses: terms rich in heterogeneity and contingency, whose varying uses in twentieth-century Chinese feminism suggest a range of ways that thinkers imagined what women might become. For Ding Ling, Maoist nationalism offered "Woman" the opportunity to become part of a revolutionary collectivity and thus a fully modern subject (Barlow 2004). Harriet Evans (1998) analyzes the language of liberation *(jiefang)* as party theorists applied it to gender from the 1920s to the 1950s, a language which promised that women were to be liberated—as responsive participants, not initiators—from the feudal past (which entailed destruction of previous class relations). Liberation was conceptualized in broad social rather than narrow individual (or even gendered) terms. To emphasize gender as primary was to take a bourgeois political position and endanger revolutionary unity based on class. Lin Chun (2001: 1284), however, calls the Chinese revolution, "notwithstanding grave limitations, simultaneously a revolution by, of, and for women."

In addition to tracing the history of a collective subject (or subject position) named "Woman," putting women into the grand narrative of revolutionary history has sometimes entailed narrating the stories of individual activists. Croll (1995) offers a survey of autobiographies by women. In the first part of the twentieth century, these autobiographies (including Pruitt 1967 and Hsieh 1986, later retranslated as Xie 2001) often portrayed their narrators as rebels against family norms: girls who chafed at their inferior status in the family, protested their increasing physical confinement as they approached adolescence, eagerly sought education, and resisted marriages arranged by their parents (see also Croll 1996). Each woman describes herself as unusual, but Croll shrewdly notes that their individual rebellions against footbinding and marriage had much in common, enabled by the larger currents of social and political critique in the world beyond their families.

Recent studies have described the travails of women who joined the Long March in 1934–35 (L. Lee and Wiles 1999; H. Young 2001, 2005; L. Lee 2004). Lily Lee and Sue Wiles, drawing on published memoirs and accounts of the march, concentrate on three women—Mao's wife He Zizhen, Zhu De's wife Kang Keqing, and Wang Quanyuan—who marched with the main contingent of Communists, following their subsequent activities into the years of the PRC. They offer stories of combat heroism as well as stark accounts of babies given away en route, extreme physical privation, the danger of being arrested if ordered to drop out of the march and stay behind, and the perils of being caught up in ongoing party struggles such as that between Mao and Zhang Guotao. They also detail Mao Zedong's emotional neglect of He Zizhen and his sexual promiscuity, and more generally Communist women's dependence upon their husbands for their political standing, which usually left them devastated by divorce. Helen Young's work is more sanguine, perhaps because it includes women who were not the companions of top leaders. Based on extensive oral history interviews with twenty-two women who were Long March veterans, including Kang Keqing and Wang Quanyuan, it focuses on children, child-birth during the march, the various types of work women performed, and the enduring relationships among them. Nicola Spakowski (2005) finds variation in women's military participation in the communist movement, along with a pervasive belief that military women should perform different tasks from men.

To date, the only high-ranking woman Communist leader to receive full-length biographical treatment in English is Mao's much-reviled fourth wife, Jiang Qing. Roxane Witke's 1977 book (see also Witke 1975) is organized around a weeklong interview that Jiang Qing gave her in 1972. After Jiang fell from power in 1976, the interview itself was criticized by the Chinese leadership as an example of her perfidy. It describes Jiang's early poverty, brief film career, desire to establish herself as a leader independent of Mao, insecurity, penchant for grudge-holding and revenge, and what Witke called her "theatrical swings of mood" (1977: 12). Ross Terrill's twice-revised biography of Jiang (1999), drawing on interviews and on news reports, memoirs, and gossip published after her fall, delineates her use of sex to gain power, but also notes the hypocrisy of the party apparatus that emphasized her alleged sexual voraciousness while blaming her personally for China's Cultural Revolution travails. Natascha Vittinghoff (2005) analyzes Jiang's 1930s film and theater career, concentrating on her portrayal of Ibsen's Nora and on the difficulties confronting a "new woman" with a highly visible career.

Recent scholarship on the base area period has begun to go beyond party policy statements to the complex local relationships that shaped variable courses of the revolution. Still, we have little sense of how most rural women understood, participated in, or reacted to party initiatives. One sketchy but intriguing exception is the Licheng Rebellion of 1941 (D. Goodman 1997, 2000), in which women in southeast Shanxi joined in a millenarian movement against local CCP authorities. An investigation conducted by the Communists after the rebellion was suppressed found that women were almost half the membership of the sectarian Li Gua Dao (Sixth Trigram), and that young women from better-off peasant backgrounds were more than one-tenth of the membership. Many were attracted to the rebellion because the Li Gua Dao allowed them to avoid or leave arranged marriages and to move around more freely outside the home—precisely the sorts of freedom that the party aimed to provide for young women. More broadly, David Goodman's work (2000) on the Taihang base area in Shanxi suggests that the CCP took different approaches to women's mobilization and won differing degrees of support in each county, depending upon land tenure patterns, preexisting local women's organizations, and other factors not easily subsumed in a single tale of revolution.

Beyond the CCP Narrative

While scholars have insisted that the grand narrative of twentieth-century revolutionary history cannot be understood without reference to gender discourse and women's participation, and have done much to establish the presence of women in revolutionary movements, they have also broadened their inquiry to take account of women whose feminist activism was conducted outside well-known revolutionary events such as the First United Front, the Northern Expedition, the Long March, or base area expansion. In a major work on the long-term significance of May Fourth thinking by and for women, Wang Zheng (1999) traces the stories of five women who lived May Fourth ideals of women's emancipation through the 1920s, 1930s, and 1940s, pursuing careers in education, law, and journalism. One was a Nationalist Party member and one a member of the Communist Party; all remained in urban settings. Wang argues that while May Fourth "liberal feminist discourse" was subsequently criticized by the Communist Party as "a bourgeois feminist fantasy," it was crucial to "constituting a new subjectivity for women in modern China" (16), although it was abruptly cut short after 1949. Liberal humanism in China, she says, unlike its Western counterpart, operated not by differentiating and excluding women but rather by demanding that they become human, that is, "the same as man" (19)—a legacy that *did* persist in Maoist approaches to "the woman question" after 1949.

From the late Qing through the Japanese occupation, conservative portrayals of woman as the authentic embodiment of Chinese national essence circulated alongside May Fourth representations of anti-Confucian nationalist women (Duara 1998, 2000, 2003). Drawing heavily on Meiji Japanese notions of women's role, Nationalist Party leaders such as Wang Jingwei assigned middle-class women the task of enacting tradition within modernity, by redirecting their capacity for self-sacrifice from the family to the nation and engaging in public service. Prasenjit Duara traces the working of these conservative representations in groups such as the Morality Society and the Red Swastika Society, which were active in the Japanese puppet state of Manchukuo during the 1930s. Although these societies were shaped by the Japanese colonial presence, Duara suggests that this conservative model of the modern woman was operative well beyond Manchukuo's borders, influencing gender-segregated institutions such as girl's schools, women's professional associations, and redemptive societies, as well as campaigns such as the Nationalist Party's New Life Movement (see also Croll 1980).

In other work on women beyond the main revolutionary story line, Maria Jaschok and Jingjun Shui (2005) trace debates among Republican-era urban Hui scholars on the role of women in a modernizing Islam. Eugenia Lean (2004) analyzes the media representation of Shi Jianqiao, a woman who assassinated the warlord Sun Chuanfang in 1935 to avenge her father's death a decade earlier. By positioning herself as a contemporary woman warrior, Lean suggests, Shi was able simultaneously to occupy the position of virtuous filial daughter, mount an indirect critique of the Guomindang for its failure to resist Japan, and exasperate leftist critics who were suspicious of an emotional, feminized urban public.

Louise Edwards (1999, 2000c, 2004a, 2005; see also Witke 1973b; Dong 2005) explores the ongoing struggle for women's suffrage from 1911 to 1936, when a draft constitution gave women the right to vote, although this provision was not implemented until 1947. She highlights the role of Tang Qunying and other women who had studied in Japan as well as the importance of campaigns to include gender equality in provincial constitutions during the 1920s. Although early women's rights activists were excoriated in the press for inappropriate behavior in public spaces (Dong 2005), ultimately anti-suffrage arguments were weakened because activists succeeded in associating women's suffrage with modernity (Edwards 2005). Edwards also examines the successful campaign feminists waged for a 10 percent quota of elected women in national legislative bodies during and after the anti-Japanese war, which marked an early shift from a politics of gender equality to one of gender difference. Attention to the suffrage movement indicates that feminists in the 1930s and 1940s did not remove themselves from politics, in spite of lukewarm or hostile responses on the part of the ruling Nationalist Party, nor did they wait to have rights handed to them by a benevolent government. Participation in the war effort helped enhance the patriotic standing of such women, involved more middle-class women in war-related welfare work, and attracted younger women to feminism. Their concerns included marriage reform, women's working conditions, and public health as well as quotas. Luo Qiong, later a prominent woman Communist official, was active in the quota movement, although its ultimate triumph in 1947 benefited only Nationalist Party members and was soon overshadowed by civil war (Edwards 1999).

Woman-Work and Women's Place in the PRC

The Women's Federation, founded in 1949, had a mandate to conduct "woman-work," which included mobilizing women for production, raising the educational level and self-confidence of women, supporting their rights, and advocating for them (Davin 1976; Croll 1979, 1980, 1985c). Whereas early reform-era scholarship tended to echo popular attitudes that dismissed the Women's Federation as a transmission belt for state directives (Honig and Hershatter 1988), more recent studies suggest that the federation under Mao was a heterogeneous and complex entity hampered by a lack of funding and status that nevertheless endeavored to keep gender issues on the wider state agenda (N. Zhang 1996; Jaschok, Milwertz, and Ping-chun Hsiung 2001; Judd 2002; Z. Wang 2005b). During the collectivization process of the 1950s, Women's Federation officials were sent to villages to identify and train local women as leaders (Hershatter 2000). Women's representative congresses, first developed in the Jiangxi Soviet (Walker 1978), became a feature of regional and national political life from the early 1950s on (Davin 1976; Croll 1985c). Training local cadres to mobilize women for production remained an important Federation task well into the 1970s (Hemmel and Sindbjerg 1984).

Women's broader participation in formal politics nevertheless remained low throughout the Mao years in spite of some gains (see Sheridan 1976), a trend that continued and even intensified in the reform period (Croll 1980, 1985c; Parish and Whyte 1978; Qi Wang 1999). Women were most active at the local level, in neighborhood committees (Davin 1976; Andors 1983; Riley 1997). At all levels in the reform period, women continued to be underrepresented in managerial and government positions. In 1992, women comprised 21 percent of National People's Congress deputies, 12 to 16 percent of its Standing Committee members, 13 percent of all party members, and in 1990 about 7 percent of all administrative cadres at all levels down to the township (Croll 1995: 131–32; see also Edwards 2000b, 2004b; Qingshu Wang 2004). Lee Feigon (1994) notes that women were likewise rare in the leadership of the 1989 protest movement, although Chai Ling, one of its most visible leaders, occasionally referred to the protesters as her "children." Gender discrimination did not figure explicitly in the list of injustices the protesters wanted redressed.

While the Cultural Revolution has been the subject of a massive amount of scholarship and memoir production, relatively little of it has focused on the gendered dimensions of state policy or Red Guard activity, or on women's changing roles in production and reproduction. This may well be because official discourses—visual as well as verbal—tended toward what Marilyn Young (1989) has called "socialist androgyny," with women portrayed as political militants and military fighters alongside men, generally under their benevolent political guidance. Harriet Evans (1999) analyzes both of these themes—woman as comrade and woman as led by revolutionary man—as they are visually expressed in Cultural Revolution posters. Cultural Revolution rhetoric extolled the Iron Girls, who were said to rival or exceed men in their capacity for heavy labor (Honig and Hershatter 1988; M. Young 1989; Honig 2000). Yet in spite of official evocations of women's achievements and ability to "hold up half the sky," Kay Ann Johnson (1983) suggests that state policy during the Cultural Revolution years neglected gender equality, particularly by abolishing the Women's Federation from 1966 to 1972. Evans (1997) points out the disjuncture between the official discourse on sexuality, which was variously silent or abstemious, and Red Guard attitudes and practices, which tended toward salacious handwritten texts and sexual promiscuity. Red Guard memoirs (see, for example, A. Min 1995; R. Yang 1997) and early post-Cultural Revolution fiction by authors such as Yu Luojin (Honig 1984) have explored the sexual feelings, experimentation, and vulnerability of young women who were sent down to the countryside, as well as their shock at the forms of gender inequality they encountered there (Honig 2000; Lin 2003). Honig (2000, 2002, 2003) suggests that scholars should not understand the Cultural Revolution as a rupture with preceding relationships and norms; violent acts perpetrated by Red Guard women, for instance, were shaped by earlier state valorizations of female militance (Honig 2002). A recent volume of essays by women of the Red Guard generation has moved away from the master question governing most of the literature on gender after 1949: was state policy good or bad for women? Instead, these authors examine the contradictory and often positive effects of state discourse on their own gendered senses of self, citing a "need to tell stories that present a less-clear-cut picture of an era and the people—in this case, women—who grew up in it" (Z. Wang 2001; Zhong, Wang, and Bai 2001: xv; see also Lin 2001, 2003).

An important element of post-1949 mobilization was the state's call that women participate fully in socialist construction. State propaganda and cultural productions offered a range of demanding models for women: the underground party worker who gave her life to bring about the revolution; the heroic laborer who worked long hours on the railroad, in the textile mill, or in the cotton fields while maintaining a harmonious family and impeccable personal conduct (Sheridan 1976; Hershatter 2000, 2002, 2005a; Chen 2005a); the Iron Girl who showed that women could do any work that men could do (Honig 2000); and the mother who cared for her own family while encouraging them to give their all for the greater social good. In post-1949 film, woman was no longer constructed by a male desiring gaze; all desire was directed toward the party, and the new woman became either a heroic woman warrior ready to sacrifice herself for the revolution or a mother who embodied the suffering of the masses and their capacity for endurance (Dai 1995). What all these icons shared was a capacity for self-sacrifice that resonated profoundly with presocialist notions of womanly virtue, even as the content of women's prescribed activities changed and the normative object of sacrifice shifted from family to nation.

Lisa Rofel (1994b) argues that this association of woman, self-sacrifice, and nation persisted well into the reform period. In the 1991 television drama "Yearnings," she suggests, the self-sacrificing wife and mother Huifang was seen by some viewers as a feudal remnant who erased recent revolutionary history of women's sacrifices on behalf of the nation, while others saw her sacrifices as making her eligible to be an icon of the nation. Both groups shared the assumption that Woman and Nation were profoundly intertwined, and sometimes identified outright. Susan Brownell (2000) notes the continued identification of female suffering with national salvation in the public reaction to two events during 1999: the NATO bombing of the Chinese embassy in Belgrade, the Chinese media coverage of which centered on the two Chinese victims who were women, and the strong showing by the Chinese women's soccer team in the World Cup, during which the women almost wrested the championship from the U.S. team. Both sets of female images, Brownell notes, point to the continuing entanglement of masculinity with nationalism. The impotent male/nation that cannot protect his/its women has a genealogy dating back more than a century, while the male as guide and master of women (athletes, soldiers, and others) who bring glory to the nation is an artifact of the Maoist and reform period (Brownell 2000).

In recent years, Susan Greenhalgh (2001) points out, state authorities have invoked the need to limit China's population in the apocalyptic terms formerly reserved for raising the status of women. If China's population is not limited, the argument now goes, the nation and its future prosperity will be imperiled. She argues that the growth in population has displaced the low status of women as a major indicator of national crisis, mandating that the population must be contained even at great cost to women individually and collectively. Greenhalgh's subsequent discussion of the dangers to women and infant girls posed by state birth planning policy, discussed in Chapter 1, suggests that while holding a place of honor at the center of national crisis may not always have served women's interests well, being removed from that place and succeeded by the specter of uncontrolled reproduction may be even worse for women.

WOMEN'S SPHERE, WOMEN'S RIGHTS, WOMEN'S STUDIES

An explosion of talk about gender difference, women's status, and attendant social problems began early in the reform era (Honig and Hershatter 1988). It was exacerbated by the maltreatment of women and girls that resulted from attempts to enforce the single-child policy in the countryside. In the wake of reports during the 1980s about wife beating, infanticide, trafficking, and a host of other problems, the Women's Federation responded with a well-publicized campaign to protect the legal rights of women and children (Z. Wang 1997). The Federation began to sponsor research on women beginning in 1984 (X. Li and Zhang 1994; Z. Wang 1997; Chow, Zhang, and Wang 2004). The same period saw the emergence of scholars, mostly university-affiliated, who began their own organizations for women's research or women's studies (Y. Chen 1994; X. Li and Zhang 1994; Croll 1995; Z. Wang 1997; Chow, Zhang, and Wang 2004; X. Li 2004).

Wang Zheng (1997; see also X. Li and Zhang 1994; Chow, Zhang, and Wang 2004) points out that women's studies in China emerges from a particular history: it is not the product of a feminist movement but, rather, is one of the main forces creating that movement in the context of the economic reforms. As the party-state moved increasingly toward market reforms, often at the expense of women, the Women's Federation and women scholars produced what they called the "Marxist theory of women"—a capacious rubric encompassing Maoist ideas about women's liberation, institutional practices, and government policies—and used it to pressure the state apparatus not to abandon gender equality as an official goal (Z. Wang 1997; Chow, Zhang, and Wang 2004).

Federation advocacy for women has taken many forms during the reform era: denouncing attempts to lay off women during times of economic contraction (Davin 1989; Jacka 1990; M. Yang 1999a; Z. Wang 2003), criticizing Daqiuzhuang village for its experiment during the late 1980s in sending all women home to become housewives (Jacka 1990; Gao 1994; Beaver, Hou, and Wang 1995), calling attention to female infanticide and domestic violence (Croll 1985c, 1995; Wong 1997; Edwards 2000b), sponsoring vocational training and legal counseling for women (Gao 1994; Croll 1995; Z. Wang 2003), forming labor service companies to recruit rural women for urban and suburban work (H. Zhang 1999a), pressuring municipal governments to establish funds covering women's maternity leaves and reproductive medical expenses so that enterprises will hire women (Z. Wang 2003), identifying women qualified to hold local political office (Judd 2002), and promoting increased economic activity by rural women in particular.

Perhaps the broadest initiative of the Women's Federation was to work for the 1992 enactment of a Women's Law that specified women's equal rights to political participation, education, work, property, freedom of the person, marital choice, and legal remedy for violation of these rights (Croll 1995; Wong 1997; Edwards 2000b). This law, however, has been criticized in China and abroad for its excessive generalities and lack of new remedies (Hom 1994; Woo 2002), and scholars acknowledge the gap between legal guarantees of equality and gendered "disparities in access to resources and social power" (Hom 1994: 1028).

From the late 1980s on, the Women's Federation actively involved itself in organizing rural women to participate in the "courtyard economy" and later the "two studies, two competitions" movement (the study of basic education and technical training, and competition among women to be economically successful and to make social contributions). Whereas a previous generation of federation activists had mobilized participation in collective labor as the means to women's liberation, in the reform era, federation officials trained women to compete in the market, at the same time attempting to strengthen the federation itself (Judd 2002; Z. Wang 2003).

Judd (2002) suggests that in taking economic development as the main task of "woman-work," the Federation enhances its legitimacy with the party-state and makes a claim on scarce state resources to be used in the advancement of women. She examines the subtleties and contradictions of the federation's attempt to raise the "quality" *(suzhi)* of rural women, calling it "the crux of the contemporary women's movement in rural China" (19). The "quality" campaign has often highlighted women's role in their own subordination (Judd 2002; on the "quality" discourse, see also Anagnost 1997; F. Xu 2000; Friedman 2004; Jacka 2005). At the same time, by participating in the state language of "quality," Federation officials reinscribe an old and still powerful linkage between the situation of women and the welfare of the Chinese nation. They seek to show that women's work has value in the cash terms of the market, and that they can add to household and community income without competing with men. Rather than criticizing a gendered division of labor, they "concentrate upon improving conditions for women in those sectors where women predominate" (Judd 2002: 36). Their explicit goal in raising women's "quality," however, is to achieve gender equality, a transformation whose relationship to the segmented labor market remains to be worked out.

For the Women's Federation, sponsoring research on women signifies a locally varied, inconsistent, and incomplete but nevertheless important change, from transmission belt for government policy to advocacy group for women (Croll 1995; Z. Wang 1997, 2003; Qi Wang 1999; D. Min 1999; Edwards 2000b; Jaschok, Milwertz, and Ping-chun Hsiung 2001). As Gao Xiaoxian aptly observes, "social modernization in and of itself will not spontaneously liberate women" (1994: 96); women scholars and women's organizations must formulate initiatives to assist women and pressure the government to act on them. Some observers argue that the Women's Federation in the past decade has begun to function like a nongovernmental organization (NGO) as well as a state organization, making alliances with smaller organizations and operating in a less hierarchical manner than it did in earlier years (Jin 2001; N. Zhang 2001).

At the same time, women scholars working outside the federation have questioned its monopoly on advocacy for women and on framing women's research. In the 1980s, Li Xiaojiang, founder of the Association for Women's Studies, openly asserted the need for self-organization on the part of women—outside the control of the Women's Federation. In practice, however, federation and nonfederation researchers share interests and approaches and have cooperated on many research projects (X. Li and Zhang 1994; Z. Wang 1997; D. Min 1999; Rofel 1999a; M. Yang 1999a; Jaschok, Milwertz, and Ping-chun Hsiung 2001). By the early 1990s, federation researchers abandoned earlier denunciations of "bourgeois" (read: Western) feminism and began to advocate a merger of feminism, itself a very flexible category, with the Marxist theory of women (Z. Wang 1997).

Many women's studies writings of the 1980s shared in the broader social rejection of the Maoist tenet that "whatever men comrades can do, women comrades can do" and the surge of interest in gender difference and femininity. In theoretical works in women's studies, "Woman" as state-endorsed revolutionary subject *(funü)* was supplanted by essential woman *(nüxing)* and woman as social category *(nüren)* (Barlow 1994a, 1994b, 1997). Li Xiaojiang wryly notes that few women think of themselves as *funü*, which carries connotations of "married," "adult," "senile," and "old-fashioned" (1999: 269), though Barlow points out that Li's notion of an "affirmative female subject" owes much to the Maoist conceptualization of Woman (1997: 518).

Much of Li Xiaojiang's work has been devoted to differentiating gender from class as an analytical category and arguing for a Marxist (and therefore scientific) investigation of sex differences, which were posited as essential and originary (Li 1999; Z. Wang 1997; Barlow 1997, 2004; M. Yang 1999a). Li has been a trenchant critic of Maoist state feminism, pointing out that it postulated gender equality without actually striving to establish it and positioned women's liberation as a completed project bestowed by the state rather than "a responsibility for every person to work on" (1999: 271; see also X. Li and Zhang 1994). She sees the state as consigning women to dependence upon the party-state; in this respect her critique converges with Stacey's 1983 discussion of "patriarchal socialism." Li (1994) has also criticized the post-Mao reforms for requiring inequality between men and women as a feature of economic development (see also Rofel 1999a). At the same time, she suggests that globalizing processes in China, even while resulting in the proliferation of exploitative factory work and sex work, offer women opportunities to improve their material lives and free themselves from familial and national strictures (X. Li 2001).

Li Xiaojiang has consistently argued that Western feminist discourses, shaped by a very different history, are of limited utility for Chinese women and may even be harmful. For instance, she says, "the personal is political" cannot open up feminist modes of analysis in a situation where personal life has been relentlessly politicized for decades (X. Li 1999; see also Shih 2005). For her, the most reliable force propelling women toward a new consciousness is that of their own lived experience, a category she regards as foundational (X. Li 1999). Barlow (1997, 2004) provides a comprehensive discussion of Li's work, situating it in the Culture Fever debates of the mid-1980s, which sought to recapture a pre-Maoist modernity and devise a post-Mao Marxism.

By the 1990s and early twenty-first century, women's studies work had become less unified, more involved in conversations with foreign and diasporic feminist scholarship (Ge and Jolly 2001; Bao and Xu 2001; Chow, Zhang, and Wang 2004), and more engaged in internationally funded development projects focused on women's health and economic empowerment (Gao 2001). China's hosting of the Fourth World Conference on Women and its associated NGO Forum in 1995, in spite of considerable anxiety and vacillation on the part of the Chinese government before the forum opened, was officially declared a success, lending women's studies scholarship unprecedented legitimacy and visibility (Z. Wang 1996; Du 2001; Chow, Zhang, and Wang 2004) and enabling the formation of a number of NGOs for women (Hershatter, Honig, and Rofel 1996; Z. Wang 1996, 1997; Ping-chun Hsiung and Wong 1998; Shang 1999; B. Liu 2001; Gao 2001; Cai, Feng, and Guo 2001; Jaschok, Milwertz, and Ping-chun Hsiung 2001; Wesoky 2002). Some of these, such as Muslim women's mosques and Protestant women's organizations, marked out areas of difference among women as well as a nascent activism among women within particular religious groups (Jaschok and Shui 2000, 2005; Shui 2001). Others, such as the periodical *Rural Women* and the Migrant Women's Club, maintained close ties to the Women's Federation while focusing their activities on the experiences of *dagong mei* in urban areas (Jacka 2005).

As Wang Zheng (1997, 2001) points out, many leading feminist scholars, women now at middle age, were themselves formed by Maoist gender discourse, which for all its limitations left them with a strong sense that being gendered female was not supposed to result in discrimination or social limitations. They have reworked and put to local use many concepts from feminist movements elsewhere, including domestic violence, sexual harassment, and gender itself (Wesoky 2002; Z. Wang 2003). What is less clear, at this writing, is what form Chinese gender critiques are taking or will take as the generation of feminists brought up "under the red flag" is joined and replaced by younger women.

Mayfair Yang and others in her edited volume (1999c) explore the gender politics of the public sphere, which Yang (1999b: 2) defines as "the space of public discourse and debate, cultural and ideological production, and mass-media representation." Yang (1999a, 1999b) sees the public sphere moving out of a period of state-sponsored "gender erasure" in the Mao years to a period of intensified attention to gender difference and awareness of new forms of gender discrimination. Lisa Rofel points out that because Maoism made women's liberation a political matter, post-Mao "efforts to create a public realm separate from the state necessarily entail a public discourse on gender" (1999a: 118). Yang and others identify specific sites of an emergent women's discourse, including a women's museum opened by Li Xiaojiang in Henan (Rofel 1999a; the museum is unfortunately now closed), women's publications and conferences, fiction and literary criticism by women writers (Dai 1999; R. Roberts 1999), telephone hotlines (Cornue 1999; Erwin 2000), media productions and media criticism (Bu 2004; Shou 2004), and attention to gender in the university curriculum (Chow, Zhang, and Wang 2004; X. Li 2004). Many of these venues, the authors point out, exist in a "blended" relationship with state feminism, as do the emergent NGOs that sponsored them (Cornue 1999; see also Ping-chun Hsiung and Wong 1998). Sharon Wesoky characterizes the relationship of an emergent women's movement to the state as "symbiotic," containing "elements of both autonomy and dependence," and operating largely within rather than in opposition to party-state institutions (2002: 4). Louise Edwards points out that the party-state continues to rely upon women's political participation to enhance its legitimacy with its own population and in the international arena, even as it continues to perpetuate "the notion of separate spheres of political work for women" (2004b: 119).

Scholars also note the emergence of less salutary discursive trends, including an anxious and assertive nationalist masculinity (both elite and popular) that replaces woman as a symbol of the nation with a cosmopolitan and desirable man, in the process obscuring Chinese women altogether (as in the television drama analyzed by Erwin 1999; also see Dai 1995). Yang (1999a) and many of the contributors to her volume (see, for example, Dai 1999; Erwin 1999) point to the intensified assertion of masculinity in the reform period as a phenomenon that also shapes media representations of women, as well as their work possibilities and the wider social environment. Meanwhile, Yang (1999a: 63) argues, "female sexuality and desire in China . . . remain for the most part submerged" as subjects of representation, and one might add as subjects of scholarly inquiry as well.

Dai Jinhua (1995, 1999, 2004) examines how literary works and films of the 1980s and 1990s position women variously as objects of men's desire, as the cause of political chaos and men's disenfranchisement, or as the embodiment of a shameful Orientalized past (see also Barlow 2004). Because the anxieties of confronting the "larger threatening world" are displaced onto women, Dai says, "the project to subvert and change the social status quo [on the part of male intellectuals] becomes an effort to perpetuate the gender order" (1999: 202). Dai (1995), along with Mayfair Yang (Dai and Yang 1995), has also explored the difficulties and possibility of a distinct women's directorial voice in film. Anxious nationalist masculinity, of course, is not exclusive to mainland intellectuals; Shu-mei Shih (1998) traces its appearance in Taiwan and Hong Kong media representations of mainland women as seductresses and invaders.

If the emergence of reform-era masculinities has provoked feminist critiques, however, it has also stimulated calls for new scholarship. In the introduction to their recent volume *Chinese Femininities/Chinese Masculinities*, Brownell and Wasserstrom (2002c) chart a move from women's studies to gender studies in the China field, a move that parallels broader scholarly developments in the humanities and social sciences. Noting that the study of men and masculinities is far less developed in the China field than the study of women, they call for increased efforts in that direction.

Given that gendered imagery has been intrinsic to nationalism, expressions of regional identity, and protest movements over the past century (Brownell and Wasserstrom 2002a), it should be uncontroversial that analysis of gender belongs at the center of work on recent Chinese history. What shape that analysis takes—the capaciousness of "gender" as a category, the degree to which "Woman" and women figure within it, and the complications introduced by attending to ethnicity, sexuality, class, region, generation, and time—remains to be worked out. Barlow (2004) argues for a new approach to the history of thinking about women in the twentieth century. Rather than focusing on the question of whether the revolution was good or bad for intellectuals or for women, she tracks the categories that thinkers devised on both sides of the 1949 divide, and examines their relationship to transnational debates about eugenics, socialism, gender, sexuality, and the psyche.

Generational difference in particular stands out within and across many of the works surveyed here. The framing circumstances of women's lives in both urban and rural locations have changed so profoundly across the twentieth century that the terms in which we would narrate a mother's life might not be at all useful when tracing the life of her daughter or daughter-in-law. While acknowledging the many ways in which the gendered division of labor has privileged and continues to privilege men in twentieth-century families and workplaces, we must note that the shift of power from senior to junior generations across the twentieth century has also benefited young women and disenfranchised older ones.

Globalization, of late, is replacing the Chinese state as the motive force of history in some, but not all, scholarly quarters. The question in much of the most recent scholarship has become: How has globalization affected, empowered, or (more often) disadvantaged women? This shift in attention away from the state has not been uniform. For women's studies scholarship in the PRC, an emergent and very lively field, it is still the state that is held to account for its policies and their effects on women (Lin 2001). Or rather, the state is still the major actor, but perhaps for the first time it is being held to account on gender grounds. In PRC scholarship, the effects of the reforms upon women are still largely framed as a national debate, albeit one profoundly influenced by transnational theories of development, empowerment, and feminism.

For scholarship based in the U.S., including that of some diasporic scholars, the critique of globalization now trumps concern with a Chinese state that no longer provides any semblance of a partner in socialist romance or an imagined beacon of women's liberation. Current scholarship on women in the workforce, on the move, in the newly transnational marriage market, and in the sex trades participates in a wider conversation about globalization, with globalizing forces often cast as the villain or at least the irresponsible force that must be called to account. Still, if the principal actors have changed, the narrative arc shows important continuities with the earlier story about the state. The controlling question in much of this scholarship remains: how has some larger force shaped the options available to women?

Perhaps it is the very zigs and zags in Chinese party-state policy, and the changing shape of China's engagement with the world, that have helped to create the scholarship boom on women in China, in contrast, for instance, to scholarly writing on Japan. The Japanese government did not make such explicit claims about or on behalf of women, present itself as a progressive beacon for world change, change course dramatically a number of times, or suddenly emerge as a powerhouse in the past twenty years. The changing configuration of the Chinese state continually compels attention by scholars of China, and we have stuck with Liang Qichao's practice of understanding women as a key indicator of state success. Even feminist scholars, who began writing social history with a mission to enlarge inquiry beyond state-centered history, are not as detached from the state-centered story as we often like to think.

In spite of the explosion of scholarship in the past several decades, silences abound—about nonrevolutionary women in the Republican years, for instance, or rural women before the 1990s, or any women for whom an extensive individual biography might be constructed (Annping Chin's 2002 account of four sisters in Hefei is an intriguing exception). Whether these silences can be addressed by the discovery of new treasures along the paper trail, or by recourse to oral narratives (which are necessarily shaped by retrospective interpretation), is unclear. It is important that we call attention to the questions that we have not found means to address. Formulation of new questions and the return to some old and intractable ones will build on a field of existing scholarship that is diverse, detailed, and no longer marginalized, but which still retains a capacity to challenge and discomfit.

Afterthoughts

This epilogue offers suggestions about the study of women in recent Chinese history, made in a spirit of creeping discomfort. The project of "engendering China" has entailed enormous excitement and inspiration for several generations of scholars, of whom I am certainly one. Gender has pried open earlier historical conventions and narratives, disrupted them, troubled them, made visible some of the integuments that enclosed a discursive world in which "human" generally meant unmarked male. Making gender visible and audible cannot be considered a finished project. I nevertheless want to caution against the impulse to define a field, assess its state, map its gaps, and sally forth to fill them. If we take seriously what we have learned in the past three decades, we cannot continue to mine "the gender field" as though it were a space with fixed boundaries. It may be more useful to regard "the field" not as a space but rather as a conjuncture.* Its emergence, intensity, and complexity are not fixed. Rather they are, and must continue to be, entangled with the tracing out of other processes of subject formation.

Ruminating on "the field" as a conjuncture requires a somewhat different approach from asking what we have learned about women in modern Chinese history over the past few decades. It entails questions not about

---

*I use the term "conjuncture" here following Gramsci's use as elaborated by Stuart Hall and others. In *Passato e Presente*, Gramsci defined the conjuncture as "the set of circumstances which determine the market in a given phase, provided that these are conceived of as being in movement, i.e. as constituting a process of ever-changing combinations. . . . Difference between 'situation' and 'conjuncture': the conjuncture is the set of immediate and ephemeral characteristics of the economic situation." Gramsci, 1971: 177, n. 79. For purposes of this discussion of women's studies, I want to loosen (not sever) the linkage to the market, while maintaining the notion of recombination, flux, and a variety of determinants.

the content of a "field," but about the conditions and shape of its emergence, about why certain questions have come to the fore while others have received less attention. In focusing on temporal change rather than spatial fixity, I may be merely reinvoking the historian's favored tools, but it seems to me necessary to insist on the temporary and contingent properties of what otherwise becomes materialized, even somatized, as a "body of knowledge."

What has this new scholarship illuminated, and what has it possibly caused us to look away from? How can we keep this area of inquiry open, even risking its dissolution, rather than delineating its borders in ways that seal it shut? And if we were to require a rigorous permeability, or imagine an object of inquiry that (like us) emerges, changes, and dissolves over time, what sorts of new questions might we bring into view?

Most of the scholarship discussed in this volume is, in my assessment, thoroughly researched and clearly argued. Some of it made me want to argue back, to be sure, and some pieces were more pleasurable to read than others. But what has interested me in the explosion of scholarship is precisely its burgeoning, sprouting, somewhat chaotic nature. One cannot easily plot the range of topics, methodologies, or even conclusions along a narrative of progress, although scholarship on women has certainly gotten broader and deeper. Rather, the multiplicity of questions, approaches, and answers suggests something else: that scholars are raising questions about gender in a broad range of conversations, many of which transcend the geographical focus of the China field. What unites this scholarship is—to borrow and twist Judith Butler's (1999) phrase—gender as a means of making trouble. Scholars have asked: How might attention to gender trouble our stories of political development, e.g., the rise of Communism? Or our stories of economic success, e.g., the market reforms? At the same time, how might attention to China trouble stories of gender that were crafted originally to explain European or North American events, or those of colonized South and Southeast Asia? Just as intriguing, how might critical attention to earlier stories about Chinese gender—the May Fourth story, for instance—alert us to the political and ideological work that these stories performed in the making of a Chinese nation-state? If we were to go back and challenge those stories of the oppressed, silent, footbound, uneducated Chinese woman suddenly bursting forth in a frenzy of subject-making and visibility, what other parts of the big national narrative might come unstuck?

This field, then, or as I have just renamed it, this conjuncture, has been characterized by gender as method, in the sense that people working in queer theory talk about "queer" as method. Asking questions about gender, coming at established China-field questions from an angle, has been enormously productive of new knowledge.

Thinking *with* gender *and* China is also a way of troubling the field of women's history and its encompassing field of women's studies, although real conversations are going to require some further serious work. The critique of Eurocentrism, colonial vestigialism, and obliviousness to race in the field of women's studies is by now well-rehearsed and has had palpable effects on institutional practices. Women's history, clearly, is no longer primarily a Euro-American enterprise. Yet the venture beyond the nation-state still commonly produces "border-crossing panels" at scholarly meetings, displaying arrays rather than carefully-thought-through relationships, and single vectors of circulating ideas rather than densely mapped intersecting fields. These are an improvement on hermetically sealed fields called (unmarked white) "women's history" or (culturally and nationally fixed) "Chinese women's history." But it would be useful to continue to pry open the categories of "gender"—multiply and locally fashioned, unevenly perceptible and important across time—and "China"—formed and reformed through encounters that often traverse national borders.

How can we move beyond the juxtaposition of national case studies to serious comparison, or, better, cross-talk? How do transnational phenomena such as medical professionalism, prostitution reform, and suffrage circulate via the movement of persons, texts, images, and other means? What is the directionality of such circulation, and specifically for China, how do we take the measure of inequalities? To name just one framing problem: should we understand such circulation as ideas that seem to flow largely one way, from metropole to semi-colony? If so, the colonizers have the knowledge advantage and set the terms. Or should we understand this circulation as involving uneven cosmopolitanisms? If so, the semi-colonized are more sophisticated and multicultural than their putative civilizational superiors. How might we trouble the nation-based framing of gender research, while still taking account of the fact that archives, narratives, social movements, and gendered subject-making are frequently organized along national lines? Is gender in a semi-colony different from gender in a colony, and if so, what are the implications for, and limitations of, postcolonial theorizing?

"Gender-as-method" has not exhausted its possibilities for people who think about China, or *from* China (in the sense of situated knowledges), or *with* China (as in using China to think with). But in my judgment, the practice of "gender-as-trouble" is useful only insofar as it is kept open to other forms of troublemaking. A field of knowledge named the "history of Chinese women," or even "Chinese women's studies," lends itself too easily to being visualized as a box, or a grid, or a map with blank spots. The scholar's job then becomes to fill in those spots or to articulate points of connection only with maps of gender elsewhere. This sort of hermetically sealed story about women fits nicely into a single lecture on the syllabus devoted to gender, or a single course on women in a history department curriculum that otherwise keeps telling an uninterrupted story about (unmarked) men. It is precisely the ability to trouble that course syllabus, however, or that history curriculum, or even more capacious knowledge domains, which interests me. Additionally, attention to gender in isolation from other questions runs the serious intellectual risk of assuming gender as stable, foundational, and fixed, therefore undermining what makes it interesting and powerful as a domain of inquiry in the first place: its profoundly historical, variable, situated character.

As feminist scholarship on China has developed, it has been constituted as a field with its own logics, agenda, and vocabulary, one whose practitioners may be tempted to talk primarily to each other. Such conversation is useful, stimulating, fun, and absolutely necessary, but it is not sufficient. It narrows the obligation to mount challenges and to consider what gender is or could be.

The uneasy feeling that the success of women's studies scholarship may actually blunt its critical edge and its receptivity to criticism parallels a broader and very heated discussion about the place of women's studies programs and departments in university curricula. Some years ago, the political theorist Wendy Brown (1997) laid out the challenges to developing a coherent women's studies curriculum. One was "the fact that contemporary feminist scholarship is not a single conversation but is instead engaged with respective domains of knowledge, or bodies of theory, that are themselves infrequently engaged with each other"; another comprised "theoretical challenges to the stability of the category of gender, and political challenges to a discourse of gender apart from race, class, and other markers of social identity" (1997: 83).* Brown went on to argue that the political and intel-

---

*Brown continues by noting the "profoundly important political moment in the academy, the moment in which women's movements challenged the ubiquitous misogyny, masculinism, and sexism in academic research, curricula, canons, and pedagogies. Indisputably, women's studies as a critique of such practices was politically important and intellectually creative. Women's studies as a contemporary institution, however, may be politically and theoretically incoherent, as well as tacitly conservative—incoherent because by definition it circumscribes uncircumscribable "women" as an object of study, and conservative because it must resist all objections to such circumscription if it is to sustain that object of study as its raison d'etre." (Brown 1997: 83).

lectual promise of women's studies lay precisely in these challenges, and that it was blunted when it became institutionalized and defined "woman" as a discrete and classifiable object of study.*

The same can, and should, be said of how the study of women—or even gender tout court —sits within "the China field," bracketing for the moment the parallel problems of "the China field" itself as a discrete domain. Gender maintains its usefulness as an analytic category only insofar as we can make it visible *while at the same time* tracing its relationship to other modes of subject formation—Chinese-ness, for instance, or identification as elite/educated, or as rural. As Brown puts it, "despite the diverse and often even unrelated formations of the subject according to race, class, nation, gender, and so forth, subject construction itself does not occur in discrete units as race, class, nation, and so forth. So the model of power developed to apprehend the making of a particular subject/ion will never accurately describe or trace the lines of a living subject" (1997: 93).

If it is living subjects we are after, in all their messy and entangled specificity, we cannot limn them with gender analysis alone, nor can we content ourselves with talking about "Chinese gender" as though either term in that phrase were a stable one. And at any given moment that a historical subject (individual or collective) is formed, it is conjunctural, not preordained or even predictable, that gender will be dominant. Several decades of fine, slowly cumulative work—the work described if not exhaustively catalogued here—has presented us with some good questions to ask *in conjunction with* other questions. It has not, and should not, give us a formula for finding the answers.

What is to be done? Shorn of its connection to a fixed domain of inquiry ("How should scholars of women in China fill in the gaps in our understanding?"), this project becomes a less prescriptive, even hapless question of temporality: "What now?" Put another way, we might continue to ask "what happened?" while also keeping in mind two other questions that situate and destabilize the first: What people, and what processes, created and left behind the material we use to answer? And why do we want to know now? Rather than prescribing topics, then, I prefer to suggest five habits of mind that might allow us to frame our topics differently.

Understand the boundaries of the state as blurry. In the context of my

---

*"Sustaining gender as a critical, self-reflexive category rather than a normative or nominal one, and sustaining women's studies as an intellectually and institutionally radical site rather than a regulatory one—in short, refusing to allow gender and women's studies to be disciplined—are concerns and refusals at odds with affirming women's studies as a coherent field of study." Brown 1997: 86.

own recent work on gendered memories of rural collectivization in China (Hershatter 2002), I have found especially useful Timothy Mitchell's work on what he calls "the state effect"—not "the effect of the state," but rather how the effect is "created that certain aspects of what occurs pertain to society, while others stand apart as the state?" (Mitchell, 1991: 89). He suggests that

> the precise specification of space and function that characterize modern institutions, the coordination of these functions into hierarchical arrangements, the organization of supervision and surveillance, the marking out of time into schedules and programs, all contribute to constructing a world that appears to consist not of a complex of social practices but of a binary order: on the one hand individuals and their activities, on the other an inert "structure" that somehow stands apart from individuals, precedes them, and contains and gives a framework to their lives. . . . We should examine it not as an actual structure, but as the powerful, apparently metaphysical effect of practices that make such structures appear to exist. (Mitchell 1999: 89)*

We need to pay consistent attention to how state discourse is modified, appropriated, and even reformulated altogether in the implementation, particularly when these activities point to the unclear boundaries of the state and the work required to produce and maintain those boundaries. For instance, the Women's Federation is usually understood as a one-way transmission belt through which party-state policies were communicated to the women masses. But Zhang Naihua (1996; see also Z. Wang 2005b) has argued that in the 1950s, women working at the highest levels of the Women's Federation in fact pushed within the higher echelons of government for more attention to women and what we would now call the gender-specific consequences of government initiatives. My own work on the 1950s (2000, 2002) shows that Women's Federation cadres at the county and village level were often operating, with very few resources and little state support, on an "uplift" model specifically directed at village women—the patient cultivation of local leadership, improvement of women's health and

---

*Mitchell's analysis is aimed at the postwar capitalist state, with interlocking connections between state and "private" institutions, on the one hand, and a naturalized separation between "state and society" or "state and economy," on the other. Although I have wrenched it from its original context, I find his work useful for thinking about the socialist party-state and the production of a sectionally differentiated entity known as "the masses," among whom women (or "woman-as-state-subject," in Tani Barlow's [1994] formulation) were an important constitutive part. For further discussion of the state effect, see Hershatter 2002.

status within the family, and so forth. Wang Zheng's recent work on urban residence committees in the 1950s shows how "women of different backgrounds and motivations all participated in producing the socialist state while being produced as new state subjects" (2005a: 207; see also 2005b). Lisa Rofel's book (1999b) on the meanings of economic reform among three generations of women silk-mill workers in Hangzhou points out how meanings of the state, and state initiatives, are reconfigured, or modified, or stymied on the ground. These activities were not opposed to state discourse—indeed, they participated fully in it, and were most effective when they articulated with larger state goals such as mobilizing women for collective rural production. They were not identical in emphasis or content, however, to state policies articulated by other agencies. Sometimes they attached themselves to state discourse, and therefore captured scarce state resources, in order to do something with directly beneficial practical consequences for women.

A recent example of this process is the *suzhi*, or human quality, discourse, briefly discussed in Chapter 3, which attributes China's economic and social woes to the low quality of its population, and calls for intensified efforts to raise that quality. In many realms—the workplace, the party, the family, the schools—*suzhi* discourse has transformed what were formerly conceived as collective social projects into matters of individual effort and responsibility. In the case of women in particular, low status and even abuse are understood as the individual's responsibility to remedy, if not entirely as her fault. The conversation about women's low *suzhi*, in some respects, picks up where Liang Qichao left off: China's ills can be explained, at least in part, by reference to the status of its women, although the privatization of *suzhi* down to the individual level is an important and not entirely salutary departure from Liang's earlier formulation. Nevertheless, by framing certain projects in terms of *suzhi*, the Women's Federation has obtained state resources for local economic activities and training projects that benefit women.

Ask who has been left out of history from below. Although Cultural Revolution memoirs have become practically a cottage industry since the mid-1980s, biographies of Chinese women who lived at any point in the twentieth century are exceedingly rare. Urban working women, and rural women of every class, have been treated by historians as collectivities, while elite and intellectual women have appeared almost not at all. Women whose agendas did not parallel that of the CCP—for example, those who worked for suffrage or in the GMD—or those whose labor or studies took them in and out of China, fade in and out (mostly out) of view. Before we hurry to dig in this underworked corner of "the field," however, we need to ask at least two questions. First, what does the relative absence of such works to date tells us about the shaping of historical inquiry (the nationalist narrative, the CCP narrative, the feminist project to rediscover subaltern heroines, the heft of the paper trail)? Second, is biography as a method possible or promising in simultaneously building on those early projects (it would be foolish to discuss suffrage without warlordism, for example) and interrupting them (by introducing modes of individual subject formation that include but do not stop with gender)?

Question chronology and narrative organized around ruptures. Work in women's history to date has had two important nodes: the imperial period, particularly from the Song on; and the twentieth-century revolutionary period. In between, largely unaddressed, is the nineteenth century, when the nation form (and its entanglement with the very writing of history) reached its first apogee. Women in the nineteenth century show up late, as stock figures in the story told by Liang Qichao and others about civilizational degeneration and the need for reform.

As noted several times in this volume, Dorothy Ko (1994) has been raising a skeptical eyebrow at the May Fourth story of Confucianism and oppression for some time now, asking modern historians whether we really want to mistake a compelling narrative, crafted at a specific conjuncture, for a usable account of gender in the late imperial past. Her work on the late Ming, as well as Susan Mann's (1997) for the long eighteenth century, have shown (among other accomplishments) how much erudition and publishing activity by literate Jiangnan women had to be forgotten in order to craft the May Fourth story. Meanwhile, scholars who have looked at late-nineteenth-century writings about courtesans have helped us see the many ways in which this particular group was represented—and maybe represented itself—as both embodiments of a world being lost and as avatars of new fashion, new commercialized sex relations, new automobiles, and other objects and practices signifying experimentation with a local version of modernity (see, for example, Zamperini 2003; C. Yeh 1998, 2005; Henriot 1997). Work by Joan Judge, Hu Ying, and others discussed in the previous chapter has pushed the generative moment of women's revolutionary activity, and women's representation as icon of the nation, back into the last decade of the Qing, or even perhaps into the last moments of the nineteenth century.

We might think of this new scholarship in the history of gender as a kind of pincer movement—extending the story of learned women forward into the nineteenth century's early years, tracing the story of modern girls and revolutionary activists back into the nineteenth century's waning years. Still, we are many monographs and a few framing devices short of a history of the nineteenth century here. When I teach a seminar on gender in China from the late imperial period to the present, about halfway into the syllabus my students and I invariably try to navigate what feels either like a black hole or a vertiginous drop where the nineteenth century ought to be.

In between the eighteenth century and the last years of the nineteenth century, surely things happened. Surely, to return to that cherished recuperative project, "women were there, too." Surely, at minimum, the arsenal-makers and self-strengtheners and frontier-settlers and language reformers and science experimenters and Taiping rebels and Nian rebels and Boxers and displaced porters and opium smugglers and compradores lived in households with some of them. (Yes, we have the Taiping move to alter the status of women and the Red Lanterns—but I think it is time to move beyond our two or three recurrent exercises in synecdoche and try to get at something more substantial, varied, and confusing.) Additionally, the move to reconfigure women as parasitic and oppressed dead weights on the body politic could not have sprung full-formed from the brain of Liang Qichao—it gestated somewhere, or several somewheres. We know that women were a powerful figuration of social crisis long before the late Qing, but what are the particularities of the nineteenth-century situation? What did women write and do? How and for what were they written and done to? As Woman (anodyne subject of History) was reformulated, what about Man, and masculinity? What might happen to our sinological truisms about key points in nineteenth-century history if gender was placed at the center, or in the picture at all?

Pay attention to moments when gender matters to the participants, and moments when it recedes. In Chinese history over the past century and a half, gender has often been a salient axis of difference or point of identification, and sometimes both. It was an axis of difference, for instance, in late Qing and May Fourth writings on the benighted status of women and the need to remedy it. It was a point of identification among women's suffrage groups in the Republican period. When the new PRC state formed branches of the Women's Federation in the 1950s, it became a different point of identification—what Tani Barlow (1994) has called "Woman as state subject." Therefore one important question when gender emerges in discourse is to ask: How and why is it erupting? Who gives it expression? Who recognizes or takes it up, with what degree of passion, and to what ends? Recognizing that people do not just take up a label, but are continually remade in the process of doing so, we need to ask how gender helps to produce political and/or personal subjectivity at particular moments. This is, of course, separate from the question of when gender emerges as a salient axis of difference or identification for historians, enabling some questions and undoubtedly obscuring others.

At the same time, we also need to attend to moments when gender as difference or gender as identification recedes, and to ask why and how that happens. After the violent suppression of the 1989 demonstrations in China, Rey Chow wrote:

> I heard a feminist ask: "How should we read what is going on in China in terms of gender?" My immediate response to that question was, and is: "We do not, because at the moment of shock Chinese people are de-gendered and become simply "Chinese." To ask how we can use gender to "read" a political crisis such as the present one is to insist on the universal and timeless sufficiency of an analytical category, and to forget the historicity that accompanies all categorical explanatory power. . . . Any analytical discourse on the Chinese situation in terms of a single category, when Chinese prodemocracy protesters are being arrested, punished, or killed for having demonstrated peacefully for freedom, is presumptuous. The problem is not how we should read what is going on in China in terms of gender, but rather: what do the events in China tell us about gender as a category, especially as it relates to the so-called Third World? What are gender's limits, where does it work, and where does it not work? (1991: 82)

To say this, I would add, is not to deny that "women were there, too" (who can forget Chai Ling?) or that "Woman was put to symbolic uses" (remember the Goddess of Democracy). Nor is it to foreclose the possibility that the post-June Fourth crackdown had gendered dimensions: the masculinism of a militarized state, for instance, or the informal and risky organization by relatives of the disappeared under the sign of maternal grief. Nor, finally, is it to regard the category of "simply Chinese" as consistent across time. Rather, it is to recognize that the movement, as its everyday dynamics unfolded and as it is remembered, was neither *about* gender in an ideological sense, nor *enacted* via gendered dynamics, nor *retold* as a moment in which gender mattered. If gender is, as Joan Scott (1999) famously put it, "a useful category of analysis," it remains so only insofar as it can be flexibly applied. To establish that "women are everywhere" or that the unmarked male, discursively speaking, is nevertheless a gendered entity is a beginning rather than an end. Too often the moments when gender recedes have been read by feminist scholars as moments of betrayal—the state sold women out—or moments devoted to a larger and more important truth: gender does not matter when the PLA opens fire;

only being Chinese, or human, matters at that moment. Rather than exco-
riating those who turn away from gender, or reproaching those who insist
on it in all times or places, I would like to see us reframe the question. If
gender is a meaning-making category, we need to track when and by whom
it is used or discarded, as well as attending to how and why it is entwined
with or displaced by other categories.

*Assess the displacement of Woman as modernity's exemplar and
Other.* The work that gender did in discourse about the state, for generations of Chinese intellectuals and for us as scholars, is still partly done by
gender in the contemporary moment. Scholars and activists ask such questions as: Are the reforms good or bad for women? Is the new ubiquity of
sexual expression, or the obvious hierarchies in sexual privilege, a sign of
resurgent patriarchy, modernity in a globalization mode, or both? Other
subaltern groups, however, are increasingly deployed in similar ways. Since
the advent of the reforms, and with more intensity in the past five years,
"the rural"—that is, the peasant—has emerged as the problematic figure
dragging China down. If Liang Qichao characterized women as parasites,
then the 1988 TV series *River Elegy* characterized toothless aged peasant men who persisted in having dozens of children as the main threat to
China's development, the embodiment of insular "yellow" (as opposed to
cosmopolitan "blue") civilization (*Heshang* 1988; Su 1991). The formulation works like this: Why did our revolution go wrong? Because the May
Fourth agenda was hijacked by an ignorant peasant, Mao, who was kept in
power by a party leadership full of peasants and, more broadly, by ignorant peasants who revered him throughout China. Although *River Elegy*
was banned by the government, in fact official discourse has shared much
of its approach. Peasants, like women in the May Fourth story, are both
the victims and the embodiment of the problem. They need uplift; they
need their quality improved; they need to change to be worthy citizens,
vessels of the nation. At the same time, in segments of the New Left, peasants—the inequalities in their status that the state has created and allowed
to stand, the injustices visited upon them—are *the* symptom for what has
gone wrong with the reforms. At the moment, one might argue that the
status of peasants, rather than that of women, has become the bellwether
in official assessments of how China is doing. Peasant weaknesses, frailties,
shortcomings, and victimization, rather than those of women, are the central sign for understanding Chinese modernity and the Chinese future.

This might not be a bad thing, both for China and for feminist scholarship. "Peasants" need the attention. Some of us are going to have to become
involved in troubling the category of peasants by asking questions that years

of doing gender research have made us practiced at: Is "peasant" a unitary category? Is it gendered? (Or, to reprise an earlier, cruder, but still useful question: Where are the women?) Is it locally differentiated? Is it historically specific? What work is this category "peasant" doing in contemporary debates, and how is that work related—if it is related—to the everyday, the material, the question of change over time?* In short, "gender as method" may be useful in troubling other scholarly paradigms and political formulations, much as it troubled an earlier narrative of unmarked-male-as-subject-of-history. But this usefulness will continue only if we recognize that "gender" and "peasant" are different methods of subjectification; we cannot reduce every form of subject production to a parallel process of creation.

Meanwhile, the displacement of Woman as the central signifier of China's national distress, or success, may open up other possibilities for thinking, scholarship, and activism. Perhaps, freed from the central symbolic burden of representing China, women—and even Woman—may turn out to have other possibilities, in new modes of scholarly analysis and activist agendas, that take full account of the state and its importance but are not propelled by it.

---

*The dissertation-in-progress of Alexander Day at the University of California, Santa Cruz, "Return of the Peasant: The Politics of Social Justice in Contemporary China," has been crucial in shaping my thinking about this topic.

Works Cited

Ahern, Emily. 1975. "The Power and Pollution of Chinese Women." In M. Wolf and Witke 1975, 193–214.

Anagnost, Ann. 1988. "Family Violence and Magical Violence: The Woman as Victim in China's One-Child Family Policy." *Women and Language* 11.2 (winter): 16–22.

———. 1989. "Transformations of Gender in Modern China." In *Gender and Anthropology: Critical Reviews for Research and Teaching,* ed. Sandra Morgen. Washington, D.C.: American Anthropological Association, 313–29.

———. 1997. *National Past-Times: Narrative, Representation, and Power in Modern China.* Durham, N.C.: Duke University Press.

Andors, Phyllis. 1983. *The Unfinished Liberation of Chinese Women, 1949–1980.* Bloomington: Indiana University Press.

Bailey, Paul J. 2001. "Active Citizen or Efficient Housewife? The Debate over Women's Education in Early Twentieth Century China." In Peterson, Hayhoe, and Lu 2001, 318–47.

———. 2003. "'Unharnessed Fillies': Discourse on the 'Modern' Female Student in Early Twentieth-Century China." In Luo and Lü 2003, 327–57.

———. 2004. "Modernizing Conservatism in Early Twentieth Century China: The Discourse and Practice of Women's Education." *European Journal of East Asian Studies* 3.2 (Nov.): 217–41.

Banister, Judith. 1987. *China's Changing Population.* Stanford, Calif.: Stanford University Press.

Bao, Xiaolan, and Wu Xu. 2001. "Feminist Collaboration between Diaspora and China." In Ping-chun Hsiung, Jaschok, and Milwertz 2001, 79–99.

Barlow, Tani E. 1989. Introduction to *I Myself Am a Woman: Selected Writings of Ding Ling,* ed. and trans. Tani E. Barlow and Gary J. Bjorge. Boston: Beacon Press, 1–45.

———, ed. 1993. *Gender Politics in Modern China: Writing and Feminism.* Durham, N.C.: Duke University Press.

———. 1994a. "Politics and Protocols of *Funü:* (Un)Making National Woman." In Gilmartin et al. 1994, 339–59.

———. 1994b. "Theorizing Woman: *Funü, Guojia, Jiating*." In Zito and Barlow 1994, 253–89.

———. 1997. "Women at the Close of the Maoist Era in the Polemics of Li Xiaojiang and Her Associates." In *The Politics of Culture in the Shadow of Capital,* ed. Lisa Lowe and David Lloyd. Durham, N.C.: Duke University Press, 506–43.

———. 2004. *The Question of Women in Chinese Feminism.* Durham, N.C.: Duke University Press.

———. 2005. "Wanting Some: Commodity Desire and the Eugenic Modern Girl." In Leutner and Spakowski 2005, 312–50.

Bauer, John, Feng Wang, Nancy E. Riley, and Xiaohua Zhao. 1992. "Gender Inequality in Urban China: Education and Employment." *Modern China* 18.3 (July): 333–70.

Bays, Daniel H., ed. 1996. *Christianity in China: From the Eighteenth Century to the Present.* Stanford, Calif.: Stanford University Press.

Beahan, Charlotte L. 1975. "Feminism and Nationalism in the Chinese Women's Press." *Modern China* 1.4 (Oct.): 379–416.

———. 1976. "The Women's Movement and Nationalism in Late Ch'ing China." Ph.D. diss., Columbia University.

———. 1981. "In the Public Eye: Women in Early Twentieth-Century China." In Guisso and Johannesen 1981, 215–38.

———. 1984. "One Woman's View of the Early Chinese Communist Movement: The Autobiography of Yang Zilie [Mme. Zhang Guotao]." *Republican China* 10.1B (Nov.): 25–35.

Beaver, Patricia D., Lihui Hou, and Xue Wang. 1995. "Rural Chinese Women: Two Faces of Economic Reform." *Modern China* 21.2 (Apr.): 205–32.

Belden, Jack. 1970. *China Shakes the World.* New York: Harper, 1949. Reprint, New York and London: Monthly Review Press.

Bell, Lynda S. 1994. "For Better, For Worse: Women and the World Market in Rural China." *Modern China* 20.2 (Apr.): 180–210.

———. 1999. *One Industry, Two Chinas: Silk Filatures and Peasant-Family Production in Wuxi County, 1865–1937.* Stanford, Calif.: Stanford University Press.

Bernhardt, Kathryn. 1994. "Women and the Law: Divorce in the Republican Period." In *Civil Law in Qing and Republican China,* ed. Kathryn Bernhardt and Philip C. C. Huang. Stanford, Calif.: Stanford University Press, 187–214.

———. 1999. *Women and Property in China, 960–1949.* Stanford, Calif.: Stanford University Press.

Berry, Chris. 1999. "Representing Chinese Women: Researching Women in the Chinese Cinema." In Finnane and McLaren 1999, 198–211.

Beynon, Louise. 2004. "Dilemmas of the Heart: Rural Working Women and Their Hopes for the Future." In Gaetano and Jacka 2004, 131–50.

Bian, Yanjie, John R. Logan, and Xiaoling Shu. 2000. "Wage and Job Inequalities in the Working Lives of Men and Women in Tianjin." In Entwisle and Henderson 2000, 111–33.

Bianco, Lucien, and Chang-ming Hua. 1988. "Implementation and Resistance: The Single-Child Family Policy." In Feuchtwang, Hussein, and Pairault 1988, 147–68.

Blake, C. Fred. 1978. "Death and Abuse in Marriage Laments: The Curse of Chinese Brides." *Asian Folklore Studies* 37.1: 13–33.

Borthwick, Sally. 1985. "Changing Concepts of Women from the Late Qing to the May Fourth Period." In *Ideal and Reality: Social and Political Change in Modern China,* ed. David Pong and Edmund Fung. Lanham, Md.: University Press of America, 63–91.

Bossen, Laurel. 1994. "Gender and Economic Reform in Southwest China." In *Femmes, Féminisme, et Développement/Women, Feminism and Development,* ed. Huguette Dagenais and Denise Piché. Montréal: McGill-Queen's University Press, 223–40.

———. 1999. "Women and Development." In Gamer 1999, 293–320.

———. 2000. "Women Farmers, Small Plots and Changing Markets in China." In *Women Farmers and Commercial Ventures: Increasing Food Security in Developing Countries,* ed. Anita Spring. Boulder, Colo.: Lynne Reinner, 171–89.

———. 2002. *Chinese Women and Rural Development: Sixty Years of Change in Lu Village, Yunnan.* Lanham, Md.: Rowman and Littlefield.

Bray, Francesca. 1997. *Technology and Gender: Fabrics of Power in Late Imperial China.* Berkeley and Los Angeles: University of California Press.

Broaded, C. Montgomery, and Chongshun Liu. 1996. "Family Background, Gender and Educational Attainment in Urban China." *China Quarterly* 145 (Mar.): 53–86.

Brook, Timothy, and Hy V. Luong, eds. 1997. *Culture and Economy: The Shaping Of Capitalism In Eastern Asia.* Ann Arbor: University of Michigan Press.

Brown, Wendy. 1997. "The Impossibility of Women's Studies." *differences: A Journal of Feminist Cultural Studies,* 9.3 (fall): 79–101.

Brownell, Susan. 1995. *Training the Body for China: Sports in the Moral Order of the People's Republic.* Chicago: University of Chicago Press.

———. 1998–99. "The Body and the Beautiful in Chinese Nationalism: Sportswomen and Fashion Models in the Reform Era." *China Information* 13.2–3 (autumn–winter): 36–58.

———. 1999. "Strong Women and Impotent Men: Sports, Gender, and Nationalism in Chinese Public Culture." In M. Yang 1999c, 207–31.

———. 2000. "Gender and Nationalism in China at the Turn of the Millennium." In *China Briefing 2000,* ed. Tyrene White. Armonk, N.Y.: M. E. Sharpe, 195–232.

———. 2001. "Making Dream Bodies in Beijing: Athletes, Fashion Models, and Urban Mystique in China." In N. Chen et al. 2001, 123–42.

Brownell, Susan, and Jeffrey Wasserstrom. 2002a. "Afterword: Putting Gender at the Center." In Brownell and Wasserstrom 2002b, 435–45.

———, eds. 2002b. *Chinese Femininities/Chinese Masculinities.* Berkeley and Los Angeles: University of California Press.

———. 2002c. "Introduction: Theorizing Femininities and Masculinities." In Brownell and Wasserstrom 2002b, 1–41.

Bu, Wei. 2004. "Chinese Women and the Mass Media: Status Quo, Interventions, and Challenges." In J. Tao, Zheng, and Mow 2004, 274–88.

Butler, Judith. 1999. *Gender Trouble: Feminism and the Subversion of Identity.* 10th anniversary ed. New York: Routledge.

Cai, Yiping, Yuan Feng, and Yanqiu Guo. 2001. "The Women's Media Watch Network." In Ping-chun Hsiung, Jaschok, and Milwertz 2001, 209–26.

Carroll, Peter. 2003. "Refashioning Suzhou: Dress, Commodification, and Modernity." *positions: east asia cultures critique* 11.2 (fall): 443–78.

Chang, Michael G. 1999. "The Good, the Bad and the Beautiful: Movie Actresses and Public Discourse in Shanghai, 1920s–1930s." In Yingjin Zhang 1999a, 128–59.

Chang, Pang-mei Natasha. 1997. *Bound Feet and Western Dress.* New York: Anchor Books.

Chang, Xiangqun. 1999. "'Fat Pigs' and Women's Gifts: Agnatic and Non-Agnatic Social Support in Kaixiangong Village." In West et al. 1999, 156–74.

Chao, Emily. 2003. "Dangerous Work: Women in Traffic." *Modern China* 29.1 (Jan.): 71–107.

Chen, Mingxia. 2004. "The Marriage Law and the Rights of Chinese Women in Marriage and the Family." In J. Tao, Zheng, and Mow 2004, 159–71.

Chen, Nancy N., Constance D. Clark, Suzanne Z. Gottschang, and Lyn Jeffery, eds. 2001. *China Urban: Ethnographies of Contemporary Culture.* Durham, N.C.: Duke University Press.

Chen, Pi-chao. 1985. "Birth Control Methods and Organisation in China." In Croll, Davin, and Kane 1985, 135–48.

Chen, Tina Mai. 2001. "Dressing for the Party: Clothing, Citizenship, and Gender Formation in Mao's China." *Fashion Theory* 5.2 (June): 143–72.

———. 2003a. "Female Icons, Feminist Iconography? Socialist Rhetoric and Women's Agency in 1950s China." *Gender and History* 15.2 (Aug.): 268–95.

———. 2003b. "Proletarian White and Working Bodies in Mao's China." *positions: east asia cultures critique* 11.2 (fall): 361–93.

Chen, Yiyun. 1994. "Out of the Traditional Halls of Academe: Exploring New Avenues for Research on Women." Trans. S. Katherine Campbell. In Gilmartin et al. 1994, 69–79.

Cheng, Weikun. 1996. "The Challenge of the Actresses: Female Performers and Cultural Alternatives in Early Twentieth Century Beijing and Tianjin." *Modern China* 22.2 (Apr.): 197–233.

―――. 2000. "Going Public through Education: Female Reformers and Girls' Schools in Late Qing Beijing." *Late Imperial China* 21.1 (June): 107–44.

Chew, Matthew. 2003. "The Dual Consequences of Cultural Localization: How Exposed Short Stockings Subvert and Sustain Global Cultural Hierarchy." *positions: east asia cultures critique* 11.2 (fall): 479–509.

Chiang, William. 1995. *We Two Know the Script, We Have Become Good Friends: Linguistic and Social Aspects of the Women's Script Literacy in Southern Hunan, China.* Lanham, Md.: University Press of America.

Chin, Angelina. 2002. "The Management of Women's Bodies: Regulating Mui Tsai and Prostitutes in Hong Kong under Colonial Rule, 1841–1935." *E-Journal on Hong Kong Cultural and Social Studies* 1 (Feb.). http://www.hku.hk/hkcsp/ccex/ehkcss01/.

―――. 2006. "Bound to Emancipate: Management of Lower-Class Women in 1920s and 1930s Urban South China." Ph.D. diss., University of California, Santa Cruz.

Chin, Annping. 2002. *Four Sisters of Hofei: A History.* New York: Scribner's.

Chow, Esther Ngan-ling, ed. 2002. *Transforming Gender and Development in East Asia.* New York: Routledge.

Chow, Esther Ngan-ling, Naihua Zhang, and Jinling Wang. 2004. "Promising and Contested Fields: Women's Studies and Sociology of Women/Gender in Contemporary China." *Gender and Society* 18.2 (Apr.): 161–88.

Chow, Rey. 1991a. "Violence in the Other Country: China as Crisis, Spectacle, and Woman." In *Third World Women and the Politics of Feminism,* ed. Chandra Talpade Mohanty, Ann Russo, and Lourdes Torres. Bloomington: Indiana University Press, 81–100.

―――. 1991b. *Woman and Chinese Modernity: The Politics of Reading between East and West.* Minneapolis: University of Minnesota Press.

Chu, Junhong. 2001. "Prenatal Sex Determination and Sex-Selective Abortion in Rural Central China." *Population and Development Review* 27.2 (June): 259–82.

Clark, Constance D. 2001. "Foreign Marriage, 'Tradition,' and the Politics of Border Crossings." In N. Chen et al. 2001, 104–22.

Cornue, Virginia. 1999. "Practicing NGOness and Relating Women's Space Publicly: The Women's Hotline and the State." In M. Yang 1999c, 68–91.

Croll, Elisabeth J. 1974. *The Women's Movement in China: A Selection of Readings, 1949–73.* Modern China Series, no. 6. London: Anglo-Chinese Educational Institute.

―――. 1979. *Women in Rural Development: The People's Republic of China.* Geneva: International Labour Office.

―――. 1980. *Feminism and Socialism in China.* London: Routledge and Kegan Paul, 1978. Reprint, New York: Schocken.

―――. 1981. *The Politics of Marriage in Contemporary China.* New York: Cambridge University Press.

―――. 1983. *Chinese Women Since Mao.* London: Zed Books.

———. 1985a. "Introduction: Fertility Norms and Family Size in China." In Croll, Davin, and Kane 1985, 1–36.

———. 1985b. "The Single-Child Family in Beijing: A First-Hand Report." In Croll, Davin, and Kane 1985, 190–232.

———. 1985c. *Women and Rural Development in China: Production and Reproduction.* Geneva: International Labour Office

———. 1994. *From Heaven to Earth: Images and Experiences of Development in China.* London and New York: Routledge.

———. 1995. *Changing Identities of Chinese Women: Rhetoric, Experience and Self-Perception in Twentieth-Century China.* Hong Kong: Hong Kong University Press. London and Atlantic Highlands, N.J.: Zed Books.

———. 1996. "Gendered Moments and Inscripted Memories: Girlhood in Twentieth-Century Chinese Autobiography." In *Gender and Memory,* ed. Selma Leydesdorff, Luisa Passerini, and Paul Thomspon. International Yearbook of Oral History and Life Stories, no. 4. Oxford: Oxford University Press, 117–31.

———. 2000. *Endangered Daughters: Discrimination and Development in Asia.* London and New York: Routledge.

———. 2001. "New Spaces, New Voices: Women Organizing in Twentieth-Century China." In Ping-chun Hsiung, Jaschok, and Milwertz 2001, 25–40.

Croll, Elisabeth, Delia Davin, and Penny Kane, eds. 1985. *China's One-Child Policy.* London: Macmillan.

Dai, Jinhua. 1995. "Invisible Women: Contemporary Chinese Cinema and Women's Film." *positions: east asia cultures critique* 3.1 (spring): 255–80.

———. 1999. "Rewriting Chinese Women: Gender Production and Cultural Space in the Eighties and Nineties." In M. Yang 1999c, 191–206.

———. 2004. "Class and Gender in Contemporary Chinese Women's Literature." In J. Tao, Zheng, and Mow 2004, 289–301.

Dai, Jinhua, and Mayfair Yang. 1995. "A Conversation with Huang Shuqing." *positions: east asia cultures critique* 3.3 (winter): 790–805.

Dal Lago, Francesca. 2000. "Crossed Legs in 1930s Shanghai: How 'Modern' the Modern Woman?" *East Asian History* 19: 103–44.

Dalsimer, Marilyn, and Laurie Nisonoff. 1987. "The Implications of the New Agricultural and One-Child Family Policies for Rural Chinese Women." *Feminist Studies* 13.3: 583–607.

Damm, Jens. 2005. "Contemporary Discourses on Homosexuality in Republican China: A Critical Analysis of Terminology and Current Research." In Leutner and Spakowski 2005, 282–311.

Davin, Delia. 1973. "Women in the Liberated Areas." In M. Young 1973, 73–91.

———. 1975a. "The Implications of Some Aspects of C.C.P. Policy toward Urban Women in the 1950s." *Modern China* 1.4 (Oct.): 363–78.

———. 1975b. "Women in the Countryside of China." In M. Wolf and Witke 1975, 243–73.

————. 1976. *Woman-Work: Women and the Party in Revolutionary China.* Oxford: Clarendon Press.

————. 1985. "The Single-Child Family Policy in the Countryside." In Croll, Davin, and Kane 1985, 37–82.

————. 1988. "The Implications of Contract Agriculture for the Employment and Status of Chinese Peasant Women." In Feuchtwang, Hussein, and Pairault 1988, 137–46.

————. 1989. "Of Dogma, Dicta, and Washing Machines: Women in the People's Republic of China." In Kruks, Rapp, and Young 1989, 354–58.

————. 1990. " 'Never Mind if It's a Girl, You Can Have Another Try.' " In *Remaking Peasant China: Problems of Rural Development and Institutions at the Start of the 1990s,* ed. Jorgen Delman, Clemens Stubbe Ostergaard, and Flemming Christiansen. Aarhus: Aarhus University Press, 81–91.

————. 1997. "Migration, Women and Gender Issues in Contemporary China." In *Floating Population and Migration in China: The Impact of Economic Reforms,* ed. Thomas Scharping. Hamburg: Institut für Asienkunde, 297–314.

————. 1999. *Internal Migration in Contemporary China.* New York: St. Martin's Press.

Davis, Deborah, ed. 2000. *The Consumer Revolution in Urban China.* Berkeley and Los Angeles: University of California Press.

Davis, Deborah, and Stevan Harrell, eds. 1993. *Chinese Families in the Post-Mao Era.* Berkeley and Los Angeles: University of California Press.

Davis-Friedmann, Deborah. 1985. "Old-Age Security and the One-Child Campaign." In Croll, Davin, and Kane 1985, 149–61.

Diamant, Neil J. 2000a. "Re-Examining the Impact of the 1950 Marriage Law: State Improvisation, Local Initiative, and Rural Family Change." *China Quarterly* 161 (Mar.): 171–98.

————. 2000b. *Revolutionizing the Family: Politics, Love, and Divorce in Urban and Rural China, 1949–1968.* Berkeley and Los Angeles: University of California Press.

Diamond, Norma. 1975. "Collectivization, Kinship, and the Status of Women in Rural China." In *Toward an Anthropology of Women,* ed. Rayna R. Reiter. New York and London: Monthly Review Press, 372–95.

Dikötter, Frank. 1995. *Sex, Culture, and Modernity in China.* Honolulu: University of Hawai'i Press.

————. 1998. *Imperfect Conceptions: Medical Knowledge, Birth Defects, and Eugenics in China.* New York: Columbia University Press.

Dirlik, Arif, and Maurice Meisner, eds. 1989. *Marxism and the Chinese Experience.* Armonk, N.Y.: M. E. Sharpe.

Dong, Madeleine Yue. 2005. "Unofficial History and Gender Boundary Crossing in the Early Chinese Republic: Shen Peizhen and Xiaofengxian." In B. Goodman and Larson 2005a, 169–87.

Dongchen District Division of the Public Security Bureau, Beijing (Dongchen

District). 1997. "An Analysis of 260 Prostitutes and Prostitute Clients." In Jeffreys 1997b, 33–44.

Dooling, Amy D., and Kristina M. Torgeson. 1998. *Writing Women in Modern China: An Anthology of Women's Literature from the Early Twentieth Century.* New York: Columbia University Press.

Drucker, Alison R. 1981. "The Influence of Western Women on the Anti-Footbinding Movement 1840–1911." In Guisso and Johannesen 1981, 179–99.

Du, Fangqin. 2001. "'Manoeuvring Fate' and 'Following the Call': Development and Prospects of Women's Studies." In Ping-chun Hsiung, Jaschok, and Milwertz 2001, 237–49.

———. 2005. "Women and Gender in the Rural Modernization Movement: A Case Study of Ding County (1912–1937)." In Leutner and Spakowski 2005, 396–421.

Duara, Prasenjit. 1995. *Rescuing History from the Nation.* Chicago: University of Chicago Press.

———. 1998. "The Regime of Authenticity: Timelessness, Gender, and National History in Modern China." *History and Theory* 37.3 (Oct.): 287–309.

———. 2000. "Of Authenticity and Woman: Personal Narratives of Middle-Class Women in Modern China." In *Becoming Chinese: Passages to Modernity and Beyond*, ed. Wen-hsin Yeh. Berkeley and Los Angeles: University of California Press, 342–64.

———. 2003. *Sovereignty and Authenticity: Manchukuo and the East Asian Modern.* Lanham, Md.: Rowman and Littlefield.

Eckholm, Erik. 2002. "Desire for Sons Drives Use of Prenatal Scans in China." *New York Times*, June 21, A3.

Edwards, Louise. 1994. "Chin Sung-Ts'en's *A Tocsin for Women:* The Dextrous Merger of Radicalism and Conservatism in Feminism of the Early Twentieth Century." *Jindai Zhongguo funü shi yanjiu/Research on Women in Modern Chinese History* 2 (June): 117–40.

———. 1999. "From Gender Equality to Gender Difference: Feminist Campaigns for Quotas for Women in Politics." *Twentieth-Century China* 24.2 (Apr.): 69–105.

———. 2000a. "Policing the Modern Woman in Republican China." *Modern China* 26.2 (Apr.): 115–47.

———. 2000b. "Women in the People's Republic of China: New Challenges to the Grand Gender Narrative." In *Women in Asia: Tradition, Modernity and Globalisation*, ed. Louise Edwards and Mina Roces. Ann Arbor: University of Michigan Press, 59–82.

———. 2000c. "Women's Suffrage in China: Challenging Scholarly Conventions." *Pacific Historical Review* 69.4 (Nov.): 617–38.

———. 2004a. "Chinese Women's Campaigns for Suffrage: Nationalism, Confucianism and Political Agency." In *Women's Suffrage in Asia: Gender, Nationalism and Democracy*, ed. Louise Edwards and Mina Roces. London and New York: RoutledgeCurzon, 59–78.

———. 2004b. "Constraining Women's Political Work with 'Women's Work': The Chinese Communist Party and Women's Participation in Politics." In McLaren 2004a, 109–30.

———. 2005. "Opposition to Women's Suffrage in China: Confronting Modernity in Governance." In Leutner and Spakowski 2005, 107–28.

Entwisle, Barbara, and Gail E. Henderson, eds. 2000. *Re-Drawing Boundaries: Work, Households, and Gender in China.* Berkeley and Los Angeles: University of California Press.

Erwin, Kathleen. 1999. "White Women, Male Desires: A Televisual Fantasy of the Transnational Chinese Family." In M. Yang 1999c, 232–57.

———. 2000. "Heart-to-Heart, Phone-to-Phone: Family Values, Sexuality, and the Politics of Shanghai's Advice Hotlines." In Davis 2000, 145–70.

———. Forthcoming. *Mobilizing Sex and Virtue: Gender and Transnational Desires in Shanghai.* Berkeley and Los Angeles: University of California Press.

Evans, Harriet. 1995. "Defining Difference: The 'Scientific' Construction of Sexuality and Gender in the People's Republic of China." *Signs: Journal of Women in Culture and Society* 20.2: 357–94.

———. 1997. *Women and Sexuality in China: Dominant Discourses of Female Sexuality and Gender Since 1949.* London: Blackwell.

———. 1998. "The Language of Liberation: Gender and *Jiefang* in Early CCP Discourse." *Intersections,* inaugural issue (Sept.). http://wwwsshe.murdoch .edu.au/intersections/. Reprinted in Wasserstrom 2003, 193–220.

———. 1999. "'Comrade Sisters': Gendered Bodies and Spaces." In *Picturing Power in the People's Republic of China: Posters of the Cultural Revolution,* ed. Harriet Evans and Stephanie Donald. Lanham, Md.: Rowman and Littlefield, 63–78.

———. 2000. "Marketing Femininity: Images of the Modern Chinese Woman." In *China Beyond the Headlines,* ed. Timothy B. Weston and Lionel M. Jensen. Lanham, Md.: Rowman and Littlefield, 217–44.

———. 2001. "What Colour Is Beautiful Hair? Subjective Interventions and Global Fashions in the Cultural Production of Gender in Urban China." *Figurationen: Gender, Literature, Culture* 2: 117–32.

———. 2002. "Past, Perfect or Imperfect: Changing Images of the Ideal Wife." In Brownell and Wasserstrom 2002b, 335–60.

———. 2003. "Sex and the Open Market." In *Sexualities and Society: A Reader,* ed. Jeffrey Weeks, Janet Holland, and Matthew Waites. Cambridge: Polity, 216–226.

Families with Children from China. 1999. "Adoption Law of the People's Republic of China, 1998." http://www.fwcc.org/china_adoption_law_98.htm.

Fan, C. Cindy. 2003. "Rural-Urban Migration and Gender Division of Labor in Transitional China." *International Journal of Urban and Regional Research* 27.1 (Mar.): 24–47.

———. 2004. "Out to the City and Back to the Village: The Experiences and

Contributions of Rural Women Migrating from Sichuan and Anhui." In Gaetano and Jacka 2004, 177–206.

Fan, C. Cindy, and Youqin Huang. 1998. "Waves of Rural Brides: Female Marriage Migration in China." *Annals of the Association of American Geographers* 88.2 (June): 227–51.

Fan, C. Cindy, and Ling Li. 2002. "Marriage and Migration in Transitional China: A Field Study of Gaozhou, Western Guangdong." *Environment and Planning A* 34.4 (Apr.): 619–38.

Fan, Hong. 1997. *Footbinding, Feminism and Freedom: The Liberation of Women's Bodies in Modern China.* London: Frank Cass.

Farquhar, Judith. 2002. *Appetites: Food and Sex in Post-Socialist China.* Durham, N.C.: Duke University Press.

Farrer, James. 2000. "Dancing through the Market Transition: Disco and Dance Hall Sociability in Shanghai." In Davis 2000, 226–49.

———. 2002. *Opening Up: Youth Sex Culture and Market Reform in Shanghai.* Chicago: University of Chicago Press.

Farrer, James, and Zhongxin Sun. 2003. "Extramarital Love in Shanghai." *China Journal* 50 (July): 1–36.

Feigon, Lee. 1994. "Gender and the Chinese Student Movement." In *Popular Protest and Political Culture in Modern China,* ed. Jeffrey N. Wasserstrom and Elizabeth J. Perry. 2nd ed. Boulder, Colo.: Westview Press, 125–35.

Feuchtwang, Stephan, Athar Hussein, and Thierry Pairault, eds. 1988. *Transforming China's Economy in the Eighties.* Boulder, Colo.: Westview Press; London: Zed Books.

Field, Andrew D. 1999. "Selling Souls in Sin City: Shanghai Singing and Dancing Hostesses in Print, Film, and Politics, 1920–49." In Yingjin Zhang 1999a, 99–127.

Finnane, Antonia. 1996. "What Should Chinese Women Wear? A National Problem." *Modern China* 22.2 (Apr.): 99–131. Reprinted in Finnane and McLaren 1999, 3–36.

———. 2003. "Yu Feng and the 1950s Dress Reform Campaign: Global Hegemony and Local Agency in the Art of Fashion." *Jindai Zhongguo de funü yu shehui (1600–1950)* [Women and Society in Modern China (1600–1950)]. Vol. 2 of *Wusheng zhi sheng* [Voices amid Silence], ed. Yu Chien-ming. Taipei: Zhongyang yanjiuyuan jindaishi yanjiusuo, 235–67.

———. 2005a. "China on the Catwalk: Between Economic Success and Nationalist Anxiety." *China Quarterly* 183 (Sept.): 587–608.

———. 2005b. "Looking for the Jiang Qing Dress: Some Preliminary Findings." *Fashion Theory* 9.1: 3–22.

Finnane, Antonia, and Anne McLaren, eds. 1999. *Dress, Sex and Text in Chinese Culture.* Clayton: Monash Asia Institute.

Fong, Grace S. 2004. "Female Hands: Embroidery as a Knowledge Field in Women's Everyday Life in Late Imperial and Early Republican China." *Late Imperial China* 25.1 (June): 1–58.

Friedman, Sara L. 2000. "Spoken Pleasures and Dangerous Desires: Sexuality,

Marriage, and the State in Rural Southeastern China." *East Asia: An International Quarterly* 18.4 (winter): 13–39.

———. 2004. "Embodying Civility: Civilizing Processes and Symbolic Citizenship in Southeastern China." *Journal of Asian Studies* 63.3 (Aug.): 687–718.

———. 2005. "The Intimacy of State Power: Marriage, Liberation, and Socialist Subjects in Southeastern China." *American Ethnologist* 62.2 (May): 312–27.

———. 2006. *Intimate Politics: Marriage, the Market, and State Power in Southeastern China.* Cambridge, Mass.: Harvard University Asia Center and Harvard University Press.

Furth, Charlotte. 1999. *A Flourishing Yin: Gender in China's Medical History, 960–1665.* Berkeley and Los Angeles: University of California Press.

Gaetano, Arianne M. 2004. "Filial Daughters, Modern Women: Migrant Domestic Workers in Post-Mao Beijing." In Gaetano and Jacka 2004, 41–79.

Gaetano, Arianne M., and Tamara Jacka, eds. 2004. *On the Move: Women in Rural-to-Urban Migration in Contemporary China.* New York: Columbia University Press.

Gamer, Robert, ed. 1999. *Understanding Contemporary China,* Boulder, Colo.: Lynne Reinner.

Gao, Xiaoxian. 1994. "China's Modernization and Changes in the Social Status of Rural Women." Trans. S. Katherine Campbell. In Gilmartin et al. 1994, 80–97.

———. 2001. "Strategies and Space: A Case Study." In Ping-chun Hsiung, Jaschok and Milwertz 2001, 193–208.

Gates, Hill. 1989. "The Commoditization of Chinese Women." *Signs: Journal of Women in Culture and Society* 14.4: 799–832.

———. 1993. "Cultural Support for Birth Limitation among Urban Capital-Owning Women." In Davis and Harrell 1993, 251–74.

———. 1996a. *China's Motor: A Thousand Years of Petty Capitalism.* Ithaca, N.Y.: Cornell University Press.

———. 1996b. "Footbinding, Handspinning, and the Modernization of Little Girls." In *South China: State, Culture and Social Change during the 20th Century,* ed. Leo Douw and Peter Post. Amsterdam and New York: North-Holland, 51–56.

———. 1999. *Looking for Chengdu.* Ithaca, N.Y.: Cornell University Press.

———. 2001. "Footloose in Fujian: Economic Correlates of Footbinding." *Comparative Studies in Society and History* 43.1 (Jan.): 130–48.

Ge, Youli, and Susan Jolly. 2001. "East Meets West Feminist Translation Group: A Conversation between Two Participants." In Ping-chun Hsiung, Jaschok, and Milwertz 2001, 61–75.

Gillette, Maris Boyd. 2000a. *Between Mecca and Beijing: Modernization and Consumption among Urban Chinese Muslims.* Stanford, Calif.: Stanford University Press.

———. 2000b. "What's in a Dress? Brides in the Hui Quarter of Xi'an." In Davis 2000, 80–106.

Gilmartin, Christina K. 1989. "Gender, Politics, and Patriarchy in China: The Experiences of Early Women Communists, 1920–27." In Kruks, Rapp, and Young 1989, 82–105.

———. 1990. "Violence against Women in Contemporary China." In *Violence in China: Essays in Culture and Counterculture,* ed. Jonathan N. Lipman and Stevan Harrell. Albany: State University of New York Press, 203–25.

———. 1993. "Gender in the Formation of a Communist Body Politic." *Modern China* 19.3 (July): 299–329.

———. 1994. "Gender, Political Culture, and Women's Mobilization in the Chinese Nationalist Revolution, 1924–1927." In Gilmartin et al. 1994, 195–225.

———. 1995. *Engendering the Chinese Revolution: Radical Women, Communist Politics, and Mass Movements in the 1920s.* Berkeley and Los Angeles: University of California Press.

———. 1999. "Introduction: May Fourth and Women's Emancipation." In Lan and Fong 1999, ix–xxv.

Gilmartin, Christina K., Gail Hershatter, Lisa Rofel, and Tyrene White, eds. 1994. *Engendering China: Women, Culture, and the State.* Cambridge, Mass.: Harvard University Press.

Gilmartin, Christina K., and Isabel Crook. 2005. "Marriage Reform, Rural Women and the Chinese State during World War II." In Leutner and Spakowski 2005, 422–49.

Gipoulon, Catherine. 1984. "Integrating the Feminist and Worker's Movement: The Case of Xiang Jingyu." *Republican China* 10.1A (Nov.): 29–41.

———. 1989–90. "The Emergence of Women in Politics in China, 1898–1927." *Chinese Studies in History* 23.3 (winter): 46–67.

Glosser, Susan L. 1995. "The Business of Family: You Huigao and the Commercialization of a May Fourth Ideal." *Republican China* 20.2 (Apr.): 80–116.

———. 2002. "'The Truths I Have Learned': Nationalism, Family Reform, and Male Identity in China's New Culture Movement, 1915–1923." In Brownell and Wasserstrom 2002b, 120–44.

———. 2003. *Chinese Visions of Family and State, 1915–1953.* Berkeley and Los Angeles: University of California Press.

Goldman, Merle, and Elizabeth J. Perry, eds. 2002. *Changing Meanings of Citizenship in Modern China.* Cambridge, Mass.: Harvard University Press.

Goldstein, Joshua. 1998. "Scissors, Surveys, and Psycho-Prophylactics: Prenatal Health Care Campaigns and State Building in China, 1949–1954." *Journal of Historical Sociology* 11.2 (June): 153–84.

Goldstein, Melvyn C., Ben Jiao, Cynthia M. Beall, and Phuntsog Tsering. 2002. "Fertility and Family Planning in Rural Tibet." *China Journal* 47 (Jan.): 19–39.

Goldstein, Sidney, Zai Liang, and Alice Goldstein. 2000. "Migration, Gender, and Labor Force in Hubei Province, 1985–1990." In Entwisle and Henderson 2000, 214–30.

Goodman, Bryna. 2005a. "The New Woman Commits Suicide: The Press, Cultural Memory, and the New Republic." *Journal of Asian Studies* 62.1 (Feb.): 67–101.

———. 2005b. "Unvirtuous Exchanges: Women and the Corruptions of the Shanghai Stock Market in the Early Republican Era." In Leutner and Spakowski 2005, 351–75.

———. 2005c. "The Vocational Woman and the Elusiveness of 'Personhood' in Early Republican China." In B. Goodman and Larson 2005a, 265–86.

Goodman, Bryna, and Wendy Larson, eds. 2005a. *Gender in Motion: Divisions of Labor and Cultural Change in Late Imperial and Modern China.* Lanham, Md.: Rowman and Littlefield.

———. 2005b. "Introduction: Axes of Gender: Divisions of Labor and Spatial Separation." In B. Goodman and Larson 2005a, 1–25.

Goodman, David S. G. 1997. "The Licheng Rebellion of 1941: Class, Gender, and Leadership in the Sino-Japanese War." *Modern China* 23.2 (Apr.): 216–45.

———. 2000. "Revolutionary Women and Women in the Revolution: The Chinese Communist Party and Women in the War of Resistance to Japan, 1937–1945." *China Quarterly* 164 (Dec.): 915–42.

———. 2004. "Why Women Count: Chinese Women and the Leadership of Reform." In McLaren 2004a, 19–41.

Gottschang, Suzanne Z. 2001. "The Consuming Mother: Infant Feeding and the Feminine Body in Urban China." In N. Chen et al. 2001, 89–103.

Gramsci, Antonio. 1971. *Selections from the Prison Notebooks of Antonio Gramsci.* Ed. and trans. Quintin Hoare and Geoffrey Nowell Smith. New York: International Publishers.

Greenhalgh, Susan. 1990. "The Evolution of the One-Child Policy in Shaanxi, 1979–88." *China Quarterly* 122 (June): 191–229.

———. 1993. "The Peasantization of the One-Child Policy in Shaanxi." In Davis and Harrell 1993, 219–50.

———. 1994. "Controlling Births and Bodies in Village China." *American Ethnologist* 21.1: 3–30.

———. 2001. "Fresh Winds in Beijing: Chinese Feminists Speak Out on the One-Child Policy and Women's Lives." *Signs: Journal of Women in Culture and Society* 26.3 (spring): 847–87.

———. 2003. "Science, Modernity and the Making of China's One-Child Policy." *Population and Development Review* 29.2 (June): 163–96.

Greenhalgh, Susan, and Jiali Li. 1995. "Engendering Reproductive Policy and Practice in Peasant China: For a Feminist Demography of Reproduction." *Signs: Journal of Women in Culture and Society* 20.3: 601–41.

Greenhalgh, Susan, and Edwin A. Winckler. 2005. *Governing China's Population: From Leninist to Neoliberal Biopolitics.* Stanford, Calif.: Stanford University Press.

Greenhalgh, Susan, Chuzhu Zhu, and Nan Li. 1994. "Restraining Population Growth in Three Chinese Villages, 1988–93." *Population and Development Review* 20.2 (June): 365–96.

Gronewold, Sue. 1984. *Beautiful Merchandise: Prostitution in China, 1840–1936.* New York: Haworth Press.

———. 1996. "Encountering Hope: The Door of Hope Mission in Shanghai and Taipei." Ph.D. diss., Columbia University.

Guisso, Richard W., and Stanley Johannesen, eds. 1981. *Women in China: Current Directions in Historical Scholarship.* Youngstown, N.Y.: Philo Press.

Han, Jialing. 2004. "Economic Growth and Women's Development in China's Western Areas: A Case Study." In J. Tao, Zheng, and Mow 2004, 242–47.

Handlin, Joanna F. 1975. "Lü Kun's New Audience: The Influence of Women's Literacy on Sixteenth-Century Thought." In M. Wolf and Witke 1975, 13–38.

Handwerker, Lisa. 1995a. "The Hen That Can't Lay an Egg: Conceptions of Female Infertility in Modern China." In *Deviant Bodies: Critical Perspectives on Difference in Science and Popular Culture,* ed. Jacqueline Urla and Jennifer Terry. Bloomington: Indiana University Press, 358–86.

———. 1995b. "Social and Ethical Implications of *In Vitro* Fertilization in Contemporary China." *Cambridge Quarterly of Healthcare Ethics* 4: 355–63.

———. 1998. "The Consequences of Modernity for Childless Women in China: Medicalization and Resistance." In *Pragmatic Women and Body Politics,* ed. Margaret Lock and Patricia A. Kaufert. Cambridge: Cambridge University Press, 178–205.

Hanser, Amy. 2005. "The Gendered Rice Bowl: The Sexual Politics of Service Work in Urban China." *Gender and Society* 19.5 (Oct.): 581–600.

Harris, Kristine. 1995. "*The New Woman:* Image, Subject, and Dissent in 1930s Shanghai Film Culture." *Republican China* 20.2 (Apr): 55–79.

Hayes, James. 1994. "San Po Tsai (Little Daughters-in-Law) and Child Betrothals in the New Territories of Hong Kong from the 1890s to the 1960s." In Jaschok and Miers 1994a, 45–76.

He, Xiaopei. 2001. "Chinese Queer *(Tongzhi)* Women Organizing in the 1990s." In Ping-chun Hsiung, Jaschok, and Milwertz 2001, 41–59.

Hemmel, Vibeke, and Pia Sindbjerg. 1984. *Women in Rural China: Policy towards Women Before and After the Cultural Revolution.* London: Curzon; Atlantic Highlands, N.J.: Humanities Press.

Henriot, Christian. 1988. "Prostitution et 'Police des moeurs' a Shanghai aux XIXe-XXe siècles" [Prostitution and "Morals Police" in Shanghai in the Nineteenth and Twentieth Centuries]. *La Femme en Asie Orientale* [Woman in East Asia], ed. Christian Henriot. Lyon: Université Jean Moulin Lyon II, 64–93.

———. 1992. "Medicine, VD, and Prostitution in Pre-Revolutionary China." *Social History of Medicine* 5.1 (Apr.): 95–120.

———. 1994. "Chinese Courtesans in Late Qing and Early Republican Shanghai." *East Asian History* 8 (Dec.): 33–52.

———. 1995. "'La Fermeture': The Abolition of Prostitution in Shanghai, 1949–58." *China Quarterly* 142 (June): 467–86.

———. 1996. "'From a Throne of Glory to a Seat of Ignominy': Shanghai Prostitution Revisited (1849–1949)." *Modern China* 22.2 (Apr.): 132–63.

———. 1997. *Belles de Shanghai: Prostitution et sexualité en Chine aux XIXe-XXe siècles* [Beauties of Shanghai: Prostitution and Sexuality in China in the Nineteenth and Twentieth Centuries]. Paris: CNRS. Trans. Nöel Castelino as *Prostitution and Sexuality in Shanghai: A Social History, 1849–1949*. Cambridge: Cambridge University Press, 2001.

Hershatter, Gail. 1986. *The Workers of Tianjin, 1900–1949*. Stanford, Calif.: Stanford University Press.

———. 1989. "The Hierarchy of Shanghai Prostitution, 1870–1949." *Modern China* 15.4 (Oct.): 463–98.

———. 1991. "Prostitution and the Market in Women in Early Twentieth-Century Shanghai." In R. Watson and Ebrey 1991, 256–85.

———. 1992a. "Courtesans and Streetwalkers: The Changing Discourses on Shanghai Prostitution, 1890–1949." *Journal of the History of Sexuality* 3.2 (Oct.): 245–69.

———. 1992b. "Regulating Sex in Shanghai: The Reform of Prostitution in 1920 and 1951." In *Shanghai Sojourners*, ed. Frederic Wakeman and Wen-hsin Yeh. China Research Monograph, no. 40. Berkeley: Institute of East Asian Studies, University of California, 147–86.

———. 1992c. "Sex Work and Social Order: Prostitutes, Their Families, and the State in Twentieth-Century Shanghai." In *Family Process and Political Process in Modern Chinese History*, ed. Zhongyang yanjiuyuan jindaishi yanjiusuo. Vol. 2. Taipei: Zhongyang yanjiuyuan jindaishi yanjiusuo, 1083–1123.

———. 1993. "The Subaltern Talks Back: Reflections on Subaltern Theory and Chinese History." *positions: east asia cultures critique* 1.1 (spring): 103–30.

———. 1994. "Modernizing Sex, Sexing Modernity: Prostitution in Early Twentieth-Century Shanghai." In Gilmartin et al. 1994, 147–74.

———. 1996. "Sexing Modern China." In *Remapping China: Fissures in Historical Terrain*, ed. Gail Hershatter, Emily Honig, Jonathan N. Lipman, and Randall Stross. Stanford, Calif.: Stanford University Press, 77–93.

———. 1997. *Dangerous Pleasures: Prostitution and Modernity in Twentieth-Century Shanghai*. Berkeley and Los Angeles: University of California Press.

———. 2000. "Local Meanings of Gender and Work in Rural Shaanxi in the 1950s." In Entwisle and Henderson 2000, 79–96.

———. 2002. "The Gender of Memory: Rural Chinese Women and the 1950s." *Signs: Journal of Women in Culture and Society* 28.1 (fall): 43–70.

———. 2003. "Making the Visible Invisible: The Fate of 'The Private' in Revolutionary China." In *Jindai Zhongguo de funü yu guojia (1600–1950)* [Women and the Nation in Modern China (1600–1950)]. Vol. 1 of *Wusheng zhi sheng* [Voices amid Silence], ed. Lü Fangshang. Taiwan: Zhongyang yanjiuyuan jindaishi yanjiusuo, 257–81.

———. 2004. "State of the Field: Women in China's Long Twentieth Century." *Journal of Asian Studies* 63.4 (November), 991–1065.

———. 2005a. "Virtue at Work: Rural Shaanxi Women Remember the 1950s." In B. Goodman and Larson 2005a, 309–328.

———. 2005b. "What's in a Field? Women, China, History, and the 'What Next?' Question," *Jindai Zhongguo funüshi yanjiu/Research on Women in Modern Chinese History* 13 (Dec.), 167–95; trans. Yu Fengzhen, Ye Yijun, and Mo Yajun as "Yanjiu lingyu nei qiankun: nüxing, Zhongguo, lishi yu 'zhihou ruhe' wenti," ibid., 197–216.

Hershatter, Gail, Emily Honig, Susan Mann, and Lisa Rofel, eds. and comps. 1998. *Guide to Women's Studies in China.* Berkeley: Institute of East Asian Studies, University of California.

Hershatter, Gail, Emily Honig, and Lisa Rofel. 1996. "Reflections on the Fourth World Conference on Women, Beijing and Huairou, 1995." *Social Justice* 23.1–2 (spring–summer): 368–75.

Heshang [River Elegy]. 1988. Videorecording. Zhongyang dianshi tai; director, Xia Jun; producers, Wang Song and Guo Baoxiang . Millbrae, Calif.: Nan Hai Co.

Hesketh, Therese, Lu Li, and Wei Xing Zhu. 2005. "The Effect of China's One-Child Family Policy after 25 Years." *New England Journal of Medicine* 353.11 (15 Sept.): 1171–76.

Hieronymus, Sabine. 2005. "Qiu Jin (1875–1907)—A Heroine for All Seasons." In Leutner and Spakowski 2005, 194–207.

Ho, Clara Wing-chung. 1999. "Toward a Redefinition of the Content of Chinese Women's History: Reflections on Eight Recent Bibliographies." *Nan Nü: Men, Women, and Gender in Early and Imperial China* 1.1 (Mar.): 145–59.

Ho, Virgil K.Y. 1993. "Selling Smiles in Canton: Prostitution in the Early Republic." *East Asian History* 5 (June): 101–32.

———. 1998–99. "Whose Bodies? Taming Contemporary Prostitutes' Bodies in Official Chinese Rhetorics." *China Information* 13.2–3 (autumn–winter): 14–35.

Holmgren, Jennifer. 1981. "Myth, Fantasy or Scholarship: Images of the Status of Women in Traditional China." *Australian Journal of Chinese Affairs* 6: 147–70.

Hom, Sharon. 1992. "Female Infanticide in China: The Human Rights Specter and Thoughts toward (An)Other Vision." *Columbia Human Rights Law Review* 23.2 (summer): 249–314.

———. 1994. "Engendering Chinese Legal Studies: Gatekeeping, Master Discourses, and Other Challenges." *Signs: Journal of Women in Culture and Society* 19.4 (summer): 1020–47.

Honig, Emily. 1983. "The Contract Labor System and Women Workers: Pre-Liberation Cotton Mills of Shanghai." *Modern China* 9.4 (Oct.): 421–54.

———. 1984. "Private Issues, Public Discourse: The Life and Times of Yu Luojin." *Pacific Affairs* 57.2 (summer): 252–65.

————. 1985. "Burning Incense, Pledging Sisterhood: Communities of Women Workers in the Shanghai Cotton Mills, 1919–1949." *Signs: Journal of Women in Culture and Society* 10.4 (summer): 700–14.

————. 1986. *Sisters and Strangers: Women in the Shanghai Cotton Mills, 1919–1949.* Stanford, Calif.: Stanford University Press.

————. 1992. *Creating Chinese Ethnicity: Subei People in Shanghai, 1850–1980.* New Haven: Yale University Press.

————. 1996. "Christianity, Feminism, and Communism: The Life and Times of Deng Yuzhi." In Bays 1996, 243–62.

————. 2000. "Iron Girls Revisited: Gender and the Politics of Work in the Cultural Revolution, 1966–76." In Entwisle and Henderson 2000, 97–110.

————. 2002. "Maoist Mappings of Gender: Reassessing the Red Guards." In Brownell and Wasserstrom 2002b, 255–68.

————. 2003. "Socialist Sex: The Cultural Revolution Revisited." *Modern China* 29.2 (Apr.): 143–75.

Honig, Emily, and Gail Hershatter. 1988. *Personal Voices: Chinese Women in the 1980s.* Stanford, Calif.: Stanford University Press.

Hooper, Beverley. 1984. "China's Modernization: Are Young Women Going to Lose Out?" *Modern China* 10.3 (July): 317–43.

————. 1999. "Researching Women's Lives in Contemporary China." In Finnane and McLaren 1999, 243–62.

Hsieh, Ping-ying. 1986. *Autobiography of a Chinese Girl.* Trans. Chi Tsui. London and New York: Pandora.

Hsiung, Ping-chen. 2005. "Seeing Neither the Past Nor the Future: The Trouble of Positioning Women in Modern China." In Leutner and Spakowski 2005, 14–39.

Hsiung, Ping-chun. 1996. *Living Rooms as Factories: Class, Gender, and the Satellite Factory System in Taiwan.* Philadelphia: Temple University Press.

Hsiung, Ping-chun, Maria Jaschok, and Cecilia Milwertz, eds. 2001. *Chinese Women Organizing: Cadres, Feminists, Muslims, Queers.* Oxford and New York: Berg.

Hsiung, Ping-chun, and Yuk-lin Renita Wong. 1998. "*Jie Gui*—Connecting the Tracks: Chinese Women's Activism Surrounding the 1995 World Conference on Women in Beijing." *Gender and History* 10.3 (Nov.): 470–97.

Hu, Chi-hsi. 1974. "The Sexual Revolution in the Kiangsi Soviet." *China Quarterly* 59: 477–90.

Hu, Ying. 1997. "Re-Configuring *Nei/Wai:* Writing the Woman Traveller in the Late Qing." *Late Imperial China* 18.1 (June): 72–99.

————. 2000. *Tales of Translation: Composing the New Woman in China, 1899–1918.* Stanford, Calif.: Stanford University Press.

————. 2001. "Naming the First New Woman: The Case of Kang Aide." *Nan Nü: Men, Women, and Gender in Early and Imperial China* 3.2: 196–231.

————. 2002. "Naming the First 'New Woman.'" In Karl and Zarrow 2002, 180–211.

————. 2004. "Writing Qiu Jin's Life: Wu Zhiying and Her Family Learning." *Late Imperial China* 25.2 (Dec.): 119–60.

Hua, Chang-ming. 1984. "Peasants, Women and Revolution—CCP Marriage Reform in the Shaan-Gan-Ning Border Area." *Republican China* 10.1B (Nov.): 1–14.

Huang, Philip C. C. 1990. *The Peasant Family and Rural Development in the Yangzi Delta, 1350–1988*. Stanford, Calif.: Stanford University Press.

———. 2001a. *Code, Custom, and Legal Practice in China: The Qing and the Republic Compared*. Stanford, Calif.: Stanford University Press.

———. 2001b. "Women's Choices under the Law: Marriage, Divorce, and Illicit Sex in the Qing and the Republic." *Modern China* 27.1 (Jan.): 3–58.

———. 2005. "Divorce Law Practices and the Origins, Myths, and Realities of Judicial 'Mediation' in China." *Modern China* 31.2 (Apr.): 151–203.

Huang, Xiyi. 1999. "Divided Gender, Divided Women: State Policy and the Labour Market." In West et al. 1999, 90–107.

Huang, Yufu. 2004. "Chinese Women's Status as Seen through Peking Opera." In J. Tao, Zheng, and Mow 2004, 30–38.

Hyde, Sandrea Teresa. 2001. "Sex Tourism Practices on the Periphery: Eroticizing Ethnicity and Pathologizing Sex on the Lancang." In N. Chen et al. 2001, 143–62.

Ip, Hung-yok. 2003. "Fashioning Appearances: Feminine Beauty in Chinese Communist Revolutionary Culture." *Modern China* 29.3 (July): 329–61.

Jacka, Tamara. 1990. "Back to the Wok: Women and Employment in Chinese Industry in the 1980s." *Australian Journal of Chinese Affairs* 24: 1–23.

———. 1992. "The Public/Private Dichotomy and the Gender Division of Rural Labour." In *Economic Reform and Social Change in China*, ed. Andrew Watson. London and New York: Routledge, 117–43.

———. 1997. *Women's Work in Rural China: Change and Continuity in an Era of Reform*. Cambridge: Cambridge University Press.

———. 1998. "Working Sisters Answer Back: The Presentation and Self-Presentation of Women in China's Floating Population." *China Information* 13.1 (summer): 43–75.

———. 1999. "Researching Women's Work and Gender Division of Labour in the PRC." In Finnane and McLaren 1999, 263–76.

———. 2000. " 'My Life as a Migrant Worker': Women in Rural-Urban Migration in Contemporary China." *Intersections* 4 (Sept.). http://wwwsshe.murdoch.edu.au/intersections/.

———. 2004. "Migrant Women's Stories." In Gaetano and Jacka 2004, 279–85.

———. 2005. *Rural Women in Urban China: Gender, Migration, and Social Change*. Armonk, N.Y.: M. E. Sharpe.

Jacka, Tamara, and Arianne M. Gaetano. 2004. "Introduction: Focusing on Migrant Women." In Gaetano and Jacka 2004, 1–38.

Jacka, Tamara, and Josko Petkovic. 1998. "Ethnography and Video: Researching Women in China's Floating Population." *Intersections,* inaugural issue (Sept.). http://wwwsshe.murdoch.edu.au/intersections/.

Jacka, Tamara, and Xianlin Song, trans. 2004. "My Life as a Migrant Worker." In Gaetano and Jacka 2004, 286–307.

Jackal, Patricia Stranahan. 1981. "Changes in Policy for Yan'an Women, 1935–1947." *Modern China* 7.1 (Jan.): 83–112.

Jankowiak, William R. 1993. *Sex, Death, and Hierarchy in a Chinese City: An Anthropological Account.* New York: Columbia University Press.

———. 2002. "Proper Men and Proper Women: Parental Affection in the Chinese Family." In Brownell and Wasserstrom 2002b, 361–80.

Jaschok, Maria. 1984. "On the Lives of Women Unwed by Choice in Pre-Communist China." *Republican China* 10.1A: 42–55.

———. 1988. *Concubines and Bondservants: A Social History.* London and Atlantic Highlands, N.J.: Zed Books.

———. 1994. "Chinese 'Slave' Girls in Yunnan-Fu: Saving (Chinese) Womanhood and (Western) Souls, 1930–1991." In Jaschok and Miers 1994a, 171–97.

Jaschok, Maria, and Suzanne Miers, eds. 1994a. *Women and Chinese Patriarchy: Submission, Servitude, and Escape.* London and Atlantic Highlands, N.J.: Zed Books.

———. 1994b. "Women in the Chinese Patriarchal System: Submission, Servitude, Escape and Collusion." In Jaschok and Miers 1994a, 1–24.

Jaschok, Maria, Cecilia N. Milwertz, and Ping-chun Hsiung. 2001. "Introduction." In Ping-chun Hsiung, Jaschok, and Milwertz 2001, 3–21.

Jaschok, Maria, and Jingjun Shui. 2000. *The History of Women's Mosques in Chinese Islam: A Mosque of Their Own.* Richmond: Curzon.

———. 2005. "Gender, Religion and Little Traditions: Henanese Women Singing *Minguo*." In Leutner and Spakowski 2005, 242–81.

Jeffreys, Elaine. 1997a. "Guest Editor's Introduction." In Jeffreys 1997b, 3–27.

———, guest ed. 1997b. *Prostitution in Contemporary China. Chinese Sociology and Anthropology* 30.1 (fall).

———. 2004a. *China, Sex and Prostitution.* London and New York: RoutledgeCurzon.

———. 2004b. "Feminist Prostitution Debates: Are There Any Sex Workers in China?" In McLaren 2004a, 83–105.

Jiang, Rongsheng. 1997. "Identifying Prostitution." In Jeffreys 1997b, 28–32.

Jiang, Yongping. 2004. "Employment and Chinese Urban Women under Two Systems." In J. Tao, Zheng, and Mow 2004, 207–20.

Jin, Yihong. 2001. "The All China Women's Federation: Challenges and Trends." In Ping-chun Hsiung, Jaschok, and Milwertz 2001, 123–40.

———. 2004. "Rural Women and Their Road to Public Participation." In J. Tao, Zheng, and Mow 2004, 221–41.

Johansson, Perry. 1998–99. "White Skin, Large Breasts: Chinese Beauty Product Advertising as Cultural Discourse." *China Information* 13.2–3 (autumn–winter): 59–84.

Johnson, Elizabeth L. 1988. "Grieving for the Dead, Grieving for the Living: Funeral Laments of Hakka Women." In J. Watson and Rawski 1988, 135–63.

Johnson, Kay Ann. 1983. *Women, the Family and Peasant Revolution in China*. Chicago: University of Chicago Press.

—————. 1993. "Chinese Orphanages: Saving China's Abandoned Girls." *Australian Jounral of Chinese Affairs* 30 (July): 61–87.

—————. 1996. "The Politics of the Revival of Infant Abandonment in China, with Special Reference to Hunan." *Population and Development Review* 22.1 (Mar.): 77–98.

—————. 2004. *Wanting a Daughter, Needing a Son: Abandonment, Adoption, and Orphanage Care in China*. Ed. and intro. Amy Klatzkin. St. Paul, Minn.: Yeong & Yeong.

Johnson, Kay Ann, Banghan Huang, and Liyao Wang. 1998. "Infant Abandonment and Adoption in China." *Population and Development Review* 24.3 (Sept.): 469–94. Reprinted in K. Johnson 2004, 76–134.

Johnson, Marshall, William L. Parish, and Elizabeth Lin. 1987. "Chinese Women, Rural Society, and External Markets." *Economic Development and Cultural Change* 35.2 (Jan.): 257–77.

Judd, Ellen R. 1989. "*Niangjia:* Chinese Women and Their Natal Families." *Journal of Asian Studies* 48.3 (Aug.): 525–44.

—————. 1990. "'Men Are More Able': Rural Chinese Women's Conceptions of Gender and Agency." *Pacific Affairs* 63.1: 40–62.

—————. 1994. *Gender and Power in Rural North China*. Stanford, Calif.: Stanford University Press.

—————. 1998. "Reconsidering China's Marriage Law Campaign: Toward a De-Orientalized Feminist Perspective." *Asian Journal of Women's Studies* 4.2 (June): 8–26.

—————. 2002. *The Chinese Women's Movement between State and Market*. Stanford, Calif.: Stanford University Press.

—————. 2005. "Women on the Move: Women's Kinship, Residence, and Networks in Rural Shandong." In B. Goodman and Larson 2005a, 97–118.

Judge, Joan. 1997. "Citizens or Mothers of Citizens?: Reimagining Femininity in Late Qing Women's Textbooks." *Transactions of the International Conference of Eastern Studies* 42: 102–14.

—————. 2000. "Meng Mu Meets the Modern: Female Exemplars in Early-Twentieth-Century Textbooks for Girls and Women." *Jindai Zhongguo funü shi yanjiu/Research on Women in Modern Chinese History* 8 (June): 129–77.

—————. 2001. "Talent, Virtue, and the Nation: Chinese Nationalisms and Female Subjectivities in the Early Twentieth Century." *American Historical Review* 106.3 (June): 765–803.

—————. 2002a. "Citizens or Mothers of Citizens? Gender and the Meaning of Modern Chinese Citizenship." In Goldman and Perry 2002, 23–43.

—————. 2002b. "Reforming the Feminine: Female Literacy and the Legacy of 1898." In Karl and Zarrow 2002, 158–79.

—————. 2003. "Beyond Nationalism: Gender and the Chinese Student Experience in Japan in the Early Twentieth Century." In Luo and Lü 2003, 359–93.

———. 2004. "Blended Wish Images: Chinese and Western Exemplary Women at the Turn of the Twentieth Century." *Nan Nü: Men, Women, and Gender in Early and Imperial China* 6.1: 102–35.

———. 2005. "Between *Nei* and *Wai:* Chinese Women Students in Japan in the Early Twentieth Century." In B. Goodman and Larson 2005a, 121–143.

Kane, Penny. 1985. "The Single-Child Family Policy in the Cities." In Croll, Davin, and Kane 1985, 83–113.

———. 1987. *The Second Billion: Population and Family Planning in China.* New York: Penguin Books.

Karl, Rebecca E. 2002. " 'Slavery,' Citizenship, and Gender in Late Qing China's Global Context." In Karl and Zarrow 2002, 212–44.

Karl, Rebecca E., and Peter Zarrow, eds. 2002. *Rethinking the 1898 Reform Period: Political and Cultural Change in Late Qing China.* Cambridge, Mass.: Harvard University Asia Center.

Kelly, Joan. 1984. *Women, History, and Theory: The Essays of Joan Kelly.* Chicago: University of Chicago Press.

Ko, Dorothy. 1994. *Teachers of the Inner Chambers: Women and Culture in Seventeenth-Century China.* Stanford, Calif.: Stanford University Press.

———. 2005. *Cinderella's Sisters: A Revisionist History of Footbinding.* Berkeley and Los Angeles: University of California Press.

Kruks, Sonia, Rayna Rapp, and Marilyn B. Young, eds. 1989. *Promissory Notes: Women in the Transition to Socialism.* New York: Monthly Review Press.

Kung, Lydia. 1995. *Factory Women in Taiwan.* New York: Columbia University Press.

Kwok, Pui-lan. 1992. *Chinese Women and Christianity, 1860–1927.* Atlanta: Scholars Press.

———. 1996. "Chinese Women and Protestant Christianity at the Turn of the Twentieth Century." In Bays 1996, 194–208.

Laing, Ellen Johnston. 2003. "Visual Evidence for the Evolution of 'Politically Correct' Dress for Women in Early Twentieth Century Shanghai." *Nan Nü: Men, Women, and Gender in Early and Imperial China* 5.1: 69–114.

Lan, Hua R., and Vanessa L. Fong, eds. 1999. *Women in Republican China: A Sourcebook.* Armonk, N.Y.: M. E. Sharpe.

Lang, Graeme, and Josephine Smart. 2002. "Migration and the 'Second Wife' in South China: Toward Cross-Border Polygyny." *International Migration Review* 36.2 (summer): 546–69.

Larson, Wendy. 1998. *Women and Writing in Modern China.* Stanford, Calif.: Stanford University Press.

———. 2005. "He Yi's *The Postman:* The Work Space of a New Age Maoist." In B. Goodman and Larson 2005a, 211–236.

Lavely, William. 1991. "Marriage and Mobility under Rural Collectivism." In R. Watson and Ebrey 1991, 286–312.

Lean, Eugenia. 2004. "The Making of a Public: Emotions and Media Sensation in 1930s China." *Twentieth-Century China* 29.2 (Apr.): 39–61.

Lee, Bernice J. 1981. "Female Infanticide in China." In Guisso and Johannesen 1981, 163–78.

Lee, Ching Kwan. 1998. *Gender and the South China Miracle: Two Worlds of Factory Women.* Berkeley and Los Angeles: University of California Press.

Lee, Gong-way. 1991. "Critiques of Ch'iu Chin: A Radical Feminist and National Revolutionary (1875–1907)." *Chinese Culture* 32.2 (June): 57–66.

Lee, Lily Xiao Hong. 2004. "The Chinese Women's Movement Before and After the Long March." In J. Tao, Zheng, and Mow 2004, 71–91.

Lee, Lily Xiao Hong, and Sue Wiles. 1999. *Women of the Long March.* St. Leonards, NSW: Allen and Unwin.

Leith, Suzette. 1973. "Chinese Women in the Early Communist Movement." In M. Young 1973, 47–71.

Leutner, Mechthild. 2002. "Women's, Gender and Mainstream Studies on Republican China: Problems in Theory and Research." *Research on Women in Modern Chinese History* 10 (Dec.): 117–45. Reprinted in Leutner and Spakowski 2005, 57–85.

Leutner, Mechthild, and Nicola Spakowski, eds. 2005. *Women in China: The Republican Period in Historical Perspective.* Münster: Lit Verlag; distributed in North America by Transaction Publishers.

Levy, Howard S. 1992. *The Lotus Lovers: The Complete History of the Curious Erotic Custom of Footbinding in China.* Buffalo, N.Y.: Prometheus Books.

Li, Danke. 2004. "Gender Inequality in Education in Rural China." In J. Tao, Zheng, and Mow 2004, 123–36.

Li, Danke, and Mun C. Tsang. 2003. "Household Decisions and Gender Inequality in Education in Rural China." *China: An International Journal* 1.2 (Sept.): 224–48.

Li, Xiaojiang. 1994. "Economic Reform and the Awakening of Chinese Women's Collective Consciousness." Trans. S. Katherine Campbell. In Gilmartin et al. 1994, 360–82.

———. 1999. "With What Discourse Do We Reflect on Chinese Women? Thoughts on Transnational Feminism in China." Trans. Yajie Zhang. In M. Yang 1999c, 261–77.

———. 2001. "From 'Modernization' to 'Globalization': Where Are Chinese Women?" Trans. Tani E. Barlow. *Signs: Journal of Women in Culture and Society* 26.4: 1274–78.

———. 2004. "The Center for Gender Studies at Dalian University." In J. Tao, Zheng, and Mow 2004, 137–55.

Li, Xiaojiang, and Xiaodan Zhang. 1994. "Creating a Space for Women: Women's Studies in China in the 1980s." *Signs: Journal of Women in Culture and Society* 20.1: 137–51.

Li, Xiaoping. 1998. "Fashioning the Body in Post-Mao China." In *Consuming Fashion: Adorning the Transnational Body,* ed. Anne Brydon and Sandra Niessen. Oxford and New York: Berg, 71–89.

Li, Yongshan. 1997. "Tears of Blood: The Path of Prostitution." In Jeffreys 1997b, 65–76.

Li, Yu-ning. 1984. "Hsu Tsung-Han: Tradition and Revolution." *Republican China* 10.1A (Nov.): 13–28.

———. 1988. "Sun Yat-Sen and Women's Transformation." *Chinese Studies in History* 21.4: 58–78.

———. 1992. *Chinese Women through Chinese Eyes.* Armonk, N.Y.: M. E. Sharpe.

Liang, Zai, and Yiu Por Chen. 2004. "Migration and Gender in China: An Origin-Destination Linked Approach." *Economic Development and Cultural Change* 52.2 (Jan.): 423–43.

Lin, Chun. 2001. "Whither Feminism: A Note on China." *Signs: Journal of Women in Culture and Society* 26.4 (summer): 1281–86.

———. 2003. "Toward a Chinese Feminism: A Personal Story." In Wasserstrom 2003, 66–80.

Liu, Bohong. 2001. "The All China Women's Federation and Women's NGOs." In Ping-chun Hsiung, Jaschok, and Milwertz 2001, 141–57.

Liu, Dalin, Man Lun Ng, Li Ping Zhou, and Erwin J. Haeberle. 1997. *Sexual Behavior in Modern China: Report on the Nationwide Survey of 20,000 Men and Women* [Zhongguo dangdai xing wenhua]. English-language edition ed. Man Lun Ng and Erwin J. Haeberle. New York: Continuum.

Liu, Fei-wen. 2001. "The Confrontation between Fidelity and Fertility: *Nüshu, Nüge,* and Peasant Women's Conceptions of Widowhood in Jiangyong County, Hunan Province, China." *Journal of Asian Studies* 60.4 (Nov.): 1051–84.

———. 2004. "Literacy, Gender, and Class: Nüshu and Sisterhood Communities in Southern Rural Hunan." *Nan Nü: Men, Women, and Gender in Early and Imperial China* 6.2: 241–82.

Liu, Huiying. 2003. "Feminism: An Organic or an Extremist Position? On *Tien Yee* as Represented by He Zhen." Trans. Yan Hairong. *positions: east asia cultures critique* 11.3 (winter): 779–800.

Liu, Judith, and Donald P. Kelly. 1996. "'Oasis in a Heathen Land': St. Hilda's School for Girls, Wuchang, 1928–1936." In Bays 1996, 228–42.

Liu, Lydia H. 1994. "The Female Body and Nationalist Discourse." In Zito and Barlow 1994, 157–77.

———. 1995. *Translingual Practice: Literature, National Culture, and Translated Modernity—China, 1900–1937.* Stanford, Calif.: Stanford University Press.

Liu, Meng. 2002. "Rebellion and Revenge: The Meaning of Suicide of Women in China." *International Journal of Social Welfare* 11.4: 300–309.

Liu, Ying. 2004. "The Lives and Needs of Elderly Women in Urban China." In J. Tao, Zheng, and Mow 2004, 193–203.

Lou, Binbin, Zhenzhen Zheng, Rachel Connelly, and Kenneth D. Roberts. 2004. "The Migration Experiences of Young Women from Four Counties in Sichuan and Anhui." In Gaetano and Jacka 2004, 207–42.

Lu, Meiyi. 2004. "The Awakening of Chinese Women and the Women's Movement in the Early Twentieth Century." In J. Tao, Zheng, and Mow 2004, 55–70.

Lu, Tonglin, ed. 1993. *Gender and Sexuality in Twentieth-Century Chinese Literature and Society.* New York: State University of New York Press.

Lu, Weijing. 1998. "Uxorilocal Marriage among Qing Literati." *Late Imperial China* 19.2 (Dec.): 64–110.

Luo, Jiurong, and Miao-fen Lü, eds. 2003. *Jindai Zhongguo de funü yu wenhua (1600–1950)* [Women and Culture in Modern China (1600–1950)]. Vol. 3 of *Wusheng zhi sheng* [Voices amid Silence]. Taipei, Taiwan: Zhongyang yanjiuyuan jindaishi yanjiusuo.

Luo, Suwen. 2005. "Gender on Stage: Actresses in an Actors' World (1895–1930)." In B. Goodman and Larson 2005a, 75–95.

Ma, Wanhua. 2004. "The Readjustment of China's Higher Education Structure and Women's Higher Education." In J. Tao, Zheng, and Mow 2004, 109–22.

Ma, Yuxin. 2003. "Male Feminism and Women's Subjectivities: Zhang Xichen, Chen Xuezhao, and *The New Woman.*" *Twentieth-Century China* 29.1: 1–37.

Makley, Cherlene E. 2002. "On the Edge of Respectability: Sexual Politics in China's Tibet." *positions: east asia cultures critique* 10.3 (winter): 575–630.

Mann, Susan. 1992. "Women's Work in the Ningbo Area, 1900–1936." In *Chinese History in Economic Perspective*, ed. Thomas G. Rawski and Lillian M. Li. Berkeley and Los Angeles: University of California Press, 243–70.

———. 1994. "The Cult of Domesticity in Republican Shanghai's Middle Class." *Jindai Zhongguo funü shi yanjiu/Research on Women in Modern Chinese History* 2 (June): 179–201.

———. 1997. *Precious Records: Women in China's Long Eighteenth Century.* Stanford, Calif.: Stanford University Press.

———. 1998. "Western Missionary Views of Educated Chinese Women at the Turn of the Twentieth Century." In *Tradition and Metamorphosis in Modern Chinese History: Essays in Honor of Professor Kwang-Ching Liu's Seventy-Fifth Birthday*, ed. Hao Yanping and Wei Xiumei. Vol. 2. Taipei: Academia Sinica Institute of Modern History, 1039–66.

Manning, Kimberley Ens. 2005. "Marxist Maternalism, Memory, and the Mobilization of Women in the Great Leap Forward." *China Review* 5.1 (spring): 83–110.

Martin, Emily. 1988. "Gender and Ideological Differences in Representations of Life and Death." In J. Watson and Rawski 1988, 164–79.

Mathieu, Christine. 1999. "History and Other Metaphors in Chinese-Mosuo Relations since 1956." In Finnane and McLaren 1999, 81–105.

Maurer-Fazio, Margaret, Thomas G. Rawski, and Wei Zhang. 1999. "Inequality in the Rewards for Holding Up Half the Sky: Gender Wages Gaps in China's Urban Labour Market, 1988–1994." *China Journal* 41 (Jan.): 55–88.

McDougall, Bonnie S. 2005. "Discourse on Privacy by Women Writers in Late Twentieth-Century China." *China Information* 19.1: 97–119.

McElderry, Andrea. 1986. "Woman Revolutionary: Xiang Jingyu." *China Quarterly* 105 (Mar.): 95–122.

McElroy, Sarah Coles. 2001. "Forging a New Role for Women: Zhili First Women's Normal School and the Growth of Women's Education in China, 1901–1921." In Peterson, Hayhoe, and Lu, 348–74.

McIntyre, Tanya. 1999. "Images of Women in Popular Prints." In Finnane and McLaren 1999, 58–80.

McLaren, Anne. 1996. "Women's Voices and Textuality: Chastity and Abduction in Chinese *Nüshu* Writing." *Modern China* 22.4 (Oct.): 382–416.

———. 1998. "Crossing Gender Boundaries in China: Nüshu Narratives." *Intersections*, inaugural issue (Sept.). http://wwwsshe.murdoch.edu.au/hum/as/intersections.

———. 1999. "On Researching Invisible Women: Abduction and Violation in Chinese Women's Script Writing." In Finnane and McLaren 1999, 164–80.

———, ed. 2004a. *Chinese Women—Living and Working*. London and New York: RoutledgeCurzon.

———. 2004b. "Women's Work and Ritual Space in China." In McLaren 2004a, 169–87.

Meijer, Marinus Johan. 1971. *Marriage Law and Policy in the Chinese People's Republic*. Hong Kong: Hong Kong University Press.

Michelson, Ethan, and William L. Parish. 2000. "Gender Differentials in Economic Suceess: Rural China in 1991." In Entwisle and Henderson 2000, 134–56.

Miers, Suzanne. 1994. "Mui Tsai through the Eyes of the Victim: Janet Lim's Story of Bondage and Escape." In Jaschok and Miers 1994a, 108–21.

Milwertz, Cecilia N. 1997. *Accepting Population Control: Urban Chinese Women and the One-Child Family Policy*. Richmond, Surrey: Curzon.

Min, Anchee. 1995. *Red Azalea*. New York: Berkley Books.

Min, Dongchao. 1999. "The Development of Women's Studies: From the 1980s to the Present." In West et al. 1999, 211–24.

Mitchell, Timothy. 1991. "The Limits of the State: Beyond Statist Approaches and Their Critics." *American Political Science Review* 85.1: 77–96.

———. 1999. "Society, Economy, and the State Effect." In *State/Culture: State Formation after the Cultural Turn*, ed. George Steinmetz. Ithaca, N.Y.: Cornell University Press, 76–97.

Mittler, Barbara. 2003. "Defy(N)ing Modernity: Women in Shanghai's Early News-Media (1872–1915)." *Jindai Zhongguo funü shi yanjiu / Research on Women in Modern Chinese History* 11 (Dec.): 215–59.

Mu, Aiping. 1999. "To Have a Son: The One-Child Family Policy and Economic Change in Rural China." In West et al. 1999, 137–55.

Mueggler, Erik. 1998. "The Poetics of Grief and the Price of Hemp in Southwest China." *Journal of Asian Studies* 57.4 (Nov.): 979–1008.

Müller, Gotelind. 2005. "Knowledge Is Easy—Action Is Difficult: The Case of

Chinese Anarchist Discourse on Women and Gender Relations and Its Practical Limitations." In Leutner and Spakowski 2005, 86–106.

Murphy, Rachel. 2004. "The Impact of Labor Migration on the Well-Being and Agency of Rural Chinese Women." In Gaetano and Jacka 2004, 243–76.

Niu, Yangzi. 1997. "Exploring the Phenomenon of 'Foreign Prostitutes.'" In Jeffreys 1997b, 90–95.

Nivard, Jacqueline. 1984. "Women and the Women's Press: The Case of *The Ladies' Journal (Funü Zazhi)*, 1915–1931." *Republican China* 10.1B (Nov.): 37–55.

———. 1986. "L'Evolution de la press feminine chinoise de 1898–1949" [The Evolution of the Chinese Women's Press, 1898–1949]. *Études Chinoises* 1–2: 157–84.

Ocko, Jonathan K. 1991. "Women, Property, and Law in the People's Republic of China." In R. Watson and Ebrey 1991, 313–46.

Ong, Aihwa. 1999. *Flexible Citizenship: The Cultural Logics of Transnationality*. Durham, N.C.: Duke University Press.

Ono, Kazuko. 1989. *Chinese Women in a Century of Revolution, 1850–1950*. Translation of *Chugoku joseishi: Taiheitengoku kara gendai made*. Tokyo: Heibonsha, 1978. Trans. Kathryn Bernhardt et al.; ed. Joshua A. Fogel. Stanford, Calif.: Stanford University Press.

Orliski, Constance. 2003. "The Bourgeois Housewife as Laborer in Late Qing and Early Republican Shanghai." *Nan Nü: Men, Women, and Gender in Early and Imperial China* 5.1: 43–68.

Ouyang, Tao. 1997. "Prostitution Offenses in Contemporary China: Characteristics and Countermeasures." In Jeffreys 1997b, 45–56.

Parish, William L., and Sarah Busse. 2000. "Gender and Work." In Tang and Parish 2000, 209–31.

Parish, William L., and James Farrer. 2000. "Gender and Family." In Tang and Parish 2000, 232–70.

Parish, William L., and Martin King Whyte. 1978. *Village and Family in Contemporary China*. Chicago: University of Chicago Press.

Pasternak, Burton, and Janet W. Salaff. 1993. *Cowboys and Cultivators: The Chinese of Inner Mongolia*. Boulder, Colo.: Westview Press.

Pearson, Veronica, and Benjamin K. P. Leung, eds. 1995. *Women in Hong Kong*. New York: Oxford University Press.

Pearson, Veronica, and Meng Liu. 2002. "Ling's Death: An Ethnography of a Chinese Woman's Suicide." *Suicide and Life-Threatening Behavior* 32.4 (winter): 347–58.

Pearson, Veronica, Michael R. Phillips, Fengsheng He, and Huiyi Ji. 2002. "Attempted Suicide among Young Rural Women in the People's Republic of China: Possibilities for Prevention." *Suicide and Life-Threatening Behavior* 32.4 (winter): 359–69.

Perry, Elizabeth J. 1993. *Shanghai on Strike: The Politics of Chinese Labor*. Stanford, Calif.: Stanford University Press.

Perry, Elizabeth J., and Mark Selden, eds. 2003. *Chinese Society: Change, Conflict, and Resistance.* 2nd ed. London and New York: RoutledgeCurzon.

Peterson, Glen, Ruth Hayhoe, and Yongling Lu, eds. 2001. *Education, Culture, and Identity in Twentieth-Century China,* Ann Arbor: University of Michigan Press.

Phillips, Michael R., Xianyun Li, and Yanping Zhang. 2002a. "Suicide Rates in China, 1995–1999." *The Lancet* 359.9309 (Mar. 9): 835–40. http://www.thelancet.com/journal.

———. "Suicide Rates in China: Authors' Reply." 2002b. *The Lancet* 359.9325 (June 29): 2274–75. http://www.thelancet.com/journal.

Pomeranz, Kenneth. 2005. "Women's Work and the Economics of Respectability." In B. Goodman and Larson 2005a, 239–63.

Potter, Sulamith Heins. 1985. *Birth Planning in Rural China: A Cultural Account.* Working Paper 103, Women in International Development, Michigan State University.

Potter, Sulamith Heins, and Jack M. Potter. 1990. *China's Peasants: The Anthropology of a Revolution.* Cambridge: Cambridge University Press.

Prazniak, Roxann. 1986. "Weavers and Sorcerers of Chuansha: The Social Origins of Political Activism among Rural Chinese Women." *Modern China* 12.2 (Apr.): 202–29.

———. 1989. "Feminist Humanism: Socialism and Neofeminism in the Writings of Zhang Jie." In Dirlik and Meisner 1989, 269–93.

———. 1997. "Mao and the Woman Question in an Age of Green Politics: Some Critical Reflections." In *Critical Perspectives on Mao Zedong's Thought,* ed. Arif Dirlik, Paul Healy, and Nick Knight. Atlantic Highlands, N.J.: Humanities Press, 23–58.

———. 1999. *Of Camel Kings and Other Things: Rural Rebels against Modernity in Late Imperial China.* Lanham, Md.: Rowman and Littlefield.

Pruitt, Ida. 1967. *A Daughter of Han: The Autobiography of a Chinese Working Woman.* Stanford, Calif.: Stanford University Press.

———. 1979. *Old Madam Yin: A Memoir of Peking Life, 1926–1938.* Stanford, Calif.: Stanford University Press.

Pun, Ngai. 1999. "Becoming *Dagongmei* (Working Girls): The Politics of Identity and Difference in Reform China." *China Journal* 42 (July): 1–18.

———. 2000. "Opening a Minor Genre of Resistance in Reform China: Scream, Dream, and Transgression in a Workplace." *positions: east asia cultures critique* 8.2 (fall): 531–55.

———. 2005. *Made in China: Women Factory Workers in a Global Workplace.* Durham, N.C.: Duke University Press; Hong Kong: Hong Kong University Press.

Qian, Changfu. 1997. "The Nature and Handling of Group Participation in Prostitution Behavior." In Jeffreys 1997b, 61–64.

Qian, Nanxiu. 2003. "Revitalizing the Xianyuan (Worthy Ladies) Tradition: Women in the 1898 Reforms." *Modern China* 29.4 (Oct.): 399–454.

———. 2004. " 'Borrowing Foreign Mirrors and Candles to Illuminate Chinese

Civilization': Xue Shaohui's Moral Vision in *The Biographies of Foreign Women.*" *Nan Nü: Men, Women, and Gender in Early and Imperial China* 6.1: 60–101.

Rankin, Mary Backus. 1975. "The Emergence of Women at the End of the Ch'ing: The Case of Ch'iu Chin." In M. Wolf and Witke 1975, 39–66.

Remick, Elizabeth J. 2003. "Prostitution Taxes and Local State Building in Republican China." *Modern China* 29.1 (Jan.): 38–70.

Riley, Nancy E. 1997. "Gender Equality in China: Two Steps Forward, One Step Back." In *China Briefing: The Contradictions of Change,* ed. William A. Joseph. Armonk, N.Y.: M. E. Sharpe, 79–108.

Roberts, Kenneth, Rachel Connelly, Zhenming Xie, and Zhenzhen Zheng. 2004. "Patterns of Temporary Labor Migration of Rural Women from Anhui and Sichuan." *China Journal* 52 (July): 49–70.

Roberts, Rosemary. 1999. "Women's Studies in Literature and Feminist Literary Criticism in Contemporary China." In Finnane and McLaren 1999, 225–40.

Robinson, Jean C. 1985. "Of Women and Washing Machines: Employment, Housework, and the Reproduction of Motherhood in Socialist China." *China Quarterly* 101 (Mar.): 32–57.

Rofel, Lisa. 1989. "Hegemony and Productivity: Workers in Post-Mao China." In Dirlik and Meisner 1989, 253–68.

———. 1992. "Rethinking Modernity: Space and Factory Discipline in China." *Cultural Anthropology* 7.1 (Feb.): 93–114.

———. 1994a. "Liberation Nostalgia and a Yearning for Modernity." In Gilmartin et al. 1994, 226–49.

———. 1994b. "'Yearnings': Televisual Love and Melodramatic Politics in Contemporary China." *American Ethnologist* 1.4 (Nov.): 700–722.

———. 1999a. "Museum as Women's Space: Displays of Gender in Post-Mao China." In M. Yang 1999c, 116–31.

———. 1999b. *Other Modernities: Gendered Yearnings in China after Socialism.* Berkeley and Los Angeles: University of California Press.

Rogaski, Ruth. 1997. "Beyond Benevolence: A Confucian Women's Shelter in Treaty-Port China." *Journal of Women's History* 8.4 (winter): 54–90.

Rong, Tiesheng. 1983. "The Women's Movement in China Before and After the 1911 Revolution." *Chinese Studies in History* 16.3–4 (spring–summer): 159–200.

Ropp, Paul S. 1976. "The Seeds of Change: Reflections on the Condition of Women in the Early and Mid-Ch'ing." *Signs: Journal of Women in Culture and Society* 2.1: 5–23.

Ross, Heidi A. 1996. "'Cradle of Female Talent': The McTyeire Home and School for Girls, 1892–1937." In Bays 1996, 209–27.

Ruan, Fang Fu. 1991. *Sex in China: Studies in Sexology in Chinese Culture.* New York and London: Plenum Press.

Ruan, Fang Fu, and Vern L. Bullough. 1992. "Lesbianism in China." *Archives of Sexual Behavior* 21.3: 217–26.

Sakamoto, Hiroko. 2004. "The Cult of 'Love and Eugenics' in May Fourth Movement Discourse." *positions: east asia cultures critique* 12.2 (fall): 329–76.

Salaff, Janet W. 1973. "Institutionalized Motivation for Fertility Limitation." In M. Young 1973, 93–144.

———. 1981. *Working Daughters of Hong Kong: Filial Piety or Power in the Family?* Cambridge: Cambridge University Press. 2nd ed. 1995.

———. 1985. "The State and Fertility Motivation in Singapore and China." In Croll, Davin, and Kane 1985, 162–89.

Salaff, Janet W., and Judith Merkle. 1973. "Women and Revolution: The Lessons of the Soviet Union and China." In M. Young 1973, 145–77.

Sang, Tze-lan D. 2003. *The Emerging Lesbian: Female Same-Sex Desire in Modern China.* Chicago: University of Chicago Press.

———. 2005. "Women's Work and Boundary Transgression in Wang Dulu's Popular Novels." In B. Goodman and Larson 2005a, 287–308.

Sankar, Andrea. 1984. "Spinster Sisterhoods." In Sheridan and Salaff 1984, 51–70.

———. 1985. "Sisters and Brothers, Lovers and Enemies: Marriage Resistance in Southern Kwangtung." *Journal of Homosexuality* 11.3–4 (summer): 69–81.

Sargeson, Sally. 2004. "Building for the Future Family." In McLaren 2004a, 147–68.

Schein, Louisa. 1997. "Gender and Internal Orientalism in China." *Modern China* 23.1 (Jan.): 69–98. Reprinted in Brownell and Wasserstrom 2002b, 385–411.

———. 2000. *Minority Rules: The Miao and the Feminine in China's Cultural Politics.* Durham, N.C.: Duke University Press.

Schwarcz, Vera. 1986. *The Chinese Enlightenment: Intellectuals and the Legacy of the May Fourth Movement of 1919.* Berkeley and Los Angeles: University of California Press.

Scott, Joan Wallach. 1999. *Gender and the Politics of History.* Rev. ed. New York: Columbia University Press.

Selden, Mark. 1993. "Family Strategies and Structures in Rural North China." In Davis and Harrell 1993, 139–64.

Shang, Xiaoyuan. 1999. "Women and the Public Sphere: Education, NGO Affiliation and Political Participation." In West et al. 1999, 195–210.

Shea, Jeanne L. 2005. "Sexual 'Liberation' and the Older Woman in Contemporary Mainland China." *Modern China* 31.1 (Jan.): 115–47.

Sheridan, Mary. 1976. "Young Women Leaders in China." *Signs: Journal of Women in Culture and Society* 2.1 (autumn): 59–88.

Sheridan, Mary, and Janet Salaff, eds. 1984. *Lives: Chinese Working Women.* Bloomington: Indiana University Press.

Shih, Shu-mei. 1996. "Gender, Race, and Semicolonialism: Liu Na'ou's Urban Shanghai Landscape." *Journal of Asian Studies* 55.4 (Nov.): 934–56.

———. 1998. "Gender and a New Geopolitics of Desire: The Seduction of

Mainland Women in Taiwan and Hong Kong Media." *Signs: Journal of Women in Culture and Society* 23.2: 287–320. Reprinted in M. Yang 1999c, 278–307.

———— 2005. "Toward an Ethics of Transnational Encounters; or, 'When' Does a 'Chinese' Woman Become a 'Feminist'?" In *Minor Transnationalisms*, ed. Françoise Lionnet and Shu-mei Shih. Durham N.C.: Duke University Press, 73–108.

Shou, Yuanjun. 2004. "*Half the Sky:* A Television Program for Women." In J. Tao, Zheng, and Mow 2004, 261–73.

Shui, Jingjun. 2001. "In Search of Sacred Women's Organizations." In Ping-chun Hsiung, Jaschok, and Milwertz 2001, 101–18.

Silber, Cathy. 1994. "From Daughter to Daughter-in-Law in the Women's Script of Southern Hunan." In Gilmartin et al. 1994, 47–68.

Sinn, Elizabeth. 1994. "Chinese Patriarchy and the Protection of Women in 19th-Century Hong Kong." In Jaschok and Miers 1994a, 141–70.

Siu, Helen F. 1990. "Where Were the Women? Rethinking Marriage Resistance and Regional Culture in South China." *Late Imperial China* 11.2: 32–62.

————. 1993. "Reconstituting Dowry and Brideprice in South China." In Davis and Harrell 1993, 165–88.

Solinger, Dorothy. 1999. *Contesting Citizenship in Urban China: Peasant Migrants, the State, and the Logic of the Market*. Berkeley and Los Angeles: University of California Press.

Song, Lina. 1999. "The Role of Women in Labour Migration: A Case Study in Northern China." In West et al. 1999, 69–89.

Spakowski, Nicola. 2005. "Women's Military Participation in the Communist Movement of the 1930s and 1940s: Patterns of Inclusion and Exclusion." In Leutner and Spakowski 2005, 129–71.

Spivak, Gayatri Chakravorty. 2000. "From Haverstock Hill Flat to U.S. Classroom, What's Left of Theory?" In *What's Left of Theory?: New Work on the Politics of Literary Theory*, ed. Judith Butler, John Guillory, and Kendall Thomas. New York: Routledge, 1–39.

Stacey, Judith. 1983. *Patriarchy and Socialist Revolution in China*. Berkeley and Los Angeles: University of California Press.

Stockard, Janice E. 1989. *Daughters of the Canton Delta: Marriage Patterns and Economic Strategies in South China, 1860–1930*. Stanford, Calif.: Stanford University Press.

Stranahan, Patricia. 1983a. "Labor Heroines of Yan'an." *Modern China* 9.2 (Apr.): 228–52.

————. 1983b. *Yan'an Women and the Communist Party*. Berkeley: Institute of East Asian Studies, University of California.

Su, Xiaokang. 1991. *Deathsong of the River: A Reader's Guide to the Chinese TV Series* Heshang. Intro., trans., and annotated by Richard W. Bodman and Pin P. Wan. Ithaca, N.Y.: East Asia Program, Cornell University.

Sun, Wanning. 2004a. "Indoctrination, Fetishization, and Compassion:

Media Constructions of the Migrant Woman." In Gaetano and Jacka 2004, 109–28.

———. 2004b. "The Maid in China: Opportunities, Challenges and the Story of Becoming Modern." In McLaren 2004a, 65–82.

Tan, Lin, and Susan E. Short. 2004. "Living as Double Outsiders: Migrant Women's Experiences of Marriage in a County-Level City." In Gaetano and Jacka 2004, 151–74.

Tan, Shen. 2000. "The Relationship between Foreign Enterprises, Local Governments, and Women Migrant Workers in the Pearl River Delta." In *Rural Labor Flows in China*, ed. Loraine A. West and Yaohui Zhao. Berkeley: Institute of East Asian Studies, University of California, 292–309.

———. 2004. "Leaving Home and Coming Back: Experiences of Rural Migrant Women." In J. Tao, Zheng, and Mow 2004, 248–58.

Tang, Wenfang, and William L. Parish, eds. 2000. *Chinese Urban Life under Reform: The Changing Social Contract*, Cambridge: Cambridge University Press.

Tao, Chia-lin Pao. 1994. "The Anti-Footbinding Movement in Late Ch'ing China: Indigenous Development and Western Influence." *Jindai Zhongguo funü shi yanjiu/Research on Women in Modern Chinese History* 2 (June): 141–78.

Tao, Jie, Zheng Bijun, and Shirley L. Mow, eds. 2004. *Holding Up Half the Sky: Chinese Women Past, Present, and Future*. New York: The Feminist Press.

Terrill, Ross. 1999. *Madam Mao: The White-Boned Demon*. Rev. ed. Stanford, Calif.: Stanford University Press.

Tien, H. Yuan. 1985. "Provincial Fertility Trends and Patterns." In Croll, Davin, and Kane 1985, 114–34.

———. 1987. "Abortion in China: Incidence and Implications." *Modern China* 13.4 (Oct.): 441–68.

Topley, Marjorie. 1975. "Marriage Resistance in Rural Kwangtung." In M. Wolf and Witke 1975, 67–88.

Tsai, Kellee S. 2000. "Banquet Banking: Gender and Rotating Savings and Credit Associations in South China." *China Quarterly* 161 (Mar.): 142–70.

Tsui, Ming and Lynne Rich. 2002. "The Only Child and Educational Opportunity for Girls in Urban China." *Gender and Society* 16.1 (Feb.): 74–92.

Unger, Jonathan. 2002. *The Transformation of Rural China*. Armonk, N.Y.: M. E. Sharpe.

Verschuur-Basse, Denyse. 1996. *Chinese Women Speak*. Trans. Elizabeth Rauch-Nolan. Westport, Conn., and London: Praeger.

Walker, Kathy Le Mons. 1978. "The Party and Peasant Women." In *Chinese Communists and Rural Society*, ed. Philip C. C. Huang, Lynda S. Bell, and Kathy Le Mons Walker. Berkeley: Center for Chinese Studies, University of California, 57–82.

———. 1993. "Economic Growth, Peasant Marginalization, and the Sexual

Division of Labor in Early Twentieth-Century China." *Modern China* 19.3 (July): 354–86.

———. 1999. *Chinese Modernity and the Peasant Path: Semicolonialism in the Northern Yangzi Delta.* Stanford, Calif.: Stanford University Press.

Walsh, Eileen Rose. 2005. "From Nüguo to Nü'er Guo: Negotiating Desire in the Land of the Mosuo." *Modern China* 31.4 (Oct.): 448–86.

Wang, Dazhong. 1997. "Some Problems Concerning the Sending of Prostitution Offenders to Be Educated through Labor and Compelling Them to Undergo Joint Detention and Education." In Jeffreys 1997b, 57–60.

Wang, Di. 2004. "'Masters of Tea': Teahouse Workers, Workplace Culture, and Gender Conflict in Wartime Chengdu." *Twentieth-Century China* 29.2: 89–136.

Wang, Feng. 2000. "Gendered Migration and the Migration of Genders in Contemporary China." In Entwisle and Henderson 2000, 231–42.

Wang, Qi. 1999. "State-Society Relations and Women's Political Participation." In West et al. 1999, 19–44.

Wang, Qingshu. 2004. "The History and Current Status of Chinese Women's Participation in Politics." In J. Tao, Zheng, and Mow 2004, 92–106.

Wang, Xingjuan. 2004. "Domestic Violence in China." In J. Tao, Zheng, and Mow 2004, 179–92.

Wang, Zheng. 1996. "A Historic Turning Point for the Women's Movement in China." *Signs: Journal of Women in Culture and Society* 22.1 (autumn): 192–99.

———. 1997. "Maoism, Feminism, and the UN Conference on Women: Women's Studies Research in Contemporary China." *Journal of Women's History* 8.4 (winter): 126–53.

———. 1999. *Women in the Chinese Enlightenment: Oral and Textual Histories.* Berkeley and Los Angeles: University of California Press.

———. 2001. "Call Me Qingnian But Not Funü: A Maoist Youth In Retrospect." *Feminist Studies* 27.1 (spring): 9–36. Reprinted in Zhong, Wang, and Bai 2001, 27–52.

———. 2003. "Gender, Employment and Women's Resistance." In Perry and Selden 2003, 158–182.

———. 2005a. "Gender and Maoist Urban Reorganization." In B. Goodman and Larson 2005a, 189–209.

——— 2005b. "'State Feminism'? Gender and Socialist State Formation in Maoist China." *Feminist Studies* 31.3 (fall), 519–51.

Wasserstrom, Jeffrey. 1984. "Resistance to the One-Child Family." *Modern China* 10.3 (July): 345–74.

———, ed. 2003. *Twentieth-Century China: New Approaches.* London and New York: Routledge.

Watson, James L., and Evelyn Rawski, eds. 1988. *Death Ritual in Late Imperial and Modern China.* Berkeley and Los Angeles: University of California Press.

Watson, Rubie S. 1984. "Women's Property in Republican China: Rights and Practice." *Republican China* 10.1A (Nov.): 1–12.

———. 1986. "The Named and the Nameless: Gender and Person in Chinese Society." *American Ethnologist* 13.4 (Nov.): 619–31.

———. 1991. "Wives, Concubines, and Maids: Servitude and Kinship in the Hong Kong Region, 1900–1940." In R. Watson and Ebrey 1991, 231–55.

———. 1994. "Girls' Houses and Working Women: Expressive Culture in the Pearl River Delta, 1900–1941." In Jaschok and Miers 1994a, 25–44.

———. 1996. "Chinese Bridal Laments: The Claims of a Dutiful Daughter." In *Harmony and Counterpoint: Ritual Music in Chinese Context,* ed. Bell Yung, Evelyn S. Rawski, and Rubie S. Watson. Stanford, Calif.: Stanford University Press, 107–29.

Watson, Rubie S., and Patricia Buckley Ebrey, eds. 1991. *Marriage and Inequality in Chinese Society.* Berkeley and Los Angeles: University of California Press.

Wesoky, Sharon. 2002. *Chinese Feminism Faces Globalization.* New York and London: Routledge.

West, Jackie, Minghua Zhao, Xiangqun Chang, and Yuan Cheng, eds. 1999. *Women of China: Economic and Social Transformation.* New York: St. Martin's Press.

White, Sydney. 1997. "Fame and Sacrifice: The Gendered Construction of Naxi Identities." *Modern China* 23.3 (July): 298–327.

White, Tyrene. 1994. "The Origins of China's Birth Planning Policy." In Gilmartin et al. 1994, 250–78.

———. 2003. "Domination, Resistance and Accommodation in China's One-Child Campaign." In Perry and Selden 2003, 183–203.

Whyte, Martin King. 1990. "Changes in Mate Choice in Chengdu." In *Chinese Society on the Eve of Tiananmen: The Impact of Reform,* ed. Deborah Davis and Ezra F. Vogel. Cambridge, Mass.: Council on East Asian Studies, Harvard University, 181–213.

———. 1993. "Wedding Behavior and Family Strategies in Chengdu." In Davis and Harrell 1993, 189–216.

———. 2000. "The Perils of Assessing Trends in Gender Inequality in China." In Entwisle and Henderson 2000, 157–67.

Whyte, Martin King, and William L. Parish. 1984. *Urban Life in Contemporary China.* Chicago: University of Chicago Press.

Wilson, Verity. 2002. "Dressing for Leadership in China: Wives and Husbands in an Age of Revolutions (1911–1976)." *Gender and History* 14.3 (Nov.): 608–28.

Witke, Roxane. 1970. "Transformation of Attitudes towards Women during the May Fourth Era of Modern China." Ph.D. diss., University of California, Berkeley.

———. 1973a. "Mao Tse-Tung, Women, and Suicide." In M. Young 1973, 7–31.

————. 1973b. "Woman as Politician in China of the 1920s." In M. Young 1973, 33–45.

————. 1975. "Chiang Ch'ing's Coming of Age." In M. Wolf and Witke 1975, 169–92.

————. 1977. *Comrade Chiang Ch'ing.* Boston and Toronto: Little Brown & Co.

Wolf, Arthur P. 1975. "The Women of Hai-Shan: A Demographic Portrait." In M. Wolf and Witke 1975, 89–110.

Wolf, Margery. 1968. *House of Lim: A Study of a Chinese Farm Family.* New York: Appleton.

————. 1972. *Women and the Family in Rural Taiwan.* Stanford, Calif.: Stanford University Press.

————. 1975. "Women and Suicide in China." In M. Wolf and Witke 1975, 111–41.

————. 1985. *Revolution Postponed: Women in Contemporary China.* Stanford, Calif.: Stanford University Press.

————. 1992. *A Thrice-Told Tale: Feminism, Postmodernism, and Ethnographic Responsibility.* Stanford, Calif.: Stanford University Press.

Wolf, Margery, and Roxane Witke, eds. 1975. *Women in Chinese Society.* Stanford, Calif.: Stanford University Press.

Wong, Yuk-Lin Renita. 1997. "Dispersing the 'Public' and the 'Private': Gender and the State in the Birth Planning Policy of China." *Gender and Society* 11.4 (Aug.): 509–25.

Woo, Margaret Y. K. 1994. "Chinese Women Workers: The Delicate Balance between Protection and Equality." In Gilmartin et al. 1994, 279–95.

————. 2002. "Law and the Gendered Citizen." In Goldman and Perry 2002, 308–29.

Woon, Yuen-fong. 2000. "Filial or Rebellious Daughters? *Dagongmei* in the Pearl River Delta Region, South China, in the 1990s." *Asian and Pacific Migration Journal* 9.2: 137–69.

Wylie, Clodagh. 2004. "Femininity and Authority: Women in China's Private Sector." In McLaren 2004a, 42–64.

Xia, Xiaohong. 2004. "New Meanings in a Classic: Different Interpretations of Ban Zhao and Her *Admonitions for Women* in the Late Qing Dynasty." In J. Tao, Zheng, and Mow 2004, 3–16.

Xie, Bingying. 2001. *A Woman Soldier's Own Story: The Autobiography of Xie Bingying.* Trans. Lily Chia Brissman and Barry Brissman. New York: Columbia University Press.

Xiong, Yu. 2004. "The Status of Chinese Women in Marriage and the Family." In J. Tao, Zheng, and Mow 2004, 172–78.

Xu, Feng. 2000. *Women Migrant Workers in China's Economic Reform.* New York: St. Martin's Press.

Xu, Xiaoqun. 1996. "The Discourse on Love, Marriage, and Sexuality in Post-Mao China: A Reading of the Journalistic Literature on Women." *positions: east asia cultures critique* 4.2 (fall): 381–414.

Yan, Hairong. 2003. "Spectralization of the Rural: Reinterpreting the Labor Mobility of Rural Young Women in Post-Mao China." *American Ethnologist* 30.4 (Nov.): 578–96.

Yan, Yunxiang. 2002. "Courtship, Love and Premarital Sex in a North China Village." *China Journal* 48 (July): 29–53.

———. 2003. *Private Life under Socialism: Love, Intimacy, and Family Change in a Chinese Village, 1949–1999.* Stanford, Calif.: Stanford University Press.

Yang, Mayfair Mei-hui. 1994. *Gifts, Favors, and Banquets: The Art of Social Relationships in China.* Ithaca, N.Y.: Cornell University Press.

———. 1999a. "From Gender Erasure to Gender Difference: State Feminism, Consumer Sexuality, and Women's Public Sphere in China." In M. Yang 1999c, 35–67.

———. 1999b. "Introduction." In M. Yang 1999c, 1–31.

———, ed. 1999c. *Spaces of Their Own: Women's Public Sphere in Transnational China.* Minneapolis: University of Minnesota Press.

Yang, Rae. 1997. *Spider Eaters.* Berkeley and Los Angeles: University of California Press.

Yang, Xiushi. 2000. "Interconnections among Gender, Work, and Migration: Evidence from Zhejiang Province." In Entwisle and Henderson 2000, 197–213.

Yang, Xiushi, and Fei Guo. 1999. "Gender Differences in Determinants of Temporary Labor Migration in China: A Multilevel Analysis." *International Migration Review* 33.4 (winter): 929–54.

Ye, Weili. 1994. "'Nüliuxuesheng': The Story of American-Educated Chinese Women, 1880s-1920s." *Modern China* 20.3 (July): 315–46.

———. 2001. *Seeking Modernity in China's Name: Chinese Students in the United States, 1900–1927.* Stanford, Calif.: Stanford University Press.

Ye, Xiaoqing. 1999. "Commercialization and Prostitution in Nineteenth Century Shanghai." In Finnane and McLaren 1999, 37–57.

Yeh, Catherine Vance. 1998. "Reinventing Ritual: Late Qing Handbooks for Proper Customer Behavior in Shanghai Courtesan Houses." *Late Imperial China* 19.2 (Dec.): 1–63.

———. 2005. "Playing with the Public: Late Qing Courtesans and Their Opera Singer Lovers." In B. Goodman and Larson 2005a, 145–68.

Yeh, Wen-hsin. 2005. "The Paradox of Autonomy: Nation, Revolution, and Women through the Chinese Looking Glass." In Leutner and Spakowski 2005, 40–56.

Young, Helen Praeger. 2001. *Choosing Revolution: Chinese Women Soldiers on the Long March.* Urbana: University of Illinois Press.

———. 2005. "Threads from Long March Stories: The Political, Economic and Social Experience of Women Soldiers." In Leutner and Spakowski 2005, 172–93.

Young, Marilyn B., ed. 1973. *Women in China: Studies in Social Change and Feminism*. Ann Arbor: Center for Chinese Studies, University of Michigan.

———. 1989. "Chicken Little in China: Women after the Cultural Revolution." In Kruks, Rapp, and Young 1989, 233–47. Reprinted in Dirlik and Meisner 1989, 253–268.

Yu, Chien-ming. 2005. "Female Physical Education and the Media in Modern China." In Leutner and Spakowski 2005, 482–506.

Yuen, Sun-pong, Pui-lam Law, and Yuk-ying Ho. 2004. *Marriage, Gender, and Sex in a Contemporary Chinese Village*. Trans. Fong-ying Yu. Armonk, N.Y.: M. E. Sharpe.

Zamperini, Paola. 2003. "On Their Dress They Wore a Body: Fashion and Identity in Late Qing Shanghai." *positions: east asia cultures critique* 11.2 (fall): 301–30.

Zang, Jian. 2005. " 'Women Returning Home'—A Topic of Chinese Women's Liberation." In Leutner and Spakowski 2005, 376–95.

Zang, Xiaowei. 1999. "Family, Kinship, Marriage, and Sexuality." In Gamer 1999, 267–92.

Zarrow, Peter. 1988. "He Zhen and Anarcho-Feminism in China." *Journal of Asian Studies* 47.4 (Nov.): 796–813.

———. 1990. *Anarchism and Chinese Political Culture*. New York: Columbia University Press.

Zeng, Jifen. 1993. *Testimony of a Confucian Woman: The Autobiography of Mrs. Nie Zeng Jifen, 1852–1942*. Athens: University of Georgia Press.

Zhang, Heather Xiaoquan. 1999a. "Female Migration and Urban Labour Markets in Tianjin." *Development and Change* 30.1 (Jan.): 21–42.

———. 1999b. "Understanding Changes in Women's Status in the Context of the Recent Rural Reform." In West et al. 1999, 45–66.

Zhang, Li. 2000. "The Interplay of Gender, Space, and Work in China's Floating Population." In Entwisle and Henderson 2000, 171–96.

———. 2001. *Strangers in the City: Reconfigurations of Space, Power, and Social Networks within China's Floating Population*. Stanford, Calif.: Stanford University Press.

Zhang, Mei. 1999. "Rural Privatisation and Women's Labour: Property Rights and Gender Concepts in Inner Mongolia and Xinjiang." In West et al. 1999, 175–92.

Zhang, Naihua 1996. *The All-China Women's Federation, Chinese Women and the Women's Movement, 1949–1993*. Ph.D. diss., Michigan State University.

———. 2001. "Searching for 'Authentic' NGOs: The NGO Discourse and Women's Organizations in China." In Ping-chun Hsiung, Jaschok, and Milwertz 2001, 159–79.

Zhang, Yanshang. 1997. "A Series of Psychological Profiles of Prostitute Clients." In Jeffreys 1997b, 77–89.

Zhang, Yingjin. 1994. "Engendering Chinese Filmic Discourse of the 1930s:

Configurations of Modern Women in Shanghai in Three Silent Films." *positions: east asia cultures critique* 2.3 (winter): 603–28.

———. 1996. *The City in Modern Chinese Literature and Film: Configurations of Space, Time, and Gender.* Stanford, Calif.: Stanford University Press.

———, ed. 1999a. *Cinema and Urban Culture in Shanghai, 1922–1943.* Stanford, Calif.: Stanford University Press.

———. 1999b. "Prostitution and Urban Imagination: Negotiating the Public and the Private in Chinese Films of the 1930s." In Yingjin Zhang 1999a, 160–180.

Zhao, Liming. 2004. "The Women's Script of Jiangyong: An Invention of Chinese Women." In J. Tao, Zheng, and Mow 2004, 39–52.

Zhao, Minghua. 1999. "From Weaving Stars to Bitter Flowers: Tradition, Reform and Their Implications for Women Textile Workers." In West et al. 1999, 108–33.

Zhao, Minghua, and Jackie West. 1999. "State and Economy in the Making of Women's Lives: An Introduction." In West et al. 1999, 1–16.

Zheng, Tiantian. "From Peasant Women to Bar Hostesses: Gender and Modernity in Post-Mao Dalian." In Gaetano and Jacka 2004, 80–108.

Zheng, Zhenzhen, Yun Zhou, Lixin Zheng, Yuan Yang, Dongxia Zhao, Chaohua Lou, and Shuangling Zhao. 2001. "Sexual Behaviour and Contraceptive Use among Unmarried, Young Women Migrant Workers in Five Cities in China." *Reproductive Health Matters* 9.17 (May): 118–27.

Zhong, Xueping, Zheng Wang, and Di Bai. 2001. *Some of Us: Chinese Women Growing Up in the Mao Era.* New Brunswick, N.J.: Rutgers University Press.

Zhou, Kate Xiao. 1996. *How the Farmers Changed China: Power of the People.* Boulder, Colo.: Westview Press.

Zito, Angela, and Tani E. Barlow, eds. 1994. *Body, Subject and Power in China.* Chicago: University of Chicago Press.

Zurndorfer, Harriet T. 2005. "Gender, Higher Education, and the 'New Woman': The Experiences of Female Graduates in Republican China." In Leutner and Spakowski 2005, 450–81.

Index

women: athletes, 42; as barometer of
revolutionary success, 5, 79, 105,
118; as barometer of social crisis, 5,
79, 81, 82, 86, 87, 97, 118; elderly,
23, 28, 32, 34, 35; as fashion models,
42–43; paired with labor, 4, 51–78;
paired with marriage, family, sexuality, and gender difference, 4, 7–50;
paired with national modernity, 4,
79–105
"Women were there, too," 4, 6, 51, 52
Women's Bell, 82
Women's Federation, 35, 77, 94–95,
96, 98, 99, 100, 102, 112, 113, 115;
and attitudes toward divorce, 20
Women's Rights Recovery Association, 83
women's script, 14
women's studies, 1, 4, 98, 98–105,
109, 110
work points, 61–62

World Cup, 97
World War II, 54
Wu Zhiying, 84
Wuhan, 53, 65
Wuxi, 58

Xi'an, 11
Xiang Jingyu, 88
Xue Shaohui, 81, 84

Yan'an, 41, 59, 90
Yangzi, 12, 57, 58, 59
Yao Lingxi, 37
Yu Luojin, 96
Yunnan, 12, 40, 57, 77, 81
YWCA, 54, 81

Zhang Guotao, 91
Zhang Jian, 56
Zhejiang, 22, 74, 77
Zhu De, 91